D1117611

ANCIENT SLAVERY AND THE IDEAL OF MAN

Joseph Vogt

ANCIENT SLAVERY AND THE IDEAL OF MAN

Translated by Thomas Wiedemann

HARVARD UNIVERSITY PRESS
CAMBRIDGE · MASSACHUSETTS
1975

Library of Congress Catalog Card Number 74–17885

ISBN 0–674–03440–6

Translated from the second German edition, *Sklaverei und Humanität: Studien zur antiken Sklaverei und ihrer Erforschung*, by arrangement with Franz Steiner Verlag, Wiesbaden.

Printed in Great Britain

Preface to the English Edition

More than twenty years have passed since I first began my studies of slavery in the ancient world with the help of the Mainz Academy of Science and Literature. During these years I have enjoyed the assistance of an impressive number of colleagues and was able to have their contributions published by the Academy. I hope that it will be possible to continue this highly attractive team-work in the years to come.

My own investigations on this subject, which had first appeared either in the *Abhandlungen* of the Mainz Academy or elsewhere, were collected and published in 1965 under the title *Sklaverei und Humanität. Studien zur antiken Sklaverei und ihrer Erforschung*. Some further articles as well as a bibliographical appendix were included in the second edition of this volume, which came out in 1972.

Both in Eastern Europe and in the Western World there has been a remarkable upsurge of interest in ancient slavery since the end of the Second World War. British and American scholars have made significant contributions in this field, and I am therefore very glad that an English translation of the second edition of my book should now be available. I would like to express my gratitude to the translator for his competence in adapting the text of these essays, and particularly the footnotes, to the conventions of English scholarship.

Tübingen, June 1974 JOSEPH VOGT

Contents

Abbreviations

1. Special Abbreviations

Bömer I, II, III, IV: F. Bömer *Untersuchungen über die Religion der Sklaven in Griechenland und Rom.*

I.: *Die wichtigsten Kulte und Religionen in Rom und im lateinischen Westen* (*Ak. d. Wiss. u. d. Lit.* 1957, 7).

II.: *Die sogenannte sakrale Freilassung in Griechenland und die* (δοῦλοι) ἱεροί (*Ak. d. Wiss. u. d. Lit.* 1960, 1).

III.: *Die wichtigsten Kulte der griechischen Welt* (*Ak. d. Wiss. u. d. Lit.* 1961, 4).

IV.: *Epilegomena* (*Ak. d. Wiss. u. d. Lit.* 1963, 10).

Finley: *Slavery in Classical Antiquity*, ed. M. I. Finley (Cambridge 1960).

Lauffer I, II: S. Lauffer *Die Bergwerkssklaven von Laureion.*

I.: *Arbeits- und Betriebsverhältnisse. Rechtsstellung* (*Ak. d. Wiss. u. d. Lit.* 1955, 12).

II.: *Gesellschaftliche Verhältnisse. Aufstände* (*Ak. d. Wiss. u. d. Lit.* 1956, 11).

Westermann *Slave Systems*: W. L. Westermann *The Slave Systems of Greek and Roman Antiquity* (*Memoirs of the American Philosophical Society* 40, Philadelphia 1955).

2. Periodicals etc. cited

Ak. d. Wiss. u. d. Lit.	*Akademie der Wissenschaft und der Literatur* (Mainz): *Abhandlungen der Geistes- und sozialwissenschaftlichen Klasse*
Arch. Pap.	*Archiv für Papyrusforschung*
Ath. Mitt.	*Mitteilungen des deutschen archäologischen Instituts, Athenische Abteilung*
BCH	*Bulletin de Correspondance Hellénique*
Bull. épigr.	*Bulletin épigraphique*
CAH	*Cambridge Ancient History*
CIL	*Corpus Inscriptionum Latinarum*
CPhil	*Classical Philology*
CSEL	*Corpus Scriptorum Ecclesiasticorum Latinorum*
GCS	*Die Griechischen Christlichen Schriftsteller der ersten drei Jahrhunderte* (Leipzig 1899–)
HSCP	*Harvard Studies in Classical Philology*
IGR	R. Cagnat *Inscriptiones Graecae ad Res Romanas pertinentes*
ILS	H. Dessau *Inscriptiones Latinae Selectae*
Jacoby *F. Gr. Hist.*	F. Jacoby *Die Fragmente der Griechischen Historiker*
JRS	*Journal of Roman Studies*
Müller *FHG*	C. & T. Müller *Fragmenta Historicorum Graecorum*
Num. Chron.	*Numismatic Chronicle*
OGIS	W. Dittenberger *Orientis Graeci Inscriptiones Selectae*
PG	*Patrologia Graeca*
PL	*Patrologia Latina*
RE	Pauly-Wissowa-Kroll *Realencyclopädie der classischen Altertumswissenschaft*
Rev. ét. gr.	*Revue des études grecques*
Rh. Mus.	*Rheinisches Museum*
Riv. Fil.	*Rivista di filologia e d'istruzione classica*
Röm. Mitt.	*Mitteilungen des deutschen archäologischen Instituts, Römische Abteilung*
SIG	W. Dittenberger *Sylloge Inscriptionum Graecarum*
VDI	*Vestnik Drevnei Istorii*
Vorsokratiker	H. Diels-W. Kranz *Fragmente der Vorsokratiker*[6]
YCS	*Yale Classical Studies*

I

Slavery and the Ideal of Man in Classical Greece

During the last few years, classical scholars have again studied the Greek conception of man, his position within the universe and his tasks in society, in an attempt to achieve a better understanding of the Greek world. From language and literature they have come to realize how sharply the Greeks distinguished the human world from that of the gods above and of animals below. It was out of this consciousness of their own special status that the Greeks first developed to the full two specifically human tendencies, abstract thought as the basis of all constructive creativity, and the ideal of the state as a common and equal commitment for all its members; and in the civic society of Athens in the fourth century, they produced a moral attitude which recognized philanthropy and education together as the highest human values.[1] Recently this idea of humanity has been shown to have existed

The original version of this chapter was first published in *Abhandlungen d. Geistes- u. sozialwiss. Kl., Ak. d. Wiss. u. d. Lit.*, 1953, 4. It is dedicated to Victor Ehrenberg.

[1] I must express my debt to the works of K. Latte *Griechentum und Humanität* (Iserlohn 1947); B. Snell 'Die Entdeckung der Menschlichkeit und unsere Stellung zu den Griechen', in *Die Entdeckung des Geistes*[3] [= *The Discovery of the Mind* (Oxford 1953), p. 246: 'The Discovery of Humanitas and Our Attitude Toward the Greeks']; R. Harder *Eigenart der Griechen* (*Herder-Bücherei* 120, Freiburg 1962); and W. Schadewaldt *Der Gott von Delphi und die Humanitätsidee* (Pfullingen 1965).

in the tragedies of Sophocles, in the realization of the blessedness brought about by man's nearness to his fellows and his striving to feel a sense of community and love for others. That feeling of sympathy which appears in the *Philoctetes* as the redeeming force of true virtue has been hailed as a milestone in the development of the moral ideas of the Athenians.[2] So it would seem that already in classical Greece we could find those humane ideals which through the Attic New Comedy of Menander and others and the philosophy of the Middle Stoa led ultimately to the opinions held by educated Romans.

But, we must ask ourselves, what was the position of slaves during the great era of Pericles and Sophocles, Euripides and Socrates? Did these slaves also reap the benefits of that spirit of humanity which the Athenians discovered? Or, because of our presupposition that Hellenism and humanitarianism go hand-in-hand, have we come to terms far too easily with the fact that slavery was an accepted institution, that is to say, that certain human beings served only as machines, as objects? To some extent, an intellectual prejudice of this kind would be understandable, as no satisfactory solution has yet been found to the problems posed by ancient slavery, in spite of the research that has been going on for over a century, and despite recent attempts to award slavery its proper place within a comprehensive picture of ancient civilization.[3] The research in this field undertaken by the Commission for Ancient History of the Academy of Science and Literature at Mainz[4] may

[2] A. Lesky 'Sophokles und das Humane' *Almanach der Österreichischen Akademie der Wissenschaften* 101 (1951), 222ff. [also in *Gesammelte Schriften* (Bern 1966), 190f.], and F. Egermann *Vom attischen Menschenbild* (Munich 1952), 5f., 123.

[3] W. L. Westermann *The Slave Systems of Greek and Roman Antiquity* (*Memoirs of the American Philosophical Society* 40, Philadelphia 1955). For the history of research on this subject, see Chapter IX below and the first part of J. A. Lentzman's book on slavery in Mycenaean and Homeric Greece (which has appeared in a German edition: J. A. Lencman *Die Sklaverei im mykenischen und homerischen Griechenland* tr. M. Bräuer-Pospelova, Wiesbaden 1966).

[4] Cf. the reports in the Journal of the Academy since 1951. The following papers have appeared in the series on social and cultural history (*Geistes- und Sozialwissenschaftliche Klasse*): J. Vogt *Sklaverei und Humanität im klassischen Griechentum* (1953, 4); *Struktur der antiken Sklavenkriege* (1957, 1); G. Micknat *Studien zur Kriegsgefangenschaft und Sklaverei in der griechischen Geschichte*. I.: *Homer* (1954, 11); S. Lauffer *Die Bergwerkssklaven von Laureion*. I.: *Arbeits- und Betriebsverhältnisse. Rechtsstellung* (1955, 12); II.: *Gesellschaftliche Verhältnisse. Aufstände* (1956, 11) henceforth cited as Lauffer I, II; F. Bömer *Untersuchungen über die Religion der Sklaven in Griechenland und Rom*. I.: *Die wichtigsten Kulte und Religionen in Rom und im lateinischen Westen* (1957, 7—a new edition is in course of

contribute towards closing a gap whose existence must be regarded as particularly striking in our present age.

The real facts are that the contemporaries of the great poets accepted without reservation that a conqueror had absolute power over the defeated. Thucydides describes without further comment how, after the conquest of a town in a war between Greeks, the adult males were killed and the women and children enslaved. By no means all Greek prisoners of war were exchanged or ransomed from captivity by their relatives or fellow-citizens. Kidnapping and slave-trading did not exist only among barbarians. Debt-bondage had long been abolished at Athens, but it continued to be practised in other Greek states. Not only in plays did parents expose their children—an occurrence that generally led to the child's being brought up as a slave if he was taken care of by someone else. In every Greek city there were human beings who in one way or another had come to be enslaved, and their condition was inherited by their descendants. They were owned by another person as a living item of his property; they had to do whatever work was set them by their master and were restricted in their freedom of movement. They differed from the Spartan Helots, the serfs of Gortyn, the Thessalian *Penestai* and other classes of bondsmen in that they were utterly and completely dependent on the will of a single individual.[5] Although killing or grossly maltreating slaves may in some places have been restricted by law,[6] they themselves enjoyed neither legal protection nor even legal recognition. They worked side by side with the free population as labourers without rights; every household

preparation); II.: *Die sogenannte sakrale Freilassung in Griechenland und die* (δοῦλοι) ἱεροί (1960, 1); III.: *Die wichtigsten Kulte der griechischen Welt* (1961, 4); IV.: *Epilegomena* (1963, 10) henceforth cited as Bömer I, II, III, IV; P. P. Spranger *Historische Untersuchungen zu den Sklavenfiguren des Plautus und Terenz* (1960, 8); H. Volkmann *Die Massenversklavungen der Einwohner eroberter Städte in der hellenistisch-römischen Zeit* (1961, 3); F. Gschnitzer *Studien zur griechischen Terminologie der Sklaverei*. I.: *Grundzüge des vorhellenistischen Sprachgebrauchs* (1963, 13); H. U. Instinsky *Marcus Aurelius Prosenes—Freigelassener und Christ am Kaiserhof* (1964, 3); [N. Himmelmann *Archäologisches zum Problem der griechischen Sklaverei* (1971, 13)].

[5] Cf. W. L. Westermann 'Between Slavery and Freedom' *American Historical Review* 50 (1945), 213ff.; D. Lotze 'Μεταξὺ ἐλευθέρων καὶ δούλων' *Deutsche Akademie der Wissenschaften zu Berlin. Schriften der Sektion für Altertumswissenschaft* 17 (1959); M. I. Finley 'The Servile Statuses of Ancient Greece' *Revue internationale des Droits de l'Antiquité* 7 (1960), 165ff., *ibid.* 'Between Slavery and Freedom' *Comparative Studies in Society and History* 6 (1964), 233ff.

[6] G. R. Morrow 'The Murder of Slaves in Attic Law' *CPhil* 32 (1937), 210ff.

depended on them, and they were indispensable both in agriculture and in industry; the mines were worked almost entirely by slaves.[7] They were present in the public services too; it was they who were the municipal workmen, served in the public offices and even acted as policemen. There is enough evidence about Athens for us to be able to deduce the relative proportions of the free and slave population with some certainty. When Athens was at the height of her influence and prosperity just before the outbreak of the Peloponnesian War, slaves may have constituted about one-third of the total population. This estimate is based on contemporary information, which constitutes the only reliable evidence for such a calculation; there were about 115,000 slaves to 172,000 citizens and 28,000 Metics.[8] From this we are entitled to conclude that material production rested to a significant extent on slave labour, and despite considerable controversy it remains an open question whether slavery should be considered one of the essential foundations of Greek society and culture.[9]

The problem which I propose to discuss here is how the existence of this institution was compatible with the Greek respect for human dignity. Hegel was surely right to say that in the servility of the serf his master also loses his humanity.[10] The investigation will be limited in particular to Athens and to the period in which this city achieved a high degree of social equality and the maximum of individual freedom. It cannot be denied that the Athenians were very mild in the way they treated their slaves—most of whom were at that time non-Greeks. One

[7] On the relationship between slaves and free men in the mines of Laureum, see Lauffer I, 4ff.

[8] This is the figure arrived at by A. W. Gomme *The population of Athens in the fifth and fourth centuries B.C.* (Oxford 1933). R. L. Sargent *The size of the slave population at Athens during the fifth and fourth centuries B.C.* (*University of Illinois Studies in the Social Sciences* XII, 3, 1924) estimates the proportion of slaves in the time of Pericles to have been up to half that of the free population. W. L. Westermann 'Athenaeus and the slaves at Athens' in *Athenian Studies presented to W. S. Ferguson* (*HSCP*, Supp. Vol. (1941), 451ff. [= Finley 73ff.]), arrives at the figure of about one-third or one-quarter of the total population. Further bibliography on this question is to be found in J. A. Lentzman *op. cit.*

[9] Several more recent studies of this problem have been collected in the volume on *Slavery in Classical Antiquity* edited by M. I. Finley (Cambridge 1960), here referred to as Finley; also P. Oliva 'Die Bedeutung der antiken Sklaverei' *Acta Antiqua* 3 (1960), 309ff., and S. Lauffer 'Die Sklaverei in der griechisch-römischen Welt' *XI. Congrès International des Sciences Historiques* (Stockholm 1960), *Rapports* II, 71ff. (reprinted in *Gymnasium* 68 (1961), 370ff.).

[10] 'In der Knechtschaft des Knechtes verliert auch der Herr seine Menschheit.'

phanes' *Ecclesiazusae* would like to see changed, namely that slave-girls should no longer be allowed to compete with free women in matters of sex.[36]

It was at this very time that philosophical criticism of the *polis* and its laws broke like a storm over this age in which the structure of society was as we have seen upheld by such rigid conventions. This was the achievement of the Sophists. With an appeal to unwritten laws, Hippias postulated the existence of a natural justice, and declared that it was contrary to such natural justice for one man to be the master of another. 'For it is only according to law and custom that one man is a slave, another free; there is no distinction in nature. Therefore it is unjust; for it is based on force alone.'[37] Antiphon put forward a belief in the equality of all mankind: 'Barbarians or Greeks, we have all been created with a nature that is identical in all respects . . . for we all breathe through our mouth and nose and use our hands to eat.'[38] The influence that the sophistic antithesis of *physis* and *nomos* had on Greek thought in general is inestimable, yet it was not able to weaken the reality of slavery. Other Sophists brought forward equally persuasive rational arguments proving the natural inequality of men, and the rule of the strong over the weak. In the fifth century there was perhaps only a single profession that required of its members almost the same obligations towards slaves as towards free men: the medical profession. In the famous Hippocratic Oath the physician vows to abstain from sexual intercourse with patients be they men or women, free or slave.[39] The medical treatment of slaves must therefore have been a fairly regular occurrence. Case-histories of slaves, and in particular of

[36] *Eccles.* 718ff.

[37] These are the words which Aristotle (*Politics* I, 3 = 1253b20ff.) uses to express the ideas of a group of Sophists which we may suppose to have included Hippias: W. Nestle *Vom Mythos zum Logos*² (Stuttgart 1942), 369ff.; *ibid.* 345 for the later use and practical application of this theory by Alcidamas. On the problem of Greek views on natural justice in general, cf. V. Ehrenberg *Archiv für Geschichte der Philosophie* 35 (1923), 119ff. (= *Polis und Imperium* (Zürich and Stuttgart 1965), 359ff.); E. Wolf *Griechisches Rechtsdenken* II (Frankfurt 1952), 76ff.

[38] *Vorsokratiker* 44 B 2 (Vol. II, 353); Nestle *op. cit.* 377.

[39] K. Deichgräber 'Die ärztliche Standesethik des hippokratischen Eides' *Quellen und Studien zur Geschichte der Naturwissenschaft und der Medizin* 3 (1933), 29ff., esp. 37f.; F. Büchner *Der Eid des Hippokrates* (Freiburg i. Br. 1945); K. Deichgräber *Professio medici. Zum Vorwort des Scribonius Largus* (*Ak. d. Wiss. u. d. Lit.* 1950, 9), 8ff.

member of the aristocratic opposition whose account of Athenian democracy survives is very critical of the excessive freedom and prosperity of city slaves, whom he mentions in the same breath as the Metics, and he grumbles that they cannot even be distinguished in public from the ordinary man by their dress or appearance.[11] There were no slave revolts during this period, and nothing in those laws that have been preserved suggests that the free citizens were permanently afraid that their slaves might revolt. So a slave's life must have been tolerable.[12] But it is exactly in this situation that the question arises how the Greeks, who followed their ideas about the problems of nature and human existence through to their logical conclusions, could reconcile themselves to the existence of slavery. The first point to note is that contemporary literature tells us far less than we today would wish about this aspect of everyday existence. But we do possess the comedies of Aristophanes and the tragedies of Euripides—and these dramas are such a rich witness of real life that we may be satisfied with them. The discussion may be limited to the extant works of these two great writers of comedy and tragedy, and so to the Athenian stage in the last third of the fifth and the beginning of the fourth century; for it was within this period that the view of man held by classical Greece reached its final form.

It is only with certain reservations that the theatre can be accepted as an accurate representation of real life. It is true that in contrast to the heroic themes of tragedy, Old Comedy is based on everyday life and the ordinary world of the Athenian citizen, but it depicts a world transformed by the poet 'in which sense and nonsense, intelligence and foolishness, reality and unreality are combined with one another in a mad, wild carnival'.[13] But the poet wants to entertain, and he knows very well that he will be most certain to achieve this if his Athenian audience can recognize themselves in his theatrical burlesque. Thus Aristophanes unites various aspects which may seem contradictory: the fantasy element in the plot, the distortion of individual personalities, and the use of a realistic background. If Old Comedy is approached with the proper questions, its rendering of this atmosphere and account of human motivation provide a unique historical source. Victor Ehrenberg based his brilliant picture of the social and economic

[11] Ps.-Xenophon *Constitution of Athens* 1, 10ff.

[12] As Frank Thiess pointed out: *Ideen zur Natur- und Leidensgeschichte der Völker* (Hamburg 1952), 84.

[13] H. Müller-Strübing *Aristophanes und die historische Kritik* (Leipzig 1873), 28.

life of Athens on the plays of Aristophanes,[14] and they may also be used with some confidence in considering the human aspect of slavery.

Aristophanes' earlier plays deal with the lofty and at the same time mean world of politics. As slaves had no political rights, he gave them only minor parts, yet in accordance with both dramatic convention and real life, he introduced them into all his plays. In several places he indeed expressly claims to have done away with the indecent and unworthy jokes by which his predecessors and rivals attempted to amuse their audiences. In this connection he mentions particularly the stock-types of coarse slaves with baskets of nuts to throw at the spectators; servants who cheat and run away and are beaten simply in order to be mocked and derided by their fellow-slaves; porters who pant and fart under their loads.[15] On a particularly solemn occasion, in the first Parabasis of the *Peace*, he describes the removal of these hollow and hackneyed characters as essential to the novelty of his own creative writing which has made comedy into a great art. That is to say, Aristophanes claims —although this claim is not always fulfilled—that his slaves are to have a share in the dignity of great art; they are to represent more civilized and at the same time more real slaves, living figures instead of mere types. And this holds just as much for those plays in which slaves are mere extras. Thus the poet himself tells us that we can use these characters in considering our problem.[16]

The slaves who appear in Aristophanes are not those of the mines or

[14] V. Ehrenberg *The People of Aristophanes. A Sociology of Old Attic Comedy*[2] (Oxford 1951); on the importance of Old Comedy as a source of historical information, see 7ff., 37ff. On the combination of realism and suprarealism in comedy see also K. Reinhardt 'Aristophanes und Athen' *Europäische Revue* 14 (1938), 754ff. (= *Tradition und Geist. Gesammelte Essays zur Dichtung* ed. C. Becker (Göttingen 1960), 257ff.); W. Schadewaldt *Griechisches Theater* (Frankfurt 1964), 518ff. On the structure of comedy in general see H. Kindermann *Meister der Komödie* (Munich 1952), 9ff.

[15] *Wasps* 54ff., *Peace* 729ff., *Frogs* 1ff. A colourful picture of Aristophanes' predecessors and rivals is painted by O. Weinreich in his introduction to Aristophanes in the *Bibliothek der alten Welt* I (1952), vii ff.

[16] The role of slaves within the structure of individual plays is considered by C. O. Zuretti 'Il servo nella comedia greca antica' *Riv. Fil.* 31 (1903), 46ff. and C. Langer *De servi persona apud Menandrum* (dissertation, Bonn 1919), 9ff. For a portrayal of the world of Athenian slaves as mirrored in Old Comedy, see Ehrenberg *op. cit.* 165ff. Cf. also S. I. Sobolevski on slaves in Aristophanes' comedies (*VDI* 1954, 4, 9ff.) and B. Bilinski's article on the battle of ideologies in Aristophanes' comedies in the collection of essays on *Arystofanes* (Warsaw 1957), 47ff.

of industry but almost exclusively domestic slaves—though they have many varied duties and different human relationships. They are members of every household; they do all the domestic work—in the case of ordinary people like Dicaeopolis, alongside his wife and daughter; they act as doormen, clean the stables, accompany their master in the street or to market to carry his luggage or goods—although there are cases where both farmer and slave carry a basket to market, or where a slave goes shopping on his own. They assist at the family's acts of worship, in which, as in some public rites, they are allowed to take part; and they naturally have to be present whenever someone is to be chased away or given a beating. Lamachus' slave is a special case, for as his shield-bearer he both does the slave's job of packing and carrying his master's baggage and then accompanies him to war.[17] Slaves have to participate according to their abilities in all of these tasks. Although they may have all kinds of different names, many of them betraying their foreign origins, they are quite simply called 'boy' (παῖ) and the replies they give their master (δεσπότης) are generally as curt as his orders. But sometimes they have come to be on intimate terms with their masters and act as their advisers; they are on particularly good terms with masters who bring themselves down to their level.[18] Quite often they are beaten, and if they have to give evidence as witnesses the rack is used. Some masters are far too dependent on their slaves to be able to whip them any longer, and instead have to persuade them by reminding them of previous kindnesses, and then imagine to themselves how nice it would be—or had been—to punish or lock up these impudent servants.[19] Female slaves are also mentioned: they were numerous in the household; they acted as call-girls at every party and could also be made to earn money as prostitutes. It goes without saying that no ordinary slave-girl could refuse her master. It is considered a great joke that old Philocleon should promise a slave flute-player that if she lets him have his way with her now he will make her his concubine.[20]

So Aristophanes does not go far in giving the slaves he has created polish or dignity. But it is only when we see the general characteristics which Aristophanes attributes to his slaves indiscriminately that we realize how lacking in dignity this slave world is. The great majority

[17] *Acharnians* 1097ff.

[18] E.g. when Trygaeus and his servant display Theoria to the Council in *Peace* 868ff.

[19] *Knights* 1129f. and 1141ff., *Wasps* 439f., 448ff., *Clouds* 6f.

[20] *Wasps* 1351ff.

of his slave-girls are described as stupid, the men are boorish; good and trustworthy slaves are overwhelmingly outnumbered by the vast crowd of their lazy, insolent, randy, cowardly, thieving and dishonest companions. A typical example of the whole class is the Scythian policeman who because of his stupidity and concupiscence is made a fool of in the most undignified way.[21] One can see the utter inferiority of these slaves by the fact that they have practically no sense of community amongst themselves. There is nothing they like better than to lower their fellow-slaves in their master's eyes by any means possible. The head slave in a household can be the worst torment the others have to put up with, and his rule may become so dreadful that his fellows are left with no alternative but to attempt to flee, beg for asylum at the shrine of a god, or contemplate suicide.[22] This is the situation depicted in the *Knights*, where the Paphlagonian slave Cleon terrorizes Demos and his whole household. Of course, this is intended in a political sense, and the servants of Demos are only pseudo-slaves, but this public situation may well have been mirrored in many a private household, where the cunning rogue who survived was the one who was the most accomplished at flattery and self-praise and the most able to hoodwink his master. Even if we suppose that Aristophanes' characterization of slaves corresponded to what his audience wanted to believe rather than to reality, we must still conclude that the class as a whole was generally despised. Though free labourers may often have worked alongside slaves, and there was no sharp distinction between the tasks of free men and those of slaves, slaves were irrevocably degraded in the eyes of the public. Nowhere is this more obvious than in the facts that they were excluded from the *palaestra*, and that a slave could never at this time become an object of homosexual love, in spite of the fact that sexual relations between free men and slave women were so numerous.

Of course, slaves who behave in an educated way sometimes appear in these comedies, but they are generally intended as a foil for their intellectual masters whom Aristophanes is ridiculing. Euripides' doorman acts like a Sophist, Agathon's slave indulges in bombastic and poetic rhetoric and Demos' pseudo-slaves seem to have some knowledge of music, literature and philosophy.[23] Because of the

[21] *Thesmophoriazusae* 1172ff. Further examples of cowardly and stupid slaves are the Scythians in *Lysistrata* 424ff.

[22] *Knights* 1–84. For the ἀγὼν κολακείας among the slaves of Demos, *op. cit.* 763ff.

[23] *Acharnians* 395ff., *Thesmo.* 39ff., *Knights* 9, 32ff.

amusing impression this produces, Aristophanes lets slaves appear in the initial scenes of some of his plays where they sometimes even make political comments.[24] On very rare occasions we can see a deeper level of meaning behind these jests, as when a slave appoints himself spokesman for mankind and criticizes the gods:[25]

> I would not care a jot about the gods
> If they keep brothels just as we mortals do.

But, in general, slaves count for nothing in the community of citizens with which all these plays concern themselves. Only the exceptional circumstances of a long war force one to take them into serious consideration. Now they can no longer be whipped or they will run away;[26] they can also sabotage Trygaeus' proposed peace-treaty by deserting to the enemy, so that he curses them in the same way as he does his war-mongering fellow-citizens.[27] And in these same years it could also happen, to the annoyance of Aristophanes and his audience, that non-Greeks like Execestides or Sacas insinuated themselves into the citizen-body.[28] And finally—as we learn from a later play—slaves were enlisted as rowers before the decisive battle of Arginusae and then given their freedom after the victory. Although Aristophanes awards this episode the recognition it deserves, it is and remains an exception.[29]

When one surveys Aristophanes' earlier works, one has to admit quite simply that in these comedies slaves are not accepted as full human beings. They have been excluded from politics; they serve as convenient tools in domestic life; they play practically no part in the social and cultural field. Although they did on occasion reap some benefits from the civilized character of the Athenians, it would not be right to say that either the practice or the idea of slavery current at Athens was humane. The later comedies do not lead us to revise this conclusion, although they generally deal with a non-political world and therefore represent a change from the earlier plays. This is certainly true of the *Frogs*, produced in 405, that sparkling literary satire which contains the contest between Aeschylus and Euripides, and the *Plutus*, a comedy about the ageless human topic of the just redistribution of wealth, which we do not have in its original version of 408

[24] *Wasps* 15ff., *Peace* 47ff. [25] *Peace* 848ff.

[26] *Clouds* 6f. On the desertion of slaves *en masse* after the occupation of Decelea see Thucydides 7, 27.5; cf. E. Ch. Welskopf *Acta Antiqua* 3 (1960), 295ff.

[27] *Peace* 450ff. [28] *Birds* 11, 31ff., 764f., 1527.

[29] *Frogs* 33, 190ff. and esp. 693ff.; cf. Ehrenberg *op. cit.* 189.

but in the revised one of 388. These two plays date from a time when the power of Athens was declining and its civic spirit was beginning to be exhausted, years in which the ageing playwright freed himself more and more from politics, and considered the questions posed by universal human and social problems to be more immediate. It is no coincidence that slaves now play more important roles, roles essential to the plot. In this way the poet seeks to express the fact that citizens who do not participate in the life of the *polis* lose an important part of their being, and consequently fall to the level of slaves. Aristophanes made a master and his servant as a close-knit pair the centre of the action in both these plays. This was a bold innovation; but one may question whether it lifted slaves from their low status to the level of full human beings.

In the *Frogs*, Dionysus and his slave Xanthias travel to Hades together, apparently as good friends, to bring back the poet Euripides. Dionysus—who stands for the 'average' Athenian, the representative of the audience—would not know what to do without his wily companion, who not only carries his luggage for him but stands beside him in the face of all the dreadful encounters in the Underworld—and generally has more wits about him than his master on these occasions. It is not surprising that when he meets with the most terrible dangers at the Gate of Hades, the all-too-human god on two occasions decides to exchange dress and roles with his slave. This leads to some hilarious situations: Xanthias, now attired as a god, offers his slave to the servants of Aeacus to testify on the rack; and when Dionysus after all appeals to the fact that he is a god, he suggests that both should be given the same number of strokes, so that the person who should cry out first would be shown not to be the god (639). However, both of them hold out: the slave because he has had past experience of beatings and the god because he cannot suffer pain. So we see here that the slave cannot possibly be allowed to benefit by changing places with his master: 'it would be ridiculous,' says Dionysus, 'if my slave here were to wallow in luxury while his ill-starred master had to take punches from him' (542ff.). And indeed this indispensable slave, who temporarily takes on his master's role, remains a completely common individual. While chatting with Aeacus, who serves as a slave in the Underworld, he finds out how similar the minds of all servants are and takes pleasure in recalling the small delights of a slave's life: cursing and grumbling, plotting, eavesdropping and gossiping (738ff.). Such a character cannot be allowed to remain on the stage when the essential part of the plot, the contest between the poets, is reached. When the play enters its climax, Xanthias leaves the stage. So the greater part that he plays does not lead to an affirmation of his dignity as a human being. Aristophanes does indeed see this society, in which Euripides appears as the spokesman of the worthless intellectuals, as declining, and is making a serious point when he compares it to the hoplite state of Aeschylus. But even under these conditions of decline, the slave—however dependent one may be on him—remains a figure who breathes, but lacks a soul.

Even in Aristophanes' last work, the much-admired and much-copied *Plutus*, the barrier between master and slave remains. The world the dramatist conjures up is the completely private existence of the poor peasant Chremylus, his family and fellow-demesmen. In such a society as this, which has no other interests but profit and a life of pleasure, the slave Carion acquires an important role. Even if he only comes at the bottom of the list of members of the peasant household (the master, his wife, children and servants, the dog, you yourself, and the sow' 1103ff.), he is nevertheless a major figure who is characterized as an individual. He participates from start to finish and is given five monologues to his master's six. His role supplements that of Chremylus, indeed, the two figures are in some respects interchangeable: master and slave agree in thinking that the only thing one cannot have enough of is money (188ff.). But the playwright is still interested first and foremost in the moral decline of the citizen-body, and he only lets slaves, who are so much at home in the material world, play such a great part in order to satirize their dependence on hopes and desires—their lack of freedom, in fact. Carion lectures his master (45ff.), he makes fun of the avaricious old farmers (253ff.), he has no respect whatsoever for his simple-minded mistress with her old-fashioned religious views, he criticizes the gods, mocks the activities that go on in the sanctuary of Asclepius (627ff.) and after Plutus recovers his sight and the gods are no longer brought any offerings, he makes the most of his victory over Hermes, who now has to be content with a position as his servant (1097ff.). But through all this he remains an ordinary vulgar slave, sly enough to know when to flatter and when to insult his master, a braggart who only takes risks when there is no danger involved, greedy and boorish. Chremylus and Carion may be equally avaricious, but they nevertheless continue to belong to two different worlds. There are some good things in life which are valued even when one has had enough of them just for the moment: in the case of the free man these are love, music, honour, heroism, ambition and status, but for the slave bread, sweets, cakes, figs, dumplings and porridge (189ff.). Slavery is an institution accepted by Chremylus as perfectly natural. Penia asks him who would submit to doing the work of smiths, shipbuilders and wheelwrights, of tailors and shoemakers, potters, launderers and tanners, and agricultural work in general, if all men were well off and could afford not to do anything they did not want to, and he answers in all innocence that the slaves would be there to do all the laborious work. Of course, he then has to admit that no wealthy man would be willing any longer to devote himself to the dangerous work of slave-hunting and trading (510–25). But however clever he may be, Carion does not even think of the possibility that slaves might be given their freedom. This is all the more striking since at the beginning of the play he bewails his lack of rights and later (147f.)[30] says of himself: 'I myself became a slave for a few pence of silver, because some people are wealthier than others.'

Whatever the reason why he fell into slavery in Caria, whether to pay off a debt, because he sold himself, or was sold as a child, he had at one time been free. It would, therefore, have been appropriate, and in harmony with the poetic purpose of this comedy, if the problem of slavery as such had been examined through the person of Carion; but this is precisely what does not happen. The humanity of slaves has yet to be discovered, and it seems that there is still a long way to go before we reach Menander's creation of the figure of a pure and noble slave.[31]

We might pause for a moment to compare Aristophanes' slaves with the servants of seventeenth- and eighteenth-century European comedy—a comedy written for a society very much dependent on class distinctions. There is perhaps a certain similarity in the dramatic function of Athenian slaves and European servants in the plot of this kind of play, and the slaves of Menander, Plautus and Terence may well

[30] The paradosis is:

ἔγωγέ τοι διὰ μικρὸν ἀργυρίδιον
δοῦλος γεγένημαι διὰ τὸ μὴ πλουτεῖν ἴσως.

Cf. scholiast on 148 in the Codex Ravennas: πρότερον ὢν ἐλεύθερος.

[31] C. Langer *De servi persona apud Menandrum* (dissertation, Bonn 1919); A. Körte 'Die Menschen Menanders' *Berichte über die Verhandlungen der Sächsischen Akademie der Wissenschaften zu Leipzig* 89 (1937), 23f.; cf. W. Schadewaldt *Griechisches Theater* 524ff.

have formed the link between them. But if we try to apply these considerations sociologically, we will immediately find huge differences between these two worlds; for while the slaves of Aristophanes stand outside society, the servants are on the lowest rung of a social system whose patriarchal structure shows that it is an association covering the whole of humanity. From this position it was possible for the barber Figaro (1784) on the eve of the French Revolution to speak on behalf of the exploited and become the herald of social upheaval.[32] In the case of Aristophanes, the exclusion of slaves from society is obvious and final; and this corresponded to the views and behaviour of most of his contemporaries.[33] According to the dominant conception, a citizen, who attained human perfection as a member of his political society, had to be liberated from hard manual labour; there were lower kinds of humanity to do work of this kind, in particular the barbarians. One must also take into account the harsh custom that was still current, of treating an enemy defeated and captured in battle as part of one's property. Fifth-century Greeks, conscious of their superiority, considered slaves as tools, and wherever possible put domestic and industrial work onto their shoulders; they deeply despised them, and treated them decently, not because they saw in them men like themselves, but because they were prudent as owners and magnanimous as masters. They could not imagine a life without servants who possessed no rights. Though some of the fairy-tale comedies of Crates and Pherecrates may, as certain fragments seem to indicate, have depicted a fool's paradise in which there was no need for slaves,[34] yet even in Aristophanes' communistic Utopia slaves are taken for granted as agricultural workers, the only difference being that in this futuristic paradise everyone would have the same number of slaves.[35] And there is one other point which Praxagora in Aristo-

[32] For the influence of ancient characters on later literature see W. Süss *Aristophanes und die Nachwelt* (Leipzig 1911), esp. 193f.; O. Rommel *Die Alt-Wiener Volkskomödie* (Vienna 1952), 153ff. On Figaro and social comedy cf. H. Kindermann *Meister der Komödie* 198ff.

[33] Cf. the detailed discussion of popular ideas about slavery in the fifth century in R. Schlaifer 'Greek theories of slavery from Homer to Aristotle' *HSCP* 47 (1936), 184ff. (= Finley 112ff.).

[34] W. Schmid–O. Stählin *Griechische Literaturgeschichte* IV (Munich 1946), 90ff., 99f.; O. Weinreich in the appendix to Aristophanes in the *Bibliothek der alten Welt* II (1953), 394f., 403; and Ch. II below.

[35] *Ecclesiazusae* 593, 651; R. von Pöhlmann *Geschichte der sozialen Frage und des Sozialismus in der antiken Welt*[3] (Munich 1925), 315ff.

phanes' *Ecclesiazusae* would like to see changed, namely that slave-girls should no longer be allowed to compete with free women in matters of sex.[36]

It was at this very time that philosophical criticism of the *polis* and its laws broke like a storm over this age in which the structure of society was as we have seen upheld by such rigid conventions. This was the achievement of the Sophists. With an appeal to unwritten laws, Hippias postulated the existence of a natural justice, and declared that it was contrary to such natural justice for one man to be the master of another. 'For it is only according to law and custom that one man is a slave, another free; there is no distinction in nature. Therefore it is unjust; for it is based on force alone.'[37] Antiphon put forward a belief in the equality of all mankind: 'Barbarians or Greeks, we have all been created with a nature that is identical in all respects . . . for we all breathe through our mouth and nose and use our hands to eat.'[38] The influence that the sophistic antithesis of *physis* and *nomos* had on Greek thought in general is inestimable, yet it was not able to weaken the reality of slavery. Other Sophists brought forward equally persuasive rational arguments proving the natural inequality of men, and the rule of the strong over the weak. In the fifth century there was perhaps only a single profession that required of its members almost the same obligations towards slaves as towards free men: the medical profession. In the famous Hippocratic Oath the physician vows to abstain from sexual intercourse with patients be they men or women, free or slave.[39] The medical treatment of slaves must therefore have been a fairly regular occurrence. Case-histories of slaves, and in particular of

[36] *Eccles.* 718ff.

[37] These are the words which Aristotle (*Politics* 1, 3 = 1253b20ff.) uses to express the ideas of a group of Sophists which we may suppose to have included Hippias: W. Nestle *Vom Mythos zum Logos*² (Stuttgart 1942), 369ff.; *ibid.* 345 for the later use and practical application of this theory by Alcidamas. On the problem of Greek views on natural justice in general, cf. V. Ehrenberg *Archiv für Geschichte der Philosophie* 35 (1923), 119ff. (= *Polis und Imperium* (Zürich and Stuttgart 1965), 359ff.); E. Wolf *Griechisches Rechtsdenken* II (Frankfurt 1952), 76ff.

[38] *Vorsokratiker* 44 B 2 (Vol. II, 353); Nestle *op. cit.* 377.

[39] K. Deichgräber 'Die ärztliche Standesethik des hippokratischen Eides' *Quellen und Studien zur Geschichte der Naturwissenschaft und der Medizin* 3 (1933), 29ff., esp. 37f.; F. Büchner *Der Eid des Hippokrates* (Freiburg i. Br. 1945); K. Deichgräber *Professio medici. Zum Vorwort des Scribonius Largus* (*Ak. d. Wiss. u. d. Lit.* 1950, 9), 8ff.

female slaves, occur in several books of the Hippocratic *Epidemics.*[40] Even if these books only date to the fourth century, the evidence seems to suggest that doctors had already at an earlier date treated slaves as their patients, not merely in order to keep the indispensable work force in good health, but because their professional ethics were truly humanitarian. It is also possible that Plato's suggestion[41] that the medical profession ought to employ slave physicians belonging to free physicians to treat those patients who were slaves may be based on the actual practice of doctors at the time. When appreciating medical ethics, one must, of course, take into account the close ties between medicine and religion; indeed a certain religious spirit can be traced in the formulation of the oath, at least in the promise to keep life and skill holy and untainted. There was on the whole a much more powerful impulse towards bringing slaves within the pale of society from the side of religion (in the cult of Dionysus and the Eleusinian Mysteries as later in the worship of foreign divinities) than from the rationalistic enlightenment. It was an accepted fact among the initiated that the godhead would sometimes take possession of a slave, and that a free man could not lose the charisma he had received from the god even when he fell into slavery: 'The divine power remains even in the heart of one enslaved.'[42]

Euripides was a dramatist who was as open to the sophistic movement as to the new religious tendencies of his time; he was an Athenian who combined a high degree of political awareness with an ability to comprehend the outside world. His view of existence enabled him as a poet to discover new areas of reality and make use of them in his tragedies. He was familiar with slavery and the problems it posed. But it is rather an oversimplification to argue, as Wilhelm Nestle does,[43]

[40] I am grateful to my colleague Dr. Diller for pointing out to me the following references: *Epidemics* 2, 4.5; 4, 9; 13 and 38; 19; 25 and 35, where we are explicitly told that she was a barbarian woman; 41; 85 and 87. On the dates of the *Epidemics* see K. Deichgräber *Abhandlungen der Berliner Akademie* 1933, 3. A study of slaves as patients and physicians has yet to be written.

[41] *Laws* 4, 720a–e and 9, 857cd; also P. Lain-Entralgo 'Die ärztliche Hilfe im Werk Platons' *Sudhoffs Archiv für Geschichte der Medizin und der Naturwissenschaft* 46 (1962), 193ff.

[42] Aeschylus *Agamemnon* 1084.

[43] W. Nestle *Euripides, der Dichter der griechischen Aufklärung* (Stuttgart 1901), 348ff. E. Wolf *Griechisches Rechtsdenken* II, 373ff., sees Euripides as the poet of δημοτικὴ ἀρετή—without considering the question of slaves; cf. 397, 428, 432, 458; the suggestion made on p. 473 that Euripides considered the validity of the principles of 'the demythologized νόμος and powerless δίκη' as applying also to non-Greeks and slaves remains unsubstantiated.

that we can recognize the poet's own voice in the many speeches about slavery delivered on the stage. We can often hear Euripides' figures say that servants are there to do the hard work and obey in silence, that their character cannot be depended upon, their meanness is inherited, their status is to be despised. It would be begging the question to say that Euripides is only reiterating popular prejudices in these utterances, while his personal convictions are to be found in those passages where the human worth of a slave is awarded recognition, and slavery as such is questioned. If it is in fact at all possible to recognize the playwright's own opinions, then it is surely only by appreciating individual utterances within their context, individual characters within the unity of a play, and individual plays within the poet's work as a whole. This method is the only adequate one and may lead to a conclusion different from that which is widely accepted.

The world we meet in tragedy is a heroic one. Heroes and royal women suffer a high fate in partnership with the gods, governed in the last resort by an inexorable necessity. Of course, their outward status is not essential to Euripides' nobles; for a contemporary audience they serve as typical representatives of mortality, who suffer and survive the destiny of human existence. But their mythical origins give them something of the semi-divine monarchy and class-structure of an earlier age, and they hand this heritage on to the world of the city-state.[44] This is the poetic reality to which we must refer our appreciation of Euripides' characterization of slaves and his speeches about slavery.

Such princes and noblewomen always need servants at their side (ὀπαδοί, οἰκέται, πρόσπολοι), who can be sent to fetch anything they need or open a door, prepare a sacrifice or tell a ship to set sail. The order is quite simply, 'let someone go and . . .', 'someone bring me . . .' or 'you go and . . .'. Here the anonymity of these servants is the surest proof that their existence and activity are taken for granted. There have to be slaves at the palace gate; if none are there, then it is a sure sign that something is wrong and a catastrophe is threatening.[45] In addition to the existence of these cyphers, the worst aspect of slavery is sometimes depicted, if not in fact, then in the imagination of one of the characters; captured women will be set to work at scrubbing, grinding corn or baking bread, and forced to sleep with some vile bought slave;[46] kidnapped men will be put to work in the galleys or

[44] As Ernst Buschor has pointed out again recently (see p. 18 n. 51 below).

[45] *Alcestis* 89f.

[46] *Hecuba* 350ff., *The Trojan Women* 190ff., 491ff.

quarries or at the treadmill.[47] Heavy physical work is always left to slaves, and when Theseus, the champion of Athenian humanity, is said personally to have carried the fallen warriors from the battlefield, washed their wounds and prepared their burial, the need for an apology is felt.[48]

The contempt the nobility feels for slaves is shown by some of the more general remarks they make about them: they are supposed to be cowardly and treacherous, and slaves from Lydia and Phrygia are particularly worthless. A slave's existence is considered so miserable that it is said to their face that death must be a relief to them.[49] But the poet does raise certain persons out of this humble population of servants and maids to give them an individual character and an important position in the structure of his plays. These are principally tutors and nurses, who can play a significant part in the plot as the confidants of princes and princesses. Already in Aeschylus slaves occur as the confidants of their aristocratic masters;[50] they are genuine figures in that mythical world of the kings in which aged servants and housemaids, men-at-arms and nurses all have their proper place. In Euripides, these trusted servants are brought nearer to their masters as human beings than they are in Aeschylus, and very much more so than in Sophocles; and quite often the nobility of their masters has a positive effect on them. A preference for characters of this kind to serve as foils to the princes and in particular princesses can be traced throughout the poet's work.

The noble Alcestis receives the deepest sympathy from her servants and maids, doubly effective in a situation that reveals that her relatives have failed her in a particularly dreadful way. It is accepted by her slaves that she herself had bound them to her by her behaviour as a mistress, in that she had been like a mother to her slaves (768ff.), and had shaken hands and taken her leave of each one as she died (192ff.). The poignancy of Medea's terrible suffering and hate-motivated behaviour is felt particularly deeply because of the respect shown to her by her faithful slaves, her nurse and the tutor of her sons (1ff.). Andromache, the king's daughter captured in war, has the slave-girl who served her in Troy by her side in her new existence. This maid overcomes her fear, helps her to face every danger and shows a loyalty

[47] *Cyclops* 238ff. [48] *Suppliants* 762ff.

[49] *Orestes* 1115, 1369ff., 1506ff., 1522f.

[50] H. Ahlers *Die Vertrautenrolle in der griechischen Tragödie* (dissertation, Giessen 1911).

and willingness to sacrifice herself which could hardly have been outdone by a free woman (87ff.). When Menelaus finds Helen again in Egypt, a servant who had been his man-at-arms at Troy comes to him as a messenger, a loyal slave of the family; he calls his master simply by name and addresses his mistress as 'daughter' (597, 700, 711). He is an old man with much experience of life, who philosophizes about God and Fate and seeks a solution for his status worthy of a human being (728ff.): 'Though I may have been born a slave, I would like to be counted among those slaves that are noble, and at least have the heart and mind of a free man, if not the name. That is better than having to suffer two evils: having to serve everyone in the house, and feeling mean as well.'

So the possibility arises here and with other characters in Euripides that someone can overcome his slavery through internal freedom. The choruses of slave-women who often appear in the poet's tragedies can also raise themselves to a level of spiritual freedom. It is in itself significant that Euripides, following the example of earlier tragedians, makes captives and slave-women represent the religious community in these plays as the chorus, and accompany the actions of the great by expressing the attitudes and opinions of the *polis*. He repeatedly makes his choruses outspoken supporters of one of the protagonists (*Hecuba*, *Helen*); the slave women of *Iphigeneia in Tauris* take part in the action of the play, and, following Sophocles, Euripides even goes so far as to make the chorus of captured Trojan women the heroines of his drama of that name. It is particularly liberating that it should be precisely the chorus of captives in *Helen* who oppose a tyrannical command and speak out on behalf of a higher justice, even to the point of offering to sacrifice their own lives (1627ff.). They are of course Greek women, who retain their Hellenic spirit in a barbarian environment, and their role as a chorus makes them very different from the individual servants who stand by their masters as real slaves.

The Euripidean figure of the noble slave is an important example of the way Greek thought tried to break through its own barriers. Yet it is questionable whether this figure in fact corresponds to reality. In the postscript to his translation of the *Medea*, Ernst Buschor says: 'It seems that it was Euripides who inspired all those figures of loyal servants on Attic gravestones that from now on surround their masters almost on a level of human equality.'[51] If this is in fact so, it would

[51] E. Buschor *Euripides Medea, Hippolytos, Herakles übertragen und erläutert* (Munich 1952), 84.

very much suggest that these loyal servants and noble slaves are the creations of literature, intended to glorify the nobility of their masters and mistresses. They generally stand at the side of the action, and even where they do play a major role in the plot—and this is decisive—they are allowed no share in tragedy. For example, Phaedra's nurse, a devoted servant and intimate confidante, is able to get her mistress to admit to her illicit love and then passes this information on to Hippolytus; through this action of hers she brings about a crisis in the plot and the ruin of the principal characters. But after she has fulfilled her task she is dismissed by her mistress (*Hippol.* 708f.): 'Get out of my sight and scheme about your own affairs alone. I can take care of mine better by myself.' At this point, where a major decision has to be taken on a serious matter, we come to a parting of ways. It would contradict the nature of tragedy—drama concerned with gods and heroes—if this slave-woman, this gossiping sophist and willing procuress, were allowed to participate in anything even remotely connected with suffering or responsibility. A subsidiary role of a similar kind is that of Creusa's confidant, an ancient slave of the family who now wants to render thanks for the sustenance he has received from his mistress, and feels himself obliged to risk his own life in order to avenge an insult to her. He takes the initiative, persuades Creusa to approve his plan to murder Ion, and undertakes the execution of the crime himself. When he is caught in the act and convicted, he betrays his mistress. He had self-consciously declared:[52] 'It is only the name that a slave should be ashamed of: apart from that he is no worse than a free man in anything, if only he is loyal.' He has now been seen not to be loyal, but as a slave he does not have to answer for it; he is incapable of a tragic existence. I think that there could have been no more impressive way for the poet to show how real the division of mankind into free men and slaves seemed to him.

However many variations there may be, the good slaves of Euripides cannot hide the fact that their characters have a positive objective: they contribute substantially towards showing up their masters' unique and unattainable positions, precisely by fulfilling an important role and representing the kind of worldly prudence that does have something to be said for it. They express their practical experience in high-sounding maxims, they know where a human being's weaknesses

[52] *Ion* 854ff. The antithesis between the external reputation and the actual worth of a slave occurs several times: Nestle *Euripides* 357ff.; *Vom Mythos zum Logos* 345.

lie, and are quick to find casuistic justifications for questionable actions. 'Always please your masters' is their first principle,[53] the other being to avoid harm to themselves when they are doing this. It is taken for granted that they will always be attracted towards the winning side, and that when their lives are at stake, they will let their masters down, no matter how attached they may be to them. They prefer a minor position to great rank, security to daring. Their sense of honour is somehow different, and they are a class of their own.

This same fact is also proclaimed by the impressive figures of nobles who have fallen into slavery by being captured in war or exposed as children—Hecuba, Cassandra and Andromache, Ion, Alexander and some others. They were born noble and remain so as slaves; they act nobly in enduring their tragic fate.

Euripides showed to shattering effect what dreadful consequences capture and enslavement could have for the free, particularly those of royal birth, in the figures of the Trojan captives in his *Hecuba* and *The Trojan Women*, written during the terrors of the Peloponnesian War. It is the women and children who have to suffer every ordeal entirely alone: while their city burns and the bodies of their menfolk lie around unburied, the conquerors cast lots for the women and girls; they are parted from their children and taken to a foreign country. There is no vestige of legal protection for them and it is hardly even accepted that those who had not been killed in the actual capture of a town could not be put to death in cold blood afterwards.[54] The captives, as the booty of their conquerors, would share their masters' beds as concubines, and do the hard tasks their mistresses set them at home. The only thing they would still have to hope for in their situation is that they might find a kind master.

Those who are most grievously affected are the women of noble rank for whom slavery is the height of disgrace, a sudden fall into the void. 'Better die than be enslaved', therefore, becomes the watchword of the strong; and even those who are barred from this course retain their nobility of character in that they overcome their degradation by reliance on themselves alone—they are scarcely ever supported by friends. Hecuba in her captivity restores herself to a position of power and respect; it is not freedom she wants, but the revenge for her son's

[53] *Alcmene* fr.93.

[54] *Hecuba* 288ff., *The Children of Heracles* 961, 966, 970, 1009ff.; cf. the Greek *nomos* referred to by Thucydides, that it was not permissible to kill people who had raised their hands in surrender: 3, 58.3; 66.2; 67.6.

murder that is her due as a person of royal rank. Although a slave, it is she who frees Agamemnon from his fears, carries out her dreadful deed, is granted a trial and justifies her action. In this way she breaks the chains of slavery in a fashion no less royal than that of her daughter Polyxena, who escapes from slavery by her sacrificial death and therefore retains her freedom even in the Underworld (*Hecuba* 404ff., 550ff., 864ff.). The prophetess Cassandra does not lose her divine inspiration when she is enslaved. The marriage-hymn she sings in her ecstasy at her forced union with Agamemnon has an air of foreboding; she prophesies the ruin of the House of Atreus, a ruin that she brings about through her own destruction, avenging herself in her slavery and triumphant at the moment of death (*The Trojan Women* 308ff.). Although enslaved and humbled, Andromache exhibits no traits of slavery and becomes a touchstone of nobility of character for everyone around her. However much she may accommodate herself to the situation that has been forced upon her, there is one thing that she is certain of: 'Far be it from me to betray myself!' Because her spirit is unsubdued, her marriage to Neoptolemus can prove the high value of human relationships and a woman's maturity to all the free men and women around her—people in reality totally dependent on the conventions of their state, class and material wishes (*Andromache* 191ff.; 184ff.).

I think we may accept that these are Euripides' own convictions: real slaves, even if they are noble according to their possibilities, never reach the full stature of individuals; nobles on the other hand retain their freedom in captivity, for they are incapable of lowering themselves. Both sides often speak about the fate of slavery, but no one suggests that slavery ought not to exist. Nor does this happen in the tragedy *Alexander*, of which only a few fragments survive, and which centres on the problem of slavery and nobility.[55] Paris/Alexander, exposed by his mother Hecuba, is taken care of by some shepherds and brought up as their slave. On coming of age, he takes part in a tournament of the free citizens of Troy, unknown to anyone, and defeats them all, including his brothers Hector and Deiphobus. A

[55] The latest edition of the fragments and reconstruction of the play as a whole is by B. Snell *Euripides Alexandros und andere Strassburger Papyri* (*Hermes Einzelschriften* 5; 1937); for an interpretation see C. Lefke *De Euripidis Alexandro* (dissertation, Münster 1936), who accepts W. Crönert's view (*Nachrichten der Göttinger Gesellschaft* 1922, 15) that Euripides attacks the institution of slavery in this play. I would like to put on record here the help of the students who took part in my Graduate Seminar during the Winter Semester 1951/2.

bitter dispute results when he is awarded the prize, and the case is taken to court for a decision. Whereas Hector, it seems, judges the slave's action only by his noble intentions, Deiphobus takes upon himself the part of the prosecution, accuses Paris of participating in the contest illegally and attacks slaves in general:[56] 'I have proved my case. That is how vulgar all slaves are—they only think about their bellies, and have no thought for the consequences of their actions.'

Paris defends himself personally and retorts scornfully to his opponent:[57] 'Vile people like you have become slaves in all but name, for Fortune has made you so.' In his view it is precisely through *Tyche*, through luck and prosperity, that a person can develop a servile nature even without being called a slave. After Priam has given judgement in favour of Paris, the chorus of shepherds chants:[58]

> It would be superfluous for us to glorify man's nobility.
> For when we took our origin and arose from the earth
> our mother, the clay gave us all the same appearance;
> we did not each create our own.
> Nature's creation is equally base and noble;
> it is Custom, and Time, which make people proud of their rank.
> True nobility lies in good sense and judgement,
> and God alone, not wealth, bestows it.

The opinion here expressed as the conclusion of a philosophical cosmogony[59] is that at the Creation all men were given the same status, and that differences of class are due to Custom (νόμος) alone. Opposed to this convention is nobility of character (εὐγένεια), recognizable in an individual's prudence (τὸ φρόνιμον) and intelligence (τὸ συνετόν) bestowed by God and not by wealth. So there is, after all, a certain nobility with which men may be endowed, and in that case we may suppose that they can also be endowed with an ignoble nature, the nature of a slave. If we are for once justified in taking the voice of the chorus as representing the poet's own opinion, this would mean that Euripides believed that nobility and servility were founded in the

[56] Fr. 33 (ed. Snell).
[57] Fr. 38 (ed. Snell):

> ὦ παγκάκιστοι καὶ τὸ δοῦλον οὐ λόγῳ
> ἔχοντες, ἀλλὰ τῇ τύχῃ κεκτημένοι.

[58] Fr. 40 (ed. Snell).
[59] S. Luria *Aegyptus* 5 (1924), 326ff., *Hermes* 64 (1929), 491ff.

god-given faculties of an individual person and not in original racial differences. Common sense and good judgement are the salient features of a nobleman marked out to govern; the unintelligent who think only in terms of material welfare and do not consider the future must obey him as his slaves. But even those who have this nobility may suffer grievously at the hands of fate, as is shown by this trilogy of which *Alexander* is, of course, only the first part. In the third part, *The Trojan Women*, noble ladies are led off to captivity, and, with their complete lack of rights, it is up to them to prove that they are slaves only in name.

Euripides, then, threw light on the human possibilities inherent in various forms of slavery; he cast a particular spotlight on domestic slaves, who were generally well intentioned despite their insuperable limitations; and he revealed the dreadful hardships of captivity in war, particularly for those endowed with nobility. The only exemplary picture he depicts is that of the activities and experiences of the temple-slave Ion. In accordance with his own preference for the contemplative life, he gives us an unparalleled example of the σεμνὸς βίος in the person of this *hierodoulos*. Abandoned as a child, Ion was brought up by the priestess of Apollo at Delphi; having grown up he looks after the temple as a slave, is supported by Apollo's altar and enjoys the protection of the shrine. The young man is deeply content in his divine duties, which are much superior to serving mortals; he prefers the god-given peace of his way of life to the restlessness of *polis* and kingship.[60] This glorification of an unfree temple-slave is doubly striking, occurring as it does in a tragedy whose dominant theme is the value of aristocratic blood and horror of servile origins. The conditions for temple-slaves, well attested at the major shrines of the Greek world,[61] will in general, of course, have been rather better than for those in domestic service or small workshops. Yet it is quite clear that Euripides intended his poetic glorification of the temple-slave to point a way out of the busy *polis* and the terrifying arena of power-politics—anticipating future generations and their preference for 'leisure, which is man's greatest boon' (*Ion* 634).[62]

These few passages from classical literature show that in Athens,

[60] Esp. *Ion* 52ff., 128ff., 585ff.

[61] Hepding *RE* VIII, 1459ff.; Bömer II, 149ff., III, 215; on the *Ion* in particular, II, 44ff.

[62] K. I. Vourveris Παιδιὰ καὶ παιδεία (Athens 1956); E. Ch. Welskopf *Probleme der Musse im alten Hellas* (Berlin 1962).

'the school of Hellas', the institution of slavery with all its shocking consequences remained inviolate. Even the most enlightened minds thought it perfectly logical that there should be people without any rights to do the servile work, with no share at all in civic life, nor indeed in that human personality which could only attain fulfilment in the social environment of the *polis*. The accident of birth, foreign origin or the misfortune of capture in war may as a result of the new ideas of the Sophists no longer have been accepted as in themselves sufficient reasons why a person should be a slave; nevertheless the belief remained that certain people existed and must exist, who because of their nature—because of their lack of insight or intelligence—could not conceivably be anything but slaves. There was no way of escaping this genuine slavery bestowed by nature. The idea that slavery was a necessity is confirmed by the remarkable rarity of manumission during this period, and the fact that when it did occur it was only on the condition that the freedman would still have certain obligations towards his former master—in other words, a liberated slave was still to some extent bound to the position and nature of a slave. The philosophers of the fourth century, who do not really come within our scope here, are in full agreement with the poets of the classical period. However much Plato opposes the enslaving of Greek prisoners of war, he clearly accepts that certain people are prevented by their nature from being anything other than slaves, and he supports an even more rigorous distinction between free men and slaves than that of the Athenian laws of the time.[63] And for Aristotle, as has often been pointed out, the relationship between master and slave is fundamental to human existence. Those men destined to rule are separated from the moment of birth from those destined to serve; the man who considers the future is a natural master, while he who acts out the essence of his life on a merely material plane is a born slave; barbarians are necessarily human beings of the inferior category. This spell that had been cast over Greek life and thought was only broken by the Macedonian Alexander and the Phoenician Zeno.

If we have become conscious of the limits of the humanitarianism of classical Greece this should not lead us either to criticize or to excuse the Greeks for their attitude to slavery. Those who are of the opinion that slavery is something entirely natural may admire the Greeks for having on the whole treated their slaves so liberally, and

[63] G. R. Morrow *Plato's Law of Slavery* (*University of Illinois Studies in Language and Literature* 25, 3; 1939).

indeed for having had doubts about the justice of the system at all. Whoever compares classical Greece with other civilizations and considers how difficult progress towards the abolition of slavery was in Western Europe, despite the fact that its civilization was moulded by Christianity and the Enlightenment, will come to appreciate the Greek approach. Nor should we lose sight of the fact that in industrialized countries today every productive person is in charge of a machine, which means that he is in charge of two or three dozen invisible technological slaves.[64] All we are concerned with here is to see this peculiarity of the Greeks in its proper perspective. We can appreciate Greek slavery as due both to that vitality which demanded that a man have a complete and active life even at the expense of others, and also to that way of thinking which looks on power not as the aimless discharge of brute force but rather as a rational instrument to bring about order. Slavery was essential to the existence both of this basic will to live and of the devotion to spiritual considerations. Even Plato's follower Heraclides Ponticus could state with all the conviction of the philosopher-ruler: 'Enjoyment and good living is reserved for free men, for this exalts and enhances the spirit. Labouring, on the other hand, is for slaves and inferior people, and that is why their character deteriorates.'[65] These forces fundamental to Hellenism succeeded in wresting the miraculous creation of the *polis* and its civilization from the poverty of the land, the inclemency of the climate and the opposition of a hostile world. Slavery and its attendant loss of humanity were part of the sacrifice which had to be paid for this achievement.

[64] H. Staudinger *Vom Aufstand der technischen Sklaven* (Essen 1947), 17.
[65] Athenaeus 12, 512a (= Müller *FHG* 2, 200 n.).

II

Slavery in Greek Utopias

In contemporary sociology and political science, the concept of Utopia has a wide range of meanings. The word is applied to a description of the perfect life which its author sees embodied on a distant island or believes to have been realized in the Golden Age at the beginning of time. But a rationally constructed blueprint for future human existence is also often put forward in the form of a Utopia, particularly when it is utopianism rather than ideology which is considered the major force towards the remodelling of existing reality.[1] This extension of the concept to include both *utopia d'evasione* and *utopia di ricostruzione*[2] is also wide enough to cover the variety of ideas which the Greeks had of a better world; and for this reason it has been widely applied in the study of antiquity, both to the interpretation of myths and festivals going back to the prehistoric age of the gods and to philosophical and literary descriptions of what human life might be like.[3]

This chapter originally appeared in *Rivista Storica dell'Antichità* 1 (1971), 19–32.

[1] Of the extensive literature on this subject, mention must be made of E. Bloch *Das Prinzip Hoffnung* I (Frankfurt a.M. 1959), esp. 107ff., 161ff.; *Säkularisation und Utopie. Ebracher Studien, E. Forsthoff zum 65. Geburtstag* (Stuttgart 1967); *Utopie. Begriff und Phänomen des Utopischen* edited and with an introduction by A. Neusüss (*Soziologische Texte* 44; 1968).

[2] The distinction is that of A. Giannini 'Mito e utopia nella letteratura greca prima di Platone' *Rendiconti dell' Istituto Lombardo, Classe di Lettere* 101 (1967), 102.

[3] H. C. Baldry *Ancient Utopias* (Southampton 1956); K. Kerenyi 'Ursinn und Sinnwandel des Utopischen' in *Vom Sinn der Utopie* (*Eranos-Jahrbuch* 1963:

In some of these representations of a perfect society, the institution of slavery, so firmly rooted in the realities of Greek life, was questioned or even explicitly rejected. This applies both to legends about the world of gods and heroes and also to fairy-tales recalling a happy life in the past or in a timeless dream-world. But the established order also comes under attack in political theory, particularly in the case of models aiming at the complete realization of justice in the human community, and in the make-believe of literature that we find in comedy and in romances; and here the question is raised whether a human society could be imagined which does not have an un-free serving class forming its lowest stratum. A survey of these visions of paradise and programmes for a utopian future may help us to perceive the extent to which Greek thought found slavery repugnant, even if these sentiments were not strong enough to put a stop to such inhumanity.

The Greeks, and later the Romans, accepted the tradition that in the good old days men had lived a happy life without slaves. There is evidence that in several places in Greece the agricultural population celebrated festivals in which masters and slaves participated together. Among the Greeks, as among other peoples, this post-harvest festival was supposed to recreate during the days of leisure the freedom and equality which had been general at the beginning of time. Then in the seventh century we find the myth that at the beginning Cronus had created a golden race of men; Hesiod says of them (*Works and Days* 109ff.) that they lived like gods, 'remote and free from toil and grief' (113: νόσφιν ἄτερ τε πόνων καὶ ὀιζύος), they had all that men might need—'of her own accord the fertile earth bore fruit in plenty and abundance' (117f. καρπὸν δ' ἔφερεν ζείδωρος ἄρουρα αὐτομάτη πολλόν τε καὶ ἄφθονον). From this time on, the traditional agricultural festival at which slave and master were placed on one level was associated with the cult of Cronus, and the idea that all men had originally been equal was expressed in a drastic fashion by the custom that master and slave should eat together or even that slaves should be served by their masters. In Greece this took place at the Cronia, at

Zurich 1964), 9ff.; M. I. Finley 'Utopianism, Ancient and Modern' in *The Critical Spirit: Essays in honor of H. Marcuse* (Boston 1967), 3ff.; A. Giannini *op. cit.* 101ff. The connections between Greek aspirations and their actual political and social experiences is stressed by H. Braunert 'Theorie, Ideologie und Utopie im griechisch-hellenistischen Staatsdenken' *Geschichte in Wissenschaft und Unterricht* 14 (1963), 145ff.; id. 'Utopia. Antworten griechischen Denkens auf die Herausforderung durch soziale Verhältnisse' *Veröffentlichungen der Schleswig-Holsteinischen Universitätsgesellschaft* N.F. 51 (1969).

Rome and in Italy at the Saturnalia, and it is not easy to decide where these feasts for slaves originated and where they were taken over from elsewhere.[4] The notion that in this blessed age of Cronus (ὁ ἐπὶ Κρόνου βίος) gods had intercourse with men, that men lived a simple and pure life without any vices or degeneracy and that there were no slaves, retained its hold in the whole of the subsequent period.[5] Even historians went so far as to assert that slavery was still unknown at the time when the tribes reached Italy and Greece to settle there. Herodotus says this in his account of the quarrel between the Athenians and the Pelasgians (6, 137); Pompeius Trogus associates the rule of Saturn, with its absence of slaves or private property, with the age when Italy was inhabited by the Aborigines (Justin 43, 1.3); Plutarch includes among the customs introduced by Numa both the dinner given to slaves at the Saturnalia and the provision that those who helped to produce the annual harvest should be allowed a share in the first-fruits of the earth (*Comparison of Lycurgus and Numa* 1, 5).

One feature that always occurs in pictures of the Golden Age is the notion that men were able to live without troubles and labours.[6] The high status that the Stoics awarded to work (φιλοπονία) suggested to them that work was already an element of human activity during the reign of Cronus (as Aratus *Phaenomena* 105ff.), but this was exceptional. The reason why in its earlier days mankind could live without heavy labour and without slaves was thought to lie in the miraculous fertility of the earth. Hesiod says that she produced her fruits 'of her own accord' (αὐτομάτη). At an early date already, this concept of automatic production was associated with machines. Homer tells of miraculous wheels which Hephaestus fixed to his tripods so that they could move around by themselves (*Iliad* 18, 373ff.); he also narrates how golden figures shaped like serving-girls were able to hold and support their master Hephaestus (*Iliad* 18, 417ff.). But this idea of automation only really came into its own at a later date when the heavy demands that the exploitation of the soil made on labour were properly appreciated, and it was no longer so easy to explain how in earlier

[4] On the myths and cults of Cronus and Saturn cf. M. P. Nilsson *Geschichte der griechischen Religion* I² (1955), 510ff.; Bömer III, 173ff. Specifically on the reversal of the social order S. Luria 'Die Ersten werden die Letzten sein' *Klio* 22 (1969), 421ff.; also L. A. El'nitzkii's article on social concepts featured in the Saturnalia, *VDI* 1946, 4, 54ff.

[5] B. Gatz *Weltalter, goldene Zeit und sinnverwandte Vorstellungen Spudasmata* 16 (1967), 114ff., esp. 127f.

[6] Hesiod *Works and Days* 118f., cf. Giannini *op. cit.* 109f.

times life had been lived without slaves. From now on, when mimes or comedies were performed to amuse the populace at the festivals of rustic divinities, or when at the festival of Dionysus Athenian choruses decked out in fantastic masks gave a representation of an inverted make-believe existence, comic poets conjured up fairy-tale worlds in which there was an unending flow of good things, with wine pouring down like rain on the house-tops; a particular feature of these stories was that magic implements of every conceivable kind performed their functions automatically. Such a paradise could be thought of as having existed in the most distant past, but could also be conceived of in a happy future; on one occasion it was even said to have been seen in the Underworld, and on another it was ascribed to a magic land in the East: in each case it was associated with an absence of slavery.

Of the fragments which Athenaeus (6, 267e–270a) has preserved of these fairy-tale comedies, I would like to make no more than a passing reference to the fantastic elements in the *Miners* (Μεταλλῆς: fr. 108 in Edmonds' *Fragments of Attic Comedy* I (Leiden 1957), 246f.) and the *Persians* (Πέρσαι: fr. 130, I, 254f.) by Pherecrates, who was particularly interested in these utopian motifs. On the other hand a dialogue from Crates' comedy *Wild Animals* (Θηρία: fr. 14f., I, 158f.) deserves some emphasis. It seems that in this passage a demagogue is promising his audience an age without slaves. When asked if this would mean that even old men will have to do their own work as best they can, the speaker replies that this would by no means be the case for they would be able to make each individual object set itself in motion:

> Each article of furniture will come to him when he calls it. Place yourself here, table! Get yourself ready for dinner! Get to work, my little kneading-trough. Fill up, ladle. Where's the cup got to? Get yourself washed, while you're about it. Over here, barley-cake. The pot ought to be serving up the beets. Get a move on, fish. 'But I'm not yet done properly on the other side.' Then be so good as to turn yourself over. With oil, please, and salt.

It is automation, therefore, that will make a life of leisure possible and slavery unnecessary—an idea that was not just left to poets to toy with. As time went on, philosophers too pointed out that life and its enjoyment require a wide variety of tools, and they came to the conclusion that, as living tools, slaves could not be dispensed with. Even Aristotle (*Politics* I, 4 = 1253b33ff.) used this argument to justify slavery:

> If every tool we had could perform its function, either at our bidding or itself perceiving the need, like the statues that were made by Daedalus or the wheeled tripods of Hephaestus, of which the poet says that 'self-moved they enter the assembly of the gods'—and if the shuttles in a loom could fly to and fro or a plectrum play on a lyre automatically, then manufacturers would have no need of assistants nor masters of slaves.

It is an argument which even today continues to be viewed with a certain degree of respect; for again and again we are faced with calculations intended to prove that we no longer need servile helpers simply because we control a large number of mechanical slaves—between fourteen and forty-two in the opinion of a German scholar,[7] or over 185, as we are informed by an American,[8] although it is pointed out that these 'power-slaves' are not generally assigned to us individually, and that they can perform only certain specific functions, so that they even have the effect of limiting our own freedom of action.

The imagination of comic poets in inventing better worlds was inexhaustible, and it is possible that these fairy-tale comedies, like the myths of the Golden Age, were particularly popular among the lower social classes and introduced them to ideas of social changes. As a writer of political comedy (in which we must generally recognize the opinions of the ruling class), Aristophanes, of course, takes great pleasure in making fun of these people with their ideas of putting right the world. His fantasies were even more radical than those of his predecessors; he could suggest that Athens might be deserted and a new world founded in the aery realm of the birds. On another occasion he confronted the Utopians with the unpleasant realities of the world of misery in which we live, and stressed that we could not do without slavery. In the *Ecclesiazusae* Praxagora describes in glowing terms the communistic society that will come about when the women have taken over the government (583ff.); no longer will one man have many slaves and another none at all, but everything will be common and equal. When asked the straightforward question, who would work the land under these conditions, she gives an even more straightforward answer: the slaves (651). It may well be that

[7] H. Staudinger *Vom Aufstand der technischen Sklaven* (Essen 1947), 17.

[8] B. de Jouvenel 'Utopia for Practical Purposes' in *Utopias and Utopian Thought* ed. F. E. Manuel (Boston 1966), 224f.

slaves were to become state property in this future society in which money would be abolished and common ownership of the land proclaimed.[9] But the institution of slavery remains, and it is ludicrous for the women's leader to go on as she does about the realization of equality. In Aristophanes' last play, the *Plutus*, poverty is depicted without qualification as the decisive spur to human activity, and slavery as a necessary concomitant. Here there is a verbal contest between the personification of poverty (Penia) and the farmer Chremylus, who wants to have sight restored to blind wealth (487ff.). Penia demonstrates that if the necessities of life were all equally distributed, no one would bother to learn a skill or acquire useful knowledge (511 f.: οὔτε τέχνην ἂν τῶν ἀνθρώπων οὔτ' ἂν σοφίαν μελετῴη οὐδείς); all labouring, ploughing and other work would cease. Penia counters Chremylus' objection that slaves would naturally do this work by remarking bluntly that in a situation where every man had become rich, no one would want to expose himself to the perils involved in kidnapping people to supply the slave-market (522ff.). Material want is here seen as a culturally creative force[10] and the problems which the slave's existence raises are ignored.

While comic poets were putting onto the stage their dream-worlds with and without slaves, the Sophists had already begun to subject the inherited order to criticism and to demand that state and society should be remodelled on a rational basis.[11] They contrasted *physis* with *nomos*, natural with artificial rules, and some, like Hippias, stated that slavery constituted an infringement of natural justice. Others appealed to the natural inequality of men and advocated the rule of the stronger. It was on these general views that philosophical blueprints of the perfect society were based; we know of some of them through fragments or excerpts. Aristotle briefly mentions the political models of Phaleas and Hippodamus in *Politics* 2, 7f. (= 1266a39–1268b22), although he does not indeed make it entirely clear what the position of slavery was in these ideal societies. The intention behind Phaleas' model was to remove the main cause

[9] J. Pečirka 'Aristophanes Ekklesiazusen und die Utopien in der Krise der Polis' *Wissenschaftliche Zeitschrift der Humboldt-Universität zu Berlin, Gesellschafts- und sprachwissenschaftliche Reihe* XI (1963), 215ff.

[10] From Protagoras to Epicurus, theories about the origin of civilization consider material need to be the motive for all innovation; cf. Gatz *op. cit.* 144ff.

[11] On the position of Greek philosophers in general cf. R. Schlaifer 'Greek Theories of Slavery' *HSCP* 47 (1936), 165ff. (= Finley 93ff.).

of revolution by establishing an equal division of property; he laid down that there should be equality in the possession of land and equality of education, and that craftsmen should work for the state, but he clearly countenanced the continued existence of slavery, as we can see from Aristotle's remark (1267b10) about the possibility of owning wealth in the form of slaves.

The Sophistic advance was arrested by Socrates and Plato. They criticized strongly the weaknesses in the Sophistic method of argumentation, and the contradictions between the leading schools were laid bare. As a reaction against the rejection of all authority which resulted from the negative doubts of the Sophists, Plato and his school turned their attention to the question of man's divinely-appointed purpose, acknowledging the duty to bring about justice in this world. All of Plato's constitutional proposals aim at perfection; the possibility of these Utopias being realized in practice varies widely.[12] In *Republic* 471c–473b, he explicitly raises the question whether the ideal state which he has described could be achieved on earth; Socrates answers that, although the place where this community is kept is in heaven, it is nevertheless necessary to describe it in detail at this point, much as an artist will give the human figure a degree of perfection which it could never have in reality: 'something which cannot be realized is not therefore pointless, but has its own particular function, which he describes with the word παράδειγμα'.[13] It follows that, although the *Republic* is a model which exists only in the world of contemplation, the extent to which it might be achieved may nevertheless be discussed. The later descriptions of primeval Athens and of Atlantis in the *Timaeus* and the *Critias* are pictures of ideal societies seen in action, like the characters of a stage-play. The prototype depicted in the *Laws*, finally, is said to be as realistic as possible. One would have thought that the problem of slavery should have been mentioned in all these designs for a perfect social system, but it is not explicitly questioned in any of them; indeed it is accepted throughout.[14]

[12] On this question see especially H. Braunert's articles mentioned in note 3 above; also H. Herter 'Platons Atlantis' *Bonner Jahrbücher* 133 (1928), 28ff.; id. 'Urathen der Idealstaat' *Politeia und Respublica: Palingenesia* 4 (1969), 108ff.; P. Vidal-Naquet 'Athènes et l'Atlantide. Structure et signification d'un mythe platonicien' *Rev. ét. gr.* 77 (1964), 420ff.

[13] V. Zuckerkandl 'Die Wahrheit des Traums und der Traum der Wahrheit' *Eranos-Jahrbuch* 32 (1963), 180f.

[14] G. R. Morrow *Plato's Law of Slavery* (*University of Illinois Studies in Language and Literature* 25, 3: 1939); G. Vlastos 'Slavery in Plato's Thought' *Philosophical*

Slaves are mentioned several times in the descriptions of the different classes of the ideal community in the *Republic.* Each section of the population is to contribute to the prosperity of the whole by performing its own particular functions (τὰ ἑαυτοῦ πράττειν). This also applies to slaves (433d). Neither here nor in any other passage is the institution as such subjected to criticism; all that Plato requires is that Greeks should refrain from enslaving fellow-Greeks (469b–471c), whereby he concedes that barbarians may be enslaved. The contrast between free man and slave, like the tension between father and son, magistrate and citizen, corresponds to differences in the essential value of particular human beings and in the functions of various social groups. All who lack λόγος are δοῦλοι, slaves; yet the notion of δουλεία is also used to describe any kind of subjection, whether to the government, to parents, or to the rule of law, and this willingness to obey is considered to be beneficial to the subject (590c,d). The body is the slave of the soul, and this relationship between ruling and serving applies beyond the limits of the human world to the cosmic world. A natural law of hierarchy applies to the structure of the soul, to the relations between status groups and to the qualities of the cosmic forces that lie behind them. Although slaves are not mentioned in the description of primeval Athens (the dramatic situation of which is to be imagined as following the rule of Cronus[15]), it is not explicitly stated that slavery has been abolished. In the *Laws*, finally, the position of slaves in civil and sacred law is described in terms similar to Attic law; yet some of the particular provisions made by Plato are stricter than the legal requirements current at that time. Perhaps this could be explained in the context of Plato's desire to return to a more primitive age; but in the last analysis this intensification of the distinct status of slaves must be based on the conviction that certain kinds of human beings are naturally inferior.[16]

Aristotle is entirely in agreement with Plato on this basic point. In the *Politics*, he does not try to describe perfect community life as he imagines it, but rather assembles a collection of data relating to political activity. One of the basic facts which politicians have to start

Review 50 (1941), 289ff. (= Finley 133ff.); id. 'Does Slavery exist in Plato's Republic?' *CPhil* 63 (1968), 291ff.

15 H. Herter *Palingenesia* 4 (see note 12 above), 132.

16 On the use of slaves as assistants by physicians, cf. F. Kudlien *Die Sklaven in der griechischen Medizin der klassischen und hellenistischen Zeit* (*Forschungen zur antiken Sklaverei* 2: 1968), 26ff.

from is that men are naturally different. This is emphatically stated at the beginning of the book (1, 1–5 = 1252a1–1255a3).[17] For the purpose of procreation, human beings have been divided into men and women, and to secure the provision of the necessities of life they have been divided into free men and slaves. It is the intellectual ability to plan rationally for the future (τὸ δυνάμενον τῇ διανοίᾳ προορᾶν) that marks a man out to rule; but the man who is merely able to carry out physically what he has been ordered to do is a slave by nature (φύσει δοῦλον). This distinction is as fundamental as the contrast between body and soul; but just as in nature, so also in social life the interdependence of slave and master has its own beneficial purpose: the slave is an animated tool belonging to the master, and thereby allows him to attain some of the perfection of the ἐπὶ Κρόνου βίος; the master is thus in a position to devote himself to εὖ ζῆν and enjoy the leisure to realize ἀρετή, while the slave, looked after by his master, can perform the work necessary to keep both of them alive (τὰ ἀναγκαῖα). Aristotle maintains this doctrine in the face of some conceptual difficulties which he does not really appreciate. Since a slave is a human being, does this not also make him a ζῷον λογικόν? Aristotle occasionally mentions the ἀρετή of slaves; is it not thereby admitted that he can have some share in λόγος? And if it is his natural disposition that makes a man a slave, one wonders whether there is any point in promising him manumission as a reward for hard work, and whether disturbances can in fact be avoided by such means.

Thus we see that the two greatest works of Greek philosophy, Plato's political utopia and Aristotle's practical handbook, are at one in their justification of slavery. It cannot be denied that this acceptance on the part of philosophers, together with their unthinking application of the notion of the imperfectibility of human nature, provided a new support for age-old injustice and suffering. Nor can one ignore the fact that it was their extreme insistence on the value of intellectual and social activity that brought about this false line of argument. For a Greek, the most valuable thing in life is to comprehend truth: and labour is generally evaluated according to the extent to which it makes rational understanding of the world possible.[18] The provision of the necessities

[17] Cf. the recent article by O. Gigon 'Die Sklaverei bei Aristoteles' *Entretiens sur l'Antiquité Classique* 11 (1965), 245ff.

[18] R. Mandolfo 'Tecnica e scienza nel pensiero antico' *Athenaeum* 43 (1965), 279ff. On the problem of leisure in Greek philosophy see e.g. E. Ch. Welskopf *Probleme der Musse im alten Hellas* (Berlin 1962), 171ff.

of life and crafts in general score very badly on such a scale of values. Instead, the greatest of the Greeks demanded the leisure to live a life of reflection, and the independence to attain ἀρετή in their own way. This makes it possible for us to understand why they found it easier in their utopian writings to do without marriage and private property than to abolish slavery, the rule of one particular class, or warfare.[19]

The dominant role ascribed to the intellect in the ethical systems of Plato and Aristotle ultimately goes back to the Socratic doctrine that virtue is knowledge. An alternative interpretation of this Socratic position led to an increased emphasis on the individual's power of moral choice—to the view that self-control was the basis of a moral independence that raised the philosopher above any political and social institutions. The beginning of this tradition is represented by Antisthenes, who was the son of a Thracian slave-woman and wrote a book Περὶ ἐλευθερίας καὶ δουλείας. The only sentence that survives from this work states that 'the man who fears others is a slave without realizing it' (Stobaeus III, 344, no. 14 in Hense's edition).[20] Slavery remained a question of personal morality even when the Cynics who succeeded Antisthenes attacked the established order outright. Indeed, this notion even maintained itself in spite of the impressive advances made by Greek thought during the Hellenistic period. After Alexander the Great had opened up Asia, and Greek and Oriental ideas were able to influence each other directly, the founders of the Stoa, Zeno and Cleanthes, proclaimed a community that would unite men of all races and social classes. In his early tract on the state, Zeno described an imaginary community in which the whole of mankind lived like a herd pasturing peacefully together, and in which there was no private property and no inequality between men and women. In later periods of his life he continued to believe that there was no such thing as a slave by nature. Later Stoic thought considered the universe as a whole to be a single entity guided by the hierarchy of the stars, a universal society (Cosmopolis) directed by the sun, all of whose citizens were united by sharing the virtues of Justice and Philanthropy.[21] Nevertheless, freedom continued to be seen in terms of moral obligation,

[19] L. Mumford 'Utopia, the City and the Machine' in *Utopias and Utopian Thought* (see note 8 above), 9; cf. also Finley 'Utopianism', Ancient and Modern' (see note 3), 14 and H. Braunert 'Utopia' (see note 3), 15f.

[20] M. Pohlenz *Griechische Freiheit* (Heidelberg 1955), 80f. [= *Freedom in Greek Life and Thought* (Dordrecht 1966), 73f.]

[21] J. Bidez 'La cité du monde et la cité du soleil chez les Stoïciens' *Académie Royale de Belgique, Bulletin de la Classe des Lettres* 18 (1932), 244ff.

required of masters in the same way as of slaves: 'Only the man who allows himself to become dependent on his appetitites and on externals is a slave.'[22] The Stoics were not able to draw the strict conclusions applicable to the real world which their view of the original form of the universe entailed—least of all during the period when their teachings began to spread among the Roman ruling class.

But the idea of a social order in which slavery would be superseded was not completely lost sight of. In the centuries when Greeks crossed continents and oceans as soldiers, traders and scholars, geographers and anthropologists embellished their reports about the unknown world with tales about fabulous lands, while historians produced stories about rulers who brought about happiness on earth: the new literary genre of the political romance was created.[23] Already in the fourth century B.C., Theopompus had conjured up in his historical work the *Philippica* a picture of a country far away in which men lived happily without having to work the land. Hecataeus of Abdera in his *Aegyptiaca*, written in the late fourth or early third century, found exemplary achievements of social organization in past Egyptian history; while Euhemerus located a community with a planned economy on the distant island of Panchaea. The surviving fragments of these utopias do not tell us if their authors recognized the urgency of the problem of slavery. But we may be confident that slavery had been excluded from the fabulous community inhabiting a dream island in the Indian Ocean which is described by Iambulus, who can probably be dated to the third century B.C.[24] (Diodorus Siculus 2, 55–60). Here the fertile soil yields food in greater quantity than the inhabitants need. The pressures of social class that were to be found in Plato's *Republic* are absent here: women and children are held in

[22] M. Pohlenz *Die Stoa* I³ (Göttingen 1964), 135ff.

[23] E. Rohde *Der griechische Roman*³ (Leipzig 1914), 178ff.; R. von Pöhlmann *Geschichte der sozialen Frage und des Sozialismus in der antiken Welt*³ ed. F. Oertel, II (Munich 1925), 274; E. Salin *Platon und die griechische Utopie* (Munich and Leipzig 1921), 199ff.; S. Mazzarino *Il pensiero storico classico* II, 1 (Bari 1966), 37ff. ('Utopia e mito, società e pensiero storico'); H. Braunert 'Staatstheorie und Staatsrecht im Hellenismus' *Saeculum*19 (1968), 54 ff.

[24] The most recent works dealing with the chronology and significance of Iambulus are W. W. Tarn *Alexander the Great* II (Cambridge, 1950), 411ff.; M. I. Finley 'Utopianism, Ancient and Modern' (see note 3 above), 10f.; Bömer III, 165ff.; F. Altheim and R. Stiehl *Die Araber in der alten Welt* I (Berlin 1964), 80ff.; H. Braunert 'Utopia' (note 3), 15ff.; C. Mossé 'Les utopies égalitaires à l'époque hellénistique' *Revue Historique* 241 (1969), 300ff.

common, and so is property in general, as we can see from Diodorus' summary. All citizens are obliged to perform the same duties, so that they go fishing, work at the crafts and occupy themselves in other useful tasks in turn. There is no place here for slavery. These people live a restrained and simple life and reach an advanced age; finally they voluntarily submit to a peaceful death. This equal division of duties was 'a provision quite unique in antiquity and in the feudal society that followed, unparalleled before or afterwards'.[25] The islanders honour the Sun and are closely united by *Homonoia*. It would seem that early Stoic thought and the religious expectations of the Orient came together in this utopian design.

It has been assumed that during the slave revolts of the Hellenistic and Roman world, one group of rebels seized upon Iambulus' utopia as a blueprint for the restructuring of the state and of society. This is supposed to have occurred when the pretender Aristonicus called on slaves to join him in the territory of the kingdom of Pergamum. But the meagre evidence we have is not sufficient to make such a hypothesis even probable.[26] It is a characteristic of slave wars wherever and whenever they occurred—from Asia Minor in the East to Italy in the West, and from Eunus' revolt to that of Spartacus—that while the rebels repeatedly tried to make their masters slaves, they never proclaimed, or held out hopes for, the complete abolition of slavery. After the Romans had put down all of these uprisings and crucified the last of the rebels, the inequality of the social order was firmly entrenched for many centuries to come.

It seems as though the Greek imagination too was now impaired in its ability to produce new visions of a better world. There are many variations on the theme of the encounter between rich and poor in Lucian's *Saturnalia*, a collection of social satires, but instead of losing himself in a dream-world, he finds satisfaction in contemplating the pleasant form taken by the Feast of Saturn. In the dialogue between the priest and the god Cronus, he makes the priest express immoderate demands for wealth, many slaves and fine clothes—yet at the god's feast, the slaves ought to be served by the rich in every way. As Cronus points out, this is the only thing left to remind him of the good old days when slaves did not exist (*Saturnalia* 7). In the next piece, called *Cronosolon*, the rules of the festival are laid down in detail: equality is to be re-established, but only for the period of the

[25] E. Bloch *op. cit.* (note 1 above), 569.

[26] Bömer III, 165ff.; cf. also 55f. and 69ff. below.

holidays and in particular during the banquet. The return to base reality comes through even more clearly in the *Correspondence with Cronus*. For these no longer even concern themselves with slaves; it is rather the poor, i.e. the free-born clients of the rich men of the Roman Empire,[27] who are to be permitted a modest share in the superfluous wealth of the rich, and in particular are to be well treated by the slaves of the rich during the Cronus-Festival—in other words, they are to be entertained 'not as they do nowadays, but in a more democratic fashion, so that each has an equal share' (*Saturnalia* 22). In his reply, Cronus points out (25ff.) that it is not up to him to make a general redistribution of property, since this is Zeus' province; but it is his intention to punish injustice or selfishness during the holidays, and those who take part in the Festival should remember that in a short time everyone will depart from this life, and some will have to give up their wealth, others their poverty (*Saturnalia* 30). With mock-seriousness he concludes: 'general equality is undoubtedly the most pleasant and appropriate thing at a banquet' (*Saturnalia* 32).

This was the way in which Greek utopian thought had its wings clipped under Roman rule. The Island of the Blessed was forgotten and there were no new proposals for a more equitable way of life. All that remained as a modest consolation was the carnival game of the Saturnalia, and as a bitter hope the expectation of death, the great leveller—except for those who turned to the promise of a salvation that could be granted only by divine grace.

[27] L. Friedländer *Darstellungen aus der Sittengeschichte Roms* II[10] (Leipzig 1922), 380f. [= *Roman Life and Manners* II (London 1909), 228.]; R. Helm *Lucian und Menipp* (Leipzig and Berlin 1906), 225.

III

The Structure of Ancient Slave Wars

Their Causes

Everyone who considers the great slave revolts of the ancient world will be struck by the fact that they all occurred in the relatively short period of time between 140 B.C and 70 B.C. There had, indeed, occasionally been conspiracies of groups of slaves both in Greece and at Rome in earlier times, but these attempts at rebellion were without exception confined to small districts and suppressed without much difficulty. But after the second Punic War disturbances of a more widespread nature occurred in Latium, Etruria and Apulia, serious enough to necessitate the use of troops by the praetors.[1] Then, after the middle of the century, there began a succession of rebellions that resulted in long-drawn-out wars: the first Sicilian revolt (136/5–132), Aristonicus' uprising in Asia (133–129), the second Sicilian revolt (104–100) and the war against Spartacus (73–71). These major conflagrations sparked off lesser revolts in several Italian cities, the mines of Attica, and at Delos, the centre of the slave-trade.[2] After the defeat of Spartacus, there were no more rebellions on this scale.

This chapter is a revised version of a paper originally published in *Abh. d. Geistes- u. sozialwiss. Kl., Ak. d. Wiss. u. d. Lit.* (1957, 1). It is dedicated 'investigatoribus servitutis antiquae tam in occidentis quam in orientis partibus assiduis'.

[1] Unrest in Latium in 198 B.C.: Livy 32, 26; war in Etruria in 196 B.C.: Livy 33, 36; risings in Apulia in 185 B.C.: Livy 39, 29. This unrest is discussed by C. M. Danov in *Godischnik Sofiiskia Universitet, Filos.-istor. Fak.* 49 (1955), 4ff.

[2] For the connections between all the uprisings that occurred during the period

If we ask what were the reasons for this large number of slave revolts, one factor can be excluded immediately. There was no doctrine current at that time among free citizens which aimed at the abolition of slavery; the idea that under certain circumstances men could be claimed as chattels by others basically remained unchallenged. The suggestions put forward by some Greek Sophists that all men had the same nature whether barbarians or Greeks,[3] and that God had set all men free and nature made a slave of no one,[4] had virtually disappeared without having achieved anything. The most influential Hellenistic school of philosophy, the Stoa, did indeed oppose the idea that being a barbarian or suffering the misfortune of capture in war could be considered valid reasons for being enslaved. It also recognized the ideal of a world-state in which mankind would be brought up according to common laws like a herd grazing together.[5] But in its strict ethical code it maintained that it was a person's moral state that showed whether he was, in fact, free or not, so that only the wise man was really free, while the ignorant and wicked were necessarily slaves.[6] This made the phenomenon of slavery a question of personal ethical behaviour. Despite this surprising identification of knowledge and virtue, Stoic teaching, particularly in its contacts with the Roman world, inculcated in its adherents the ideal of a philanthropic character and the principle of doing good to others. Yet when it came to real life, the most that this philosophy dared to aim at in particular cases was an improvement in the slave's conditions. Its advice was, more or less, that a slave ought to be treated as a hired worker who was employed for life.[7] This did not lead to any change in the legal situation. In the ancient world, the fact that among the Jews an Israelite who had been enslaved on account of his debts was treated like a hired worker,

of the Sicilian slave revolts, see Lauffer II, 240ff. I will leave aside Saumacus' uprising, since the researches of S. Shebelev and W. Gaidukevich have shown that the question of slavery and serfdom in the kingdom of the Bosphorus requires further examination. Cf. E. L. Kasakevic's article on Saumacus' revolt in *VDI* 1963, 1, 57ff.

[3] E.g. Antiphon (*Vorsokratiker* 44 B 2 = vol. II, 353); see P. Merlan 'Alexander the Great or Antiphon the Sophist?' *CPhil* 45 (1950), 161ff. Cf. p. 14 above.

[4] Alcidamas (*Vorsokratiker* Fr. 5); cf. W. Nestle *Vom Mythos zum Logos*[2] Stuttgart 1942), 345.

[5] Zeno *Stoicorum veterum fragmenta* (ed. H. von Arnim) I No. 262.

[6] Chrysippus *Stoicorum veterum fragmenta* III No. 354ff.; cf. M. Pohlenz *Die Stoa* I[3] (Göttingen 1960), 136; Westermann *Slave Systems* 40.

[7] Chrysippus *Stoicorum veterum fragmenta* III No. 351f.

and then had to be set free when the Sabbatical year came round, was still the exception.[8] But not even the wisdom of Joshua Ben-Sirach (33, 25–33) saw fit to recommend anything more than food and discipline and hard work for gentile slaves, and if they were recalcitrant, chains or torture.

So this unrest among slaves cannot have been the result of any new social doctrine. If we want to understand the reactions of the slave population we will have to consider the political and social background of this period and the conditions in which slaves lived, in a similar way, if with wider terms of reference, to that by which Posidonius approaches the subject in his introduction to the story of the first Sicilian uprising, preserved for us in the 34th book of Diodorus.[9]

The first thing to be noted is the great quantitative increase in slavery, particularly in eastern countries, and the large numbers of slaves who flooded into the Roman economy. Since the battle of Pydna, the Hellenistic system of states as a whole had been heading towards total dissolution. The kingdom of Macedon had been overthrown, the republic of Rhodes had been humbled, the Ptolemies were suffering from internal unrest in Egypt, and the Seleucid empire, which until recently had been Asia's major power, was disintegrating under the incessant pressure from every direction of the Parthians and the Romans, as well as because of struggles between rival members of the royal family,

[8] W. Lauterbach *Der Arbeiter in Recht und Rechtspraxis des Alten Testaments und des Alten Orients* (dissertation, Heidelberg 1936), 3ff.; S. W. Baron *Social and Religious History of the Jews* I (New York 1937), 197f.; R. de Vaux *Les Institutions de l'Ancien Testament* I (Paris 1958), 125ff., 328f.; E. E. Urbach 'The Laws regarding Slavery' *Annual of Jewish Studies* 1 (1963), 1ff.; I. Ch. Shifman on the legal status of slaves in Judaea according to the evidence of the biblical tradition in *VDI* 1964, 3, 54ff.

[9] Jacoby *F. Gr. Hist.* 87 F 108. I have used Jacoby's text in this chapter; the quotations are from Dindorf's edition of Diodorus. I am only incidentally concerned here with problems of sources and chronology, and would refer the reader to the works of G. Rathke *De Romanorum bellis servilibus* (dissertation, Berlin 1904); E. Ciaceri *Roma e le guerre servili in Sicilia, Processi politici e relazioni internazionali* (Rome 1918), 55ff.; L. Pareti *Riv. Fil.* 55 (1927), 44ff.; Lauffer II, 227ff., and also a study that appeared at the same time as this article was first published, V. Vavřínek *La révolte d'Aristonicos* (*Rozpravy Československé Akademie VED* 67: 1957), and an essay by M. Capozza 'Le rivolte servili di Sicilia nel quadro della politica agraria romana' *Atti dell' Istituto Veneto di Scienze, Lettere ed Arti, Classe di Scienze morali e Lettere* 115 (1956/7), 79ff. Mention should also be made of a book aimed at a wider readership, which lacks scholarly references to individual sources, J.-P. Brisson's *Spartacus* (Paris 1959): cf. the review by M. Capozza *Paideia* 16 (1961), 179ff.

rebellious satraps and revolts of subject nations. Strabo (14, 5.2) thinks that the uprising of Diodotus Tryphon, who rebelled against King Demetrius II in the year 145, was one of the causes of Cilician piracy and the brisk slave trade it entailed. There was no protection any more for town or country when the pirates attacked—indeed, nearly all belligerent states employed them to plunder neutral cities. Inscriptions show that banditry was being put on an organized footing in the interior of Asia Minor; young men were kidnapped, taken up into the mountains, and either freed in return for a large ransom or sold off elsewhere.[10] Human beings became a much sought after commodity. At the start of their campaigns against their rebellious subjects, kings and their generals summoned the slave-traders to them in their camps to offer for sale in advance the large number of prisoners they felt sure they would capture.[11] On the Greek mainland and in the Aegean area, the impoverishment of the middle classes and the disintegration of urban society continued. The exposure of infants and voluntary birth-control were, as Polybius says (36, 17.5ff.), expressions of bourgeois selfishness, but just as often they were also desperate measures of self-preservation. The particularly frequent references to manumissions among the inscriptions lining the walls of the Temple of Apollo at Delphi dating to the first half of the second century are more likely to point to the impoverishment than to the prosperity of the population. This would also explain why certain duties were so often imposed on former slaves as a condition for manumission, namely that they should continue to carry out their previous tasks or accept some responsibility for supporting their masters or other persons.[12]

The Romans at first benefited from this decline of the Hellenistic world. They brought back from their campaigns the treasures of kings, works of art from the cities, payments of reparations for many years

[10] On Cilician piracy see H. A. Ormerod *Piracy in the Ancient World* (London 1924), 190ff.; E. Maróti 'Die Rolle der Seeräuberei zur Zeit der römischen Bürgerkriege' *Das Altertum* 7 (1961), 33f.; M. K. Trofimova on piracy in the Hellenistic world in *VDI* 1963, 4, 53ff.

[11] I *Macc.* 3, 41; II *Macc.* 8, 11; see H. Volkmann *Die Massenversklavungen* (*Ak. d. Wiss. u. d. Lit.* 1961, 3), 106.

[12] W. L. Westermann 'Slave Maintenance and Slave Revolts' *CPhil* 40 (1945), 1ff. Bömer II, 29ff. is basic to a study of the certificates of manumission found at Delphi. On social and economic distress in Greece, see J. A. O. Larsen *Economic Survey of Ancient Rome* IV (1938), 418ff.; M. Rostovtzeff *Social and Economic History of the Hellenistic World* II, 603ff.

in advance and large numbers of prisoners. It has been estimated that about 250,000 prisoners of war were imported from the Hellenistic world during the period from 200 to 150 B.C.—an enormous number by ancient standards.[13] Most of them found their way onto the *latifundia* of the Roman upper classes in Italy and Sicily. All the conditions for a disastrous situation already existed. Wars had destroyed the prosperity of the free inhabitants of southern Italy and Sicily and had put cheap agricultural land into the hands of the landlords; now further wars were supplying everything that was required in the way of a labour force. In the world-wide economic system that Rome was now dominating, the cultivation of olives and vines proved to be more advantageous for Italy than the cereals which had been grown previously. The use of slave labour must have been most profitable precisely in the cultivation of these new types of crops—as in nineteenth-century America the slave-system proved most advantageous in the cultivation of sugar and rice crops. Where there is only a single harvest per year and there are only minor interruptions to work, an unfree labourer is more profitable than a free one, as experience both in the Old World and the New has shown. The advantages of slave labour are most fully realized and the use of slaves most profitable, if a landowner employs large numbers of slaves, working systematically under a single overseer; slave workers will not be called up for military service; they can be moved quickly from one place of work to another; they cannot leave their place of employment and they cannot strike.[14] This is the Roman method as it is taught in the treatises of Cato and Varro. When they were situated on private land, there was nothing to limit the size of the *latifundia* of the great landowners, worked by large numbers of slaves under a *vilicus*, and there were only minor restrictions when they were on public land.[15] Skilled workers who had become prisoners of war would find their way into the urban

[13] T. Frank *Economic Survey of Ancient Rome* I, 188; Westermann *RE* Suppl. VI (s.v. 'Sklaverei'), 954; ibid. *Slave Systems* 62. On the position of the unfree population in earlier times see L. A. El'nitzkii's volume on the origins and development of slavery at Rome from the eighth to the third centuries (Moscow 1964).

[14] See the comparative study of this topic by C. A. Yeo 'The Economics of Roman and American Slavery' *Finanz-Archiv* 13 (1952), 445ff.

[15] G. Tibiletti 'Lo sviluppo del latifondo in Italia dall'epoca Graccana al principio dell'impero' *X Congresso internazionale di Scienze Storiche, Relazioni* II (1955), 235ff.; see also S. L. Uttschenko *VDI* 1953, 4, 157ff. On the role of the *vilicus*, see M. E. Sergeyenko's article in *VDI* 1956, 4, 46ff. and P. Thielscher *Des Marcus Cato Belehrung über die Landwirtschaft* (Berlin 1963).

households, and, from the second century, to an increasing extent also into industry, particularly the shipyards and weapons factories.[16]

It is in trade and commerce that we can see most clearly how the Romans profited at the expense of Greek countries; here too slaves came to play an important role as a commodity. The whole of the Orient was now open to Roman and Italian traders. Delos was established as a depot for the trade between East and West; it was theoretically an Athenian colony, but in practice it was an international trade-centre under Roman administration. Alongside settlers from Phoenicia, Syria, Alexandria and Asia Minor there was the largest of these colonies, that of the Romans and Italians, although the majority of the Roman population at Delos consisted of freedmen, and even slaves were to be found as business managers.[17] Apart from goods brought along the oriental caravan routes, the main commodity handled at Delos was slaves; thousands, even, according to Strabo's exaggerated claim (14, 5.2), tens of thousands of slaves could be landed and packed off again without difficulty every day.[18] They were acquired from Syria, Bithynia, Pontus and Cappadocia, countries where kidnapping was a well-organized business and where even the kings now proceeded to take part. Roman traders and tax-farmers were also concerned in this none too respectable trade.

Thus there were at the same time many different sources for slaves; those who had been captured in war or kidnapped, children exposed by their parents, those enslaved for debts and those whose status was inherited. The huge concentrations of slaves in the West, especially in agriculture, resulted in slave labour being particularly harshly treated. Cato's advice that old or sick slaves should be sold like superfluous tools is notorious.[19] Posidonius reports that Sicilian slave-owners had their slaves branded as soon as they bought them, and he emphasizes that this was particularly resented by free-born slaves (Diod. 34, 2.36). We are quite justified in trying to explain these uprisings by stressing the general worsening of the lot of slave workers and referring to the

[16] W. L. Westermann 'Industrial slavery in Roman Italy' *Journal of Economic History* 2 (1942), 149ff.

[17] P. Roussel *Délos, Colonie Athénienne* (*Bibliothèque de l'école française d'Athènes et de Rome* 111; 1916), 82ff.; W. A. Laidlaw *A History of Delos* (Oxford 1933), 170, 190ff. On Delos' position in the world economic system, see Rostovtzeff *op. cit.* II, 786ff.

[18] J. A. Lentzman on the Delian slave-market: *VDI* 1950, 1, 53ff.

[19] Cato *De agri cultura* 2, 7: *Servum senem, servum morbosum et si quid aliut supersit, vendat.*

role played by the numerous new slaves, people who had been free men before they came to be enslaved and wished to regain their liberty.[20] I think that an even more important factor for the understanding of the situation as a whole was that the great increase in the numbers of slaves in the towns and in the country had the effect of giving them wide room for manoeuvre. Everywhere and at all times slave herdsmen were rough customers,[21] and they had always carried weapons to protect their herds or flocks from attack. And since in Sicily the arrogance and short-sightedness of their miserly masters now failed to provide them even with food and clothing, they had to fend for themselves by murdering wayfarers and plundering farms, and were forced to turn to robbery and terrorism of the open countryside with their bands 'like scattered groups of soldiers' as Posidonius puts it (Diod. 34, 2.30). But robbery gave them a taste of freedom. In the urban centres, slaves were allowed to join religious associations, and here they stood side by side with free men and contributed to the spread of foreign cults in Italy.[22] Educated slaves became secretaries and tutors to distinguished Roman families; they had as much freedom of movement as the hostages of foreign states like the group of Achaeans to which Polybius belonged, or the Carthaginian nobles involved in a conspiracy of the slaves of Setia in Latium in 198 B.C. Meanwhile their masters were laughing at the character of the sly and insolent slave appearing in comedies which Roman playwrights had adapted from Greek originals.[23] Slaves were ubiquitous, and they were fast becoming indispensable. Many indications show how hazardous it was for the rebellious Achaeans to set free and arm twelve thousand house-born slaves as a measure of self-defence in the last stages of their unsuccessful war for independence (Polyb. 38, 15.3). But it was not long before it was to happen in a civil war at Rome itself that Gaius Gracchus and his

[20] A. W. Mischulin *Spartacus. Abriss der Geschichte des grossen Sklavenaufstandes* (German edn. published and introduced by S. L. Uttschenko, Berlin 1952), 26ff. The role of those who were newly enslaved is stressed by E. Meyer 'Die Sklaverei im Altertum' *Kleine Schriften* I^2, 206; F. Oertel *Klassenkampf, Sozialismus und organischer Staat im alten Griechenland* (Bonn 1942), 51; Lauffer *op. cit.* 246.

[21] Cf. L. Robert 'Bergers Grecs' *Hellenica* VII (1949), 152ff.

[22] Material concerning the relationship between gods and slaves and the position of the unfree in religious cults has been collected, discussed and interpreted in the studies by Bömer I–IV referred to above; there is a summary of his conclusions in IV, 243ff.

[23] P. P. Spranger *Historische Untersuchungen zu den Sklavenfiguren des Plautus und Terenz* (*Ak. d. Wiss. u. d. Lit.*, 1960, 8).

colleague Flaccus were to call upon slaves to fight for their freedom (Appian *Bell. Civ.* 1, 115).

As we have seen, this period was one in which the state and free society in general were being shaken to their very foundations, while outlawry was on the increase. The Hellenistic states were suffering from dynastic upheavals and civil wars, and piracy and the slave trade were allowed to thrive on their borders. The Roman Empire destroyed ancient states and independent peoples, and at the same time gave its support to any unrest that could be stirred up against the Eastern monarchs; it was quick to grant the group of religious freedom-fighters in Palestine recognition as a state.[24] The intervention of the world's major power was violent, while at the same time its basis was insecure. In 162 B.C., Cnaeus Octavius, the head of a Roman delegation that had been sent out to undermine the kingdoms of the East still further, was murdered in the gymnasium of Laodicea by a Syrian fanatic called Leptines: the assassin was extradited to Rome, defended his action as divinely ordained and was released unpunished.[25] While the slaves on the *latifundia* were being branded and put in chains, some of their comrades were summoned to join distinguished families as tutors or personal physicians, or were managing trading enterprises at Delos. Tottering governments tolerated organized groups of brigands in the mountains; the Roman Senate, which for far too long followed a policy that was merely destructive, allowed the pirates to become the major naval power of the Eastern Mediterranean. It was this combination of violence and weakness, authority and lawlessness, that created a revolutionary atmosphere.

This will enable us to understand the occurrences that are reported to have triggered off the great slave revolts. They may themselves at first seem unimportant, but the political and social crisis had already provided the material for a violent explosion. In the case of the first Sicilian revolt, Posidonius himself (Diod. 34, 2.2ff.; 25ff.) rightly puts great emphasis on the events that sparked off the rebellion. But his moralizing generalizations about the *hybris* of owners which slaves could no longer tolerate neglect political elements, as well as giving a slanted view of the island's economy.[26] However important pasturage

[24] In Strabo's view (16, 2.37), the Hasmonean state had developed features characteristic of tyranny and brigandage as well as religious reverence.

[25] Appian *Syr.* 46f.; Polybius 32, 3.

[26] See R. Scalais 'La prospérité agricole et pastorale de la Sicile' *Musée Belge* 28 (1924), 87ff.; V. M. Scramuzza 'Roman Sicily' *Economic Survey of Ancient Rome*

and the raising of cattle, sheep and horses may have been, Cicero's *Verrines* make it impossible to doubt that cereals (and also the cultivation of olives and vines) and trade were the principal sources of wealth. This cannot have been very different two generations earlier, even if the Roman government, having learnt the lessons of these revolts, had done something to restrict the proportion of pasturage. Cicero represents traders and farmers as the most influential section of the Sicilian population: *negotiatores, aratores, commune Siciliae, quod est aliud in illa provincia genus hominum? Nullum* (*Verr.* 2, 2.168). Slaves are not, of course, mentioned in this list, despite the fact that on the *latifundia* the whole work-force right up to the *vilicus* and *magister pecoris* consisted of slaves. Slaves were also to be found in the households of wealthy Roman *equites*, Italians, and native Greeks and Sicels (who were probably in the majority), both as domestic servants and to provide an atmosphere of luxury. The shrine of Venus on Mount Eryx owned a number of temple-slaves, the *Venerii*, who according to Cicero could be hired as messengers and bodyguards, ushers and policemen, musicians and tax-collectors. These sacred slaves are not mentioned in the story of the Sicilian rebellion, but it seems probable that in the ancient and highly respected cult of Ceres at Enna, which Cicero (*Verr.* 2, 4.111) describes as more like a sanctuary than a city, the slaves to some extent participated in the festivals and mysteries of the goddess and thereby acquired some freedom of movement. It was in this city that the revolt began. Damophilus, a parvenu who had made a great deal of money, aspired to the role of a 'grand seigneur', in which he was emulated by his wife Megallis; between them they terrorized their slaves so cruelly that these slaves decided to kill their masters. Damophilus, who was both brutal and neglectful, had for his part done all he could to ensure the success of the uprising by turning his herdsmen into robbers and having an escort of armed slaves accompany him on his princely progress through the country. A different but equally dangerous game had been played by one Antigenes. He had a slave called Eunus, an adherent of the cult of the Syrian goddess with supposed divinatory and miraculous powers who had foretold that he would become king, and kept calling this slave to his parties in order to make fun of him by asking what he would do to his master and the

III, 240ff.; a somewhat different view is taken by L. Pareti *Storia di Roma* III (Turin 1953), 294f.; M. Capozza *op. cit.* 85ff.; S. Calderone 'Il problema delle città censorie e la storia agraria della Sicilia Romana' *Kokalos* 6 (1960), 3ff.

other guests present when he had taken over his kingdom.[27] However amusing it may have seemed to make fun of this holy idiot, it turned the Saturnalia into an everyday event, and it was not long before the slave really did become a king. For Damophilus' insurgent slaves now turned to this extraordinary prophet, and the robbers joined the followers of the goddess to achieve a violent revolution which their masters themselves were responsible for having provoked.

In the kingdom of Pergamum it was the ill-intentioned will of the last ruler, Attalus III, and the bad reputation of Roman policy as a whole in Asia that created the conditions for Aristonicus' revolt.[28] It was not unusual in the Hellenistic East at this time for an illegitimate member of the royal family to lay claim to the crown. The fact that it was the poor and the slaves to whom Aristonicus had to turn for help was inevitable in view of the terms of the will, which declared the royal residence of Pergamum a free city and confirmed the freedom of the other Greek towns, while leaving to the Romans all royal property, both movable and immovable, thereby including the lands of the Asiatic subjects. The Romans could be expected not to let anything slip out of their clutches, and the cities would clearly accept the new deal. What alternative was left open to the pretender (whom for the moment the army was not obeying either) but to appeal to the proletariat, the unfortunate serfs on the estates of the king, the temples and the cities, and the masses of slaves working in the fields, woodlands, quarries and mines in the interior of the country?[29] It could be said that this was a case of a disinherited prince joining forces with the class of the disinherited as a whole, after a combination of royal servility and Roman avarice had created a state of anarchy.

The outbreak of the second Sicilian revolt is a typical example of how the rebels had in the first instance been incited by the government's weakness in the face of the illegal practices of slave-traders and owners (Diod. 36, 3.1–3). In their greed for slave labour, Roman capitalists had often bought slaves who had been carried off by robbers from their Asiatic homes where they had been free, and had been sold

[27] Diod. 34, 2.8. The parallel with Luke 23, 42 has been pointed out several times; cf. R. Eisler *Jesus Basileus* (*Religionswissenschaftliche Bibliothek* 9) II (1930), 724.

[28] See Chapter IV on the situation that developed in Pergamum after the death of Attalus III.

[29] On social conditions in western Asia Minor see T. R. S. Broughton *Economic Survey of Ancient Rome* IV (1938), 505ff.; Rostovtzeff *op. cit.* II, 806; D. Magie *Roman Rule in Asia Minor* (Princeton 1950).

through the mediation of tax-farmers. When, during the course of his campaign against the Cimbri, the consul Marius sent a request to the Bithynian king, Nicomedes III, for a contingent of troops, the latter openly stated that most Bithynians of military age had been abducted by tax-farmers and were now being held as slaves in the various provinces of the Roman Empire. As a result, the Senate instructed provincial governors to set free persons who had been forcibly enslaved in this way. In Sicily, the praetor P. Licinius Nerva began to conduct investigations as he had been ordered, and within a few days had declared eight hundred slaves to be free. But then he brought his investigations to an abrupt end, bribed or intimidated by the capitalists, and sent the slaves who had come pouring to his tribunal at Syracuse back to their masters. Soon after, riots suddenly broke out in various parts of the island, and this at a time when the Empire found itself seriously threatened elsewhere.

Shortly before this slave war in Sicily, there had also been some conspiracies among slaves in Italy (Diod. 36, 2 and 2a). It was symptomatic of the general disarray of the ruling classes that in one case an impoverished Roman *eques*, T. Vettius, gave his slaves their freedom and declared himself to be their king. During the following years the Italic revolt and the civil war between Marius and Sulla raged throughout Italy. Even after the Sullan restoration, the government was in no position to keep the peace in the southern regions of Italy, where the great landowners were again employing large numbers of slaves, and respectable aristocrats went around murdering and pillaging with the help of armed bands of retainers.[30] The edict against crimes of violence issued by the praetor M. Licinius Lucullus in 76 B.C. (Cicero *pro M. Tullio* 8ff.) could only expose the evil effects of this practice; it could not eradicate it. Civil disturbances created by capitalists with their hordes of slaves on the territory of Roman citizens were typical of the atmosphere of Italy at the time when Spartacus broke out of the gladiatorial barracks at Capua with his companions to try to achieve freedom for himself and his fellow-sufferers. Once again it was because of the way in which the ruling class had acted that this enterprise came to be the greatest of the slave wars—the inhumanity with which gladiators had been trained to kill men as a sport, and the criminal

[30] M. Zeller *Die Rolle der unfreien Bevölkerung Roms in den politischen Kämpfen der Bürgerkriege* (typewritten dissertation, Tübingen 1962); E. M. Shtajerman on slaves and freedmen in the social struggles of the late republic in *VDI* 1962, 1, 24ff.

negligence with which the setting-up of robber-bands had been tolerated or even encouraged among rural workers. Italy was ripe for the gladiators' undertaking.

Mass Movements and Government Countermeasures

What use did the slaves make of their opportunity when they were given the chance to act? They found themselves in a very difficult situation, for although their numbers had increased greatly, they were dispersed over town and country with no cohesion, no conscious feeling of solidarity. It was only to a limited extent that they had been formed into groups—in the slave-gangs of individual farms and enterprises, in religious associations, working parties and occasionally robber-bands that were tolerated or even formed by their masters. The government and the society of free citizens stood united against this barely organized rabble. When the inhabitant of an ancient city thought of unrest among slaves, the first thing that came into his mind was that there might be an enemy in his own house,[31] and it was taken for granted that a rich man stood to lose all he possessed in such a revolt.[32] Under these circumstances, the actions of the slaves, in so far as we are told about them, would be seen as inarticulate mass movements. The stories about disturbances among slaves, whether they refer to the uprisings of this period or to earlier cases of insurrection, have certain themes in common, which is understandable given that the underlying situation did not essentially change. We are told how in their bitterness the oppressed slaves came together in secrecy and discussed the possibility of revolt,[33] an occurrence the Romans called *conspiratio*. We cannot yet be certain what language, which concepts and symbols they may have used for this in such a colourfully mixed society, which purposely contained members of different national origins. Our sources, who without exception belong to the citizen class, know that the slaves wanted revenge for the ill-treatment they had suffered, and that they were out to murder their masters,

[31] Livy 3, 16.3: *Terror servilis, ne suus cuique domi hostis esset* (with reference to the supposed *coup* of Appius Herdonius in 460 B.C.).

[32] Cicero *Verr.* 2, 5.18 and 20.

[33] Diod. 34, 2.4: συνελάλουν περὶ ἀποστάσεως ('discussed the possibility of revolt') and *ibid.* 10: συνέθεντο πρὸς ἀλλήλους ὑπὲρ ἀποστάσεως καὶ φόνου τῶν κυρίων ('conspired to revolt and murder their masters').

make free with their property and womenfolk, plunder and destroy.[34] This theme of murder, pillage and rape is also to be found in the later descriptions of slave revolts, and is often painted in extremely vivid colours, as when it is said of the first Sicilian war that in the slaughter which ensued after slaves had forced their way into a house, they even tore babies from their mothers' breasts and dashed them against the floor (Diod. 34, 2.11f.), and that when they took prisoners, they not only cut off their hands but the whole of their arms too (Diod. 34, 8). Sallust evokes the brutality of the war against Spartacus by the example of the capture of Forum Anni: *neque sanctum aut nefandum quicquam fuit irae barbarorum et servili ingenio* (*Hist.* 3, fr. 98B in Maurenbrecher's edition). But then a small group of slaves went beyond the simple desire for revenge which marked the beginnings of the revolt and proceeded to plan action of a more lasting kind; they assembled at a nocturnal sacrifice to take a common oath (*coniuratio*), grabbed any weapons they could lay their hands on on the spur of the moment, and rushed into the local town (Diod. 34, 2.24b).

This first success of theirs completely transformed the situation. Now they would have to act according to a plan of some sort; they had to decide what their long-term aims were to be and to provide some kind of political structure for their rebellion. While the first phase had the egalitarian characteristics of any spontaneous movement, the personality of a leader now appeared and the main outlines of the situation could be seen more clearly.

It is, admittedly, true that the Syrian Eunus led the first Sicilian revolt right from the beginning. His powers of magic and prophecy had caused a sensation, and he had announced that the Syrian goddess had appeared to him and promised that he would become a king. This made the oppressed and discontented slaves in Damophilus' household look to him as their leader, and it was through him that they received the approbation of the gods and were impelled to act. They occupied the town of Enna and took Damophilus and Megallis into custody. Next, the insurgents gathered in the town's theatre. It is as if the very nature of the place imposed a different procedure upon them; the slaves wanted to make their decision as a popular court like the *demos* of any Greek *polis*. But two slaves who felt particularly bitter towards Damophilus struck him dead without awaiting a formal judgement of the people (οὐκ ἀναμείναντες τὴν ἀκριβῆ τοῦ δήμου κρίσιν). The assembly

[34] This is how Dionysius of Halicarnassus (12, 6.6) describes a slave-conspiracy of 419 B.C. in terms of his own age.

had now reached the stage of political consciousness, and took a decision of major importance: 'They chose Eunus to be their King, not because of his courage or military ability, but expressly because of his magical powers and because he had started the revolt, and also because his name was a guarantee of goodwill towards his subjects' (Diod. 34, 2.10–14).

So it is clear that this mob of slaves formed itself into a People along Hellenistic lines, and, like a military assembly in the Seleucid or Ptolemaic empires, chose for itself a ruler whose very name guaranteed a virtue that was highly regarded in a prince, *Eunoia*; he was to be 'the Kindly King'.[35] The emphasis laid on the miraculous powers of the man chosen also points to the idea of the Messianic King about which we shall have more to say later. The fact that 'Eunus called himself Antiochus and gave his insurgent people the name of Syrians' (Diod. 34, 2.24) makes the Seleucid character of this monarchy absolutely clear; by using this title, the new king wanted to enrol himself in this famous dynasty. The fact that he came from Apamea in Syria suggests that he may have heard or perhaps even himself seen how, about ten years before this, the king-maker Diodotus Tryphon had put Alexander Balas' young son on the throne at Apamea as Antiochus Epiphanes Theos.[36] In any case, he laid claim to the Syrian kingdom (βασιλεία τῶν Σύρων), which was the usual way at that time of describing the Seleucid empire. As to whether, in this foreign country, he considered his people to be a national or a religious community, that is a question which cannot at present be answered.

The government's activity began forthwith. As sole ruler of the insurgents, Eunus summoned a new assembly and had all the prisoners captured at Enna put to death, with the exception of those who were able to produce weapons for him; he had Megallis handed over to the women slaves for punishment and personally killed his masters Antigenes and Python; but he set free those who in earlier days had believed his prophecies and had treated him well when he had been present at his master's table (Diod. 34, 2.15 and 41). He had himself crowned, decked himself out with the insignia and dress of monarchy,

[35] On *Eunoia* see W. Schubart 'Das hellenistische Königsideal nach Inschriften und Papyri' *Arch. Pap.* 12 (1937), 8ff.

[36] References in B. Niese *Geschichte der griechischen und makedonischen Staaten* III (Gotha 1903), 277f.; W. Hoffmann *RE* VII A, 716f. (s.v. 'Tryphon'). With particular reference to Apamea, see Strabo 16, 2.10. Cf. also H.-W. Ritter *Diadem und Königsherrschaft* (*Vestigia* 7: Munich 1965), 139f. and 169.

made his wife queen and chose a council of judicious men; in this council, the Greek Achaeus was rewarded for his outspoken criticism (Diod. 34, 2.16 and 42). The story of the last days of his rebellion shows that Eunus had a bodyguard of a thousand *somatophylakes*, and among his courtiers we find a cook, a baker, a masseur and a jester (Diod. 34, 2.22). All these institutions could also be found at the Seleucid court.[37] King Eunus also minted his own coins. The British Museum and the Museum at Syracuse each possess one small bronze coin with a veiled head of Demeter on the obverse and an ear of corn on the reverse. together with the inscription ΒΑΣΙ ΑΝΤΙ. Both these coins were found in Sicily, and the best authorities suggest that they were minted by the slave-king Antiochus.[38] It would have been some time before Eunus could have made use of the royal prerogative of coining money. Our reports suggest that the first thing that happened after he had organized his court was that the insurgents were given makeshift arms and that their numbers increased greatly, an occurrence elsewhere described by the term *congregatio*. Thus the campaign against the Romans began to gain momentum.

At the same time as Eunus' insurrection, another uprising, led by a slave called Cleon, was taking place in the south-west of the island. We are not given so many details about the first stage of this revolt, whose leader was a Cilician brigand who had come from the vicinity of the Taurus Mountains and was now employed as a herdsman and highwayman in the countryside around Agrigentum. The conditions which led him to form his gang were therefore quite similar to the situation at Enna; and it was, indeed, a common characteristic of the Sicilian insurrections that they formed around two main centres. What surprised our ancient commentators most as the situation unfolded was that the two groups did not fight one another, but that Cleon and his followers went to Enna and put themselves under Eunus' command (Diod. 34, 2.17 and 43). We can understand Posidonius' amazement, shared by his ancient copyist Diodorus, if we remember that ancient

[37] E. Bikerman *Institutions des Séleucides* (Paris 1938), 26ff.

[38] E. S. G. Robinson 'Antiochus King of the Slaves' *Num. Chron.* 20 (1920), 175f.; illustrated in *CAH*, Plates IV, 1/2 (a). G. K. Jenkins, the curator, kindly confirmed the ascription of this coin to Eunus in reply to a request of mine. The example at Syracuse, to which my attention was kindly drawn by G. Manganaro, is discussed by A. de Agostino 'Le Monete di Henna' *Bolletino Storico Catanese* 4 (1939), 84f., who comes to the conclusion that it was struck at Enna. There can be no doubt that there was a mint at Enna both before and after this date: cf. K. Christ *Jahrbuch für Numismatik und Geldgeschichte* 5/6 (1954/5), 226.

historians had certain preconceptions about these uprisings—they saw them as revolts of the type that regularly occurred in Hellenistic power-struggles, and this led them to ignore the fact that in the underworld politics of brigands, it is the rule for only a single chieftain to be recognized.

Generally speaking, Eunus' government was, outwardly, a state with a Seleucid constitution that had been transplanted to the West. The absence of a royal cult was the only noticeable deviation from the monarchy of the real Antiochi, and perhaps this may have had something to do with Eunus' singular position as the minister of the Syrian goddess. We are not told anything about the administration of this western kingdom of Syria, and we must conceive of its territory as interspersed with the numerous enclaves of the cities which took no part in the revolt, much as Syria was fragmented whenever there was a struggle for the throne, or Italy after the state of the rebel Italian allies had been set up. There is no evidence for any fundamentally new social structure; rather, slaves took over the rights and property of their defeated masters. Achaeus, for example, was given the house of his previous masters by King Eunus (Diod. 34, 2.42). This may also explain why the free proletariat of the towns neither joined the new movement nor supported the old regime, but rather tried to gain the greatest possible advantages both from its previous and its present masters. While the slaves spared granaries and estates and the peasants who worked them, the proletariat unrestrainedly plundered and burnt farms and their contents (Diod. 34, 2.48). It is clear that the first slave-state aimed only to invert society, not to achieve a communistic social system.

The military course of Aristonicus' uprising is relatively well known to us from literary sources and from inscriptions, but its political and social character is less easy to understand. What was exceptional here was that it was an illegitimate member of the ruling dynasty who claimed the crown and fought for his claim against the Romans, the heirs of the last king, and against those of his own countrymen who opposed him. In other words, the course of revolutionary activity was planned by him from the very beginning. The conditions of Attalus' will already forced Aristonicus, in his search for supporters, to turn to the oppressed population of the towns and the countryside, who had nothing to hope for from the Romans, just as it had previously been they who had had to suffer from the alliance between the royal administration and the urban bourgeoisie. News of the Sicilian rebellion could only have strengthened him in his resolve to make his attempt with the support of the poor and the slaves (Diod. 34, 2.26). There can be no doubt that Aristonicus, the son of Eumenes II by the daughter of an Ephesian lyre-player, who was not much younger than the childless Attalus III, had already had hopes of achieving power during the king's lifetime. Hellenistic customs regarding the rights of succession did not stand in his way since by the middle of the second century it had become commonplace in the decadent Syrian and Egyptian dynasties for illegitimate or supposititious sons of their predecessors to be set up against reigning kings as pretenders.[39] What is certain is that Aristonicus put forward his claim to the throne as soon as the king died; he took the royal name *Eumenes* and introduced a new chronology, reckoning by the years of his own rule.[40] It is extremely probable that he called upon the slaves to fight for their freedom from the very beginning. The decree with which the city of Pergamum tried to counter the new situation included, among other things, the provision that aliens resident in the city were to be granted citizenship, while freedmen and slaves of the king and of the people were to receive the status of Residents.[41] This unparalleled grant, made without any preconditions, indicates that there was a grave threat to the city and its territories, and suggests that at this moment slaves had already been promised their freedom from some other quarter. This is consistent with Strabo's statement (14, 1.38) that after his defeat at the naval battle of Cyme, Aristonicus went inland and 'quickly gathered about him a crowd of poor people and slaves to whom he had promised their

[39] E.g. Alexander Balas, the supposititious son of Antiochus IV, who was crowned by Attalus II (Niese *op. cit.* III, 259); a supposititious son of Ptolemy IV Philometor was set up as a candidate for the throne as a rival to Ptolemy VII Physkon (*ibid.* III, 269); and Alexander Zabinas, a reputed son of Alexander Balas, was sent to Syria by Physkon (*ibid.* III, 271f., 305ff.).

[40] E. S. G. Robinson 'Cistophori in the Name of King Eumenes' *Num. Chron.* 6th series no. 14 (1954), 1ff. and Plate I, ascribes the much-discussed cistophori with the legend *BA EY* and the numerals B, Γ, Δ, on the reverse not to Eumenes II but to his son Aristonicus, who also called himself by the name Eumenes after his *coup*. These cistophori were minted at Thyateira in the second year of the new king's reign and at Apollonia and Stratonicea in his third and fourth years. Previous attempts to explain these coins can be found in the index to D. Kienast 'Cistophoren' *Jahrbuch für Numismatik und Geldgeschichte* 11 (1961), s.v. 'Eumenes'. Robinson's interpretation is supported by L. Robert *Villes d'Asie Mineure*[2] (Paris 1962), 252, who also draws the historical and geographical conclusions that follow from recognizing this.

[41] *OGIS* 338 l.20ff.; see p. 94f. below.

freedom; he called them *Heliopolitai*'.[42] So his appeal to slaves had gone out long before this, and what he was now doing was giving final shape to his proletarian state. If the pretender had from the beginning looked to the lower classes for support, this would explain, firstly, why the Greek cities were unwilling to take any part in the movement (only Phocaea joined him of her own accord) and also the significant zeal with which the neighbouring kings of Bithynia, Paphlagonia, Pontus and Cappadocia, clients of Rome and the owners of great numbers of slaves, supported the overthrow of Aristonicus. We can only vaguely imagine what kind of social structure the new state would have had. As we shall see (below, pp. 69ff.), the designation of its members as *Heliopolitai* combines religious and nationalistic pretensions. The fact that Blossius, a supporter of the policies of the Gracchi at Rome, fled to Aristonicus in Asia after the death of Tiberius Gracchus, does not really help us to understand the social structure of the Heliopolitan community,[43] but it does prove quite clearly that opponents of senatorial policy and enemies of Rome had high hopes of Aristonicus, or at least greater hopes than of Eunus. As far as we are concerned, the insurgent slaves of Asia were no more than the passive instruments of a pretender, and only the way their struggle went on after the death of their leader gives us some inkling of their hopes for a better world.

The second Sicilian revolt is more informative from a political point of view. Here the phase of widespread violence was quickly superseded by vigorous political activity. After those slaves who were hoping to be given back their freedom had been turned away by the praetor Nerva, they gathered in the precincts of the shrine of the Palici, the traditional bastion of Sicilian independence, and discussed preparations for a revolt; but, at the same time, disturbances began 'in many places'. In the district of Halicyae in the extreme west of the island, they started when slaves on a large villa murdered their masters, were joined by

[42] εἰς δὲ τὴν μεσόγαιαν ἀνιὼν ἤθροισε διὰ ταχέων πλῆθος ἀπόρων τε ἀνθρώπων καὶ δούλων ἐπ' ἐλευθερίᾳ κατακεκλημένων, οὓς Ἡλιοπολίτας ἐκάλεσε. Vavřínek *op. cit.* 30f. also places the appeal to the slaves at the beginning of Aristonicus' rising. A different view is suggested by Bömer III, 154ff., whose argument is not, however, entirely convincing; he deals with the political and religious factors of the rising in detail.

[43] Blossius' policies seem to arise more from the traditional attitudes of his family—supporting Campanian independence and later also anti-Roman—than from Stoicism. Cf. D. R. Dudley 'Blossius of Cumae' *JRS* 31 (1941), 94ff.

slaves from neighbouring farms and occupied a defensible position near by (Diod. 36, 3.3–6). The uprising at first followed a similar course in another locality in the south-west, but the defeat of a Roman levy led to a great increase in numbers and quickly inspired long-term political action. The insurgents met as an *ekklesia* and elected one of their number, Salvius, as king. There is good contemporary evidence for slaves with this name, one of the many popular names signifying luck, but it does not necessarily follow that Salvius had been born in the Italian area. He was a soothsayer and flute-player at women's festivals, which again points to the religious basis of his suitability for leadership. It was this Salvius who directed that the cities were to be avoided as seats of idleness and debauchery, divided the insurgents into three separate groups under their own commanders, and ordered them to raid the countryside to recruit supporters and obtain better equipment. After the three divisions had reassembled in the vicinity of Morgantine in the south-east of the island,[44] operations began in earnest (Diod. 36, 4.1–5).

Meanwhile Athenion, a Cilician who was well versed in astrology, had courageously collected together a band of slaves in the vicinity of Segesta and Lilybaeum, had been chosen king and had himself crowned with the diadem. His organization of the labour-force in the area under his authority was quite surprising; he employed only the ablest men as soldiers, and obliged the rest to remain in their previous employment and position, an arrangement which also guaranteed the upkeep of the troops. He declared in an edict that the gods had shown him by means of the stars that the whole of Sicily would fall into his hands, and that the land, its cultivation and its produce were therefore to be treated with as much respect as if they belonged to himself (Diod. 36, 5.1–3). So here a stop had been put to the murdering and pillaging by a man who had been employed as a bailiff while a slave and had been in charge of two hundred labourers. It is possible that Athenion claimed as a royal prerogative that his subjects had an obligation to serve him, as did the Hellenistic rulers in the East. It could also be held that this command to spare the countryside as if it belonged to himself was intended to suggest to slaves that land would be communally owned in this new state.

As in the case of the first war, the two most important revolutionary cells coalesced—this duality may in the last analysis be due to the

[44] On the question of the site of Morgantine see M. T. Piraino 'Morgantina e Murgentia nella topografia dell' antica Sicilia Orientale' *Kokalos* 5 (1959), 174ff.

Punic and Greek origins of the Sicilian economy—and it was again the Cilician who submitted to the other's authority. Salvius, who had successfully established himself in the most fertile regions of the East, proclaimed himself king after a solemn sacrifice of thanksgiving to the Palici, and was given the name *Tryphon* by his followers (Diod. 36, 7.1). This must refer to the ceremony of the coronation, as he had already been elected king. The royal name Tryphon, which he bore from now on, points to the Hellenistic East. There are instances of its use which suggest that this name expressed the *Tryphē* or revelry of a Persian King of Kings as a formal aim in life,[45] but this would only be valid if *Tryphon* were used as a cognomen. In any case, the original meaning of the name had faded from popular memory so completely that *Tryphon* and *Tryphaina* were used as ordinary personal names.[46] Any suggestion of a connection with oriental luxury would be utterly misplaced so far as Salvius was concerned, since he had wanted the towns to be avoided because of their debauchery. Perhaps he was thinking of some particular bearer of that name. We know of one king who called himself by this name alone, the Seleucid usurper who first put the child Antiochus Epiphanes Theos on the throne, and then removed his creature and made himself ruler (probably in 142/141 B.C.). As king, his coins show that he broke with custom by using the years of his own reign as dates instead of those of the usual Seleucid Era, and by expressly placing the title *Autokrator* beside that of *Basileus*; this shows his awareness of the military basis of his power.[47] The personality of this man, who started off as a captain, then became a robber, an officer again, and finally a king, was never forgotten at Apamea, near which he had been born and within whose walls he died by leaping into a fire.[48] Perhaps the memory of this dazzling individual lived on among slaves from the East, and perhaps it was the revolutionary traits and the autocratic power of his regime that made him an example to the Sicilian insurgents.

King Tryphon set to work to create a definite constitutional form for his government, and to build himself a royal residence (Diod. 36,

[45] A. Alföldi 'Die Geschichte des Throntabernakels' *La Nouvelle Clio* 1/2 (1949/50), 556f.

[46] Cf. E. Meyer *Ursprung und Anfänge des Christentums* II (Stuttgart and Berlin 1921), 258, n. 5.

[47] W. Hoffmann *RE* VII A, 720f.; H. Seyrig *Notes on Syrian Coins* (*Numismatic Notes and Monographs* 119; 1950), 12ff. (on the date).

[48] This is suggested by Strabo's account, 16, 2.10.

7.2–4). He summoned Athenion to him as a king would summon his general. Athenion obeyed and accommodated himself to demotion from king to *strategos*; he ranked next after the king and would become his successor after his death. Tryphon equipped the lofty citadel of Triokala as his residence in the style of a Hellenistic royal foundation; it had a wall and moat in its capacity as a fortress, and as an urban centre a palace and a spacious market-place. He created a council (συνέδριον) as Eunus had done before him, but his attire was that of a Roman ruler; he had lictors accompany him and wore a wide-bordered tunic covered by a purple mantle, corresponding to the senatorial *tunica laticlavia* and the *toga purpurea* worn by the highest Roman magistrate, the *triumphator*. During one of the minor Italian insurrections which preceded the Sicilian revolt, the Roman *eques* T. Vettius, an adventurer whose enterprise had no chance of succeeding, had worn both the diadem and the purple cloak and had lictors accompany him (Diod. 36, 2.4). One might well connect Tryphon's official attire with the military stamp of the Seleucid *Basileus Autokrator*.

To pause for a moment to survey this second attempt to found a state in Sicily, it must be said that there was certainly no shortage of political ideas. But the resultant product, as it is described in our sources, is on the whole extremely amorphous, if not an assortment of rejected concepts stemming from the Eastern and the Western worlds. The greatest degree of originality is to be found in Athenion's division of his followers into soldiers and civilians, and his indication that the whole land might at some stage be held in common. If there were any communistic tendencies here, they did not stop the free proletariat from plundering and murdering even on this occasion (Diod. 36, 11), and there was no solidarity among the poor and oppressed as a whole. Tryphon's monarchy comprised both Hellenistic and Roman elements, and he was the first important leader to make the highest Roman magistracy symbolize the kingship. This strange combination of triumphal garb and monarchy anticipates the dictatorship of Caesar.

In the case of Spartacus, every facet of his life and activity that we are told about was determined by the needs of military service, the gladiatorial profession, and leadership in war, so that the quest for any political plans that may have played a role in his uprising must be inconclusive. This seems natural both because of his own origins and character and also because of the national characteristics of the larger sections of his sizeable army. He himself is said to have been a Thracian, and his name also points to a Thracian origin (so does the fact that the name *Spartokos* occurs in the ruling dynasty of the Kingdom of the Bosphorus). As a *Sparticus* of the tribe of the Bessi is mentioned in a military diploma of the Emperor Claudius,[49] it is, indeed, possible that the gladiator also came from this wild and warlike people. According to Strabo (7, 5.12), the Bessi were considered brigands even by the robbers who infested Mount Rhodope, and they therefore counted as thieves to the second degree. Admittedly, the character of this courageous and prudent warrior does not lack elements of nobility and kindness; but Hellenistic culture, which in one form or another had influenced the Syrian and Cilician slaves, remained totally alien to him, and theoretical thinking did not interest him. This is also true of the Thracians, Celts and Germans who constituted the major forces among his supporters, and against whom those men of Greek and Italic origin who came to join him were never able to prevail.[50]

The escape from the gladiatorial school had been preceded by a conspiracy. But as soon as the plot was discovered, personal decisions had to be taken about an immediate escape, hasty mobilization and the taking up of positions on Mount Vesuvius. There, three leaders were chosen, of whom Spartacus was the first, with the Gauls Crixus and Oenomaus as his lieutenants.[51] Spartacus proved his superior intelligence during the course of the rebellion, but his leadership was not of such a kind as to exclude opposition; on the contrary, his own better judgement often had to give way before that of the other chieftains and the rank and file. There is no evidence that there were any outward marks of leadership. When the insignia and lictors of the praetor Varinius were captured in battle, they were brought to Spartacus as booty,[52] but it is not said whether he ever made any use of them. His problem was to wage war under the most difficult conditions for the highest of aims, and the few measures of a political nature of which we are told were in line with this task. His attempts to put a limit to the murder and pillaging and the equal allotment of booty[53] were intended to conserve all energy for the struggle in hand. We are told that

[49] *CIL* III, 844 = *CIL* XVI, 1 = *ILS* 1986.

[50] On the Thracian and Germano-Celtic elements in Spartacus' following, see M. Capozza 'Spartaco e il sacrificio del cavallo' *Critica Storica* 2 (1963), 251ff.

[51] Plut. *Crass.* 8, 3, also Appian *Bell. Civ.* 1, 540; the tradition followed by Livy recognizes three leaders of equal rank.

[52] Plut. *Crass.* 9, 7; Flor. 2, 8.7f.

[53] Sall. *Hist.* 3, fr. 98A and C (Maurenbrecher); Appian *Bell. Civ.* 1, 541.

during the last days of the revolt, when he was near Thurii trying to make contact with Sicily, he forbade merchants to import any gold or silver, and forbade his men to possess any.[54] Even this demand was not related to any Greek social theory, but, rather, was clearly intended to make it easier to acquire essential war materials such as iron and other metals and to prevent his warriors from becoming normal citizens. The way of life of Spartacus' army was certainly one of war-time communism, but, on the other hand, there is no hint of any plans to remodel society. His aims were to bring the crowds of slaves back to their homelands, to carry on the fight against Rome and to try to make contact with Sicily. Italy was merely the theatre of war, not a country whose society had to be reformed. So the inhabitants of the towns remained indifferent and even hostile to the slave revolt, although the insurgents were joined by a stream of impoverished peasants and hired workers from the land, some of them from the same areas from which Catiline was to draw his support some years later.[55] The outlandish behaviour of these northern warriors who in slavery had learnt nothing and forgotten nothing almost seems to support Aristotle's contention (*Politics* 7, 6.1 = 1327b23f.) that the peoples of the European interior surpassed others in courage, but lacked understanding, so that they might well be free and independent, but were nevertheless unfit to build a state or to rule over others.

Religious and National Motivations

Although slaves were completely excluded from politics, the religion and cults of the Greeks and particularly of the Romans did give them a certain amount of recognition and ultimate protection as human beings. In the general air of unrestrained festivity of the Greek festivals of Cronos and the Roman Saturnalia class distinctions were forgotten, at least for this one day, which was considered a revival of the original Golden Age, and slaves were even waited upon by their own masters.[56] In cases of extreme oppression slaves could place themselves under the

[54] Appian *Bell. Civ.* 1, 547. [55] Pareti *Storia di Roma* III, 690, 814f.

[56] M. P. Nilsson *Geschichte der griechischen Religion* I^2 (Munich 1955), 512f. id. *RE* II A, 201ff.; cf. S. Luria 'Die letzten werden die ersten sein' *Klio* 22 (1929), 406f., 421ff.; W. B. Kristensen 'De antieke opvatting van Dienstbaarheid' *Meded. Kon. Ak. Afd. Letterk.* 78B (1934), 95ff. and in particular Bömer III, 173ff. Cf. also Ch. II above.

protection of certain shrines. Although this did not ultimately make them the property of the particular divinity to whom they had turned, the sanctuary would support them until their master had at least given them better conditions.[57] Various divinities were particularly closely associated with slaves, especially the Chthonic deities, the Lares and Silvanus, but also Artemis and Diana; Zeus Eleutherios was originally the god of free men, but in Hellenistic times he began to be more intimately connected with slaves, together with his Latin counterpart, Iuppiter Liber; to these must also be added Helios, who lets his light shine on all men equally and so became the protector of Justice.[58] In the ancient Semitic East, the sun-god already had the same function, and when in Hellenistic times the Syrian religion was disseminated in the West by merchants and slaves, the god Hadad of Baalbek came to have a dominant position in it. In the Graeco-Roman world, he was furnished with the symbols of the sun-god, and in the West was called Iuppiter Heliopolitanus.[59] In 128/7 B.C. a temple was built on Delos for Hadad and his consort Atargatis, the goddess of Hierapolis in Syria. At this time they were still being addressed by their Syrian titles, but later they were also given the names Zeus or Helios and Aphrodite.[60] Slaves were also admitted to the ritual associations of these gods; and there were probably mystery rites linked to the cult. But there were, otherwise, no doctrines about the social structure of the human race, and no programmes for revolution connected with these secret initiation ceremonies. On the other hand, we do know of religious associations of Hellenistic and especially Roman times which had an extremely materialistic eschatology. The idea that the world to come would bring universal satisfaction often led to revolutionary agitation at the festivals and banquets of these clubs.[61]

So, to some extent, religion was a bastion of freedom for slaves, particularly in the case of the oriental cults which had loosened their

[57] On the rights of slaves to sanctuary in Rome and ancient Italy see F. Altheim *Römische Religionsgeschichte* I (Baden-Baden 1951), 175ff.

[58] Cf. in particular Bömer I, 110ff., III, 154ff., who in some important respects corrects the views of J. Bidez 'La cité du monde et la cité du soleil chez les Stoïciens' *Académie Royale de Belgique, Bulletins de la Classe des Lettres* 18 (1932), 275ff.

[59] Dussaud *RE* VIII, 50ff.

[60] Roussel *op. cit.* 252ff.; G. Goossens *Hiérapolis de Syrie* (Université de Louvain *Receuil de travaux d'histoire et de philologie* 3, 12: 1943), 94ff.

[61] B. Reicke 'Diakonie, Festfreude und Zelos' *Upps. Univ. Årsskr.* 1951, 5, 186ff., 310f., 325ff.

ties with a particular city or people and turned to all men in their universal missionary activity, addressing each person as an individual. In the rituals and symbolism of these cults, slaves who had been systematically uprooted from their native lands could express their common experience as outcasts among men, and find refuge with the gods. It is quite understandable that they sought extreme forms of religious experience and looked for visible tokens of divine aid, and that they should try to discover the future through any possible means. Those slaves who were of oriental origin were already given to orgiastic types of worship by their upbringing, and they were now also afflicted by the severe strain of lifelong servitude. We know from the experiences of many people in our own times what the spiritual conditions of a prison camp are like, how willing people are to believe any tokens of hope for the future, and how ready they are to clutch at the slightest prospect of freedom. We may assume that this kind of tension existed among the large slave-gangs on farms and other enterprises in Asia and Greece, Sicily and Italy. Once the signal for freedom had been given and the first steps towards revolt had been taken, there began an extremely dangerous existence; so it is hardly surprising that, when these momentous decisions were being made, they should have looked for a lucky omen or a few words of prophecy. Upper-class Greeks and Romans also looked into the future when they decided to overthrow a tyrant or seize power in an autocratic state. This was so widespread that in the Roman Empire claims that someone had interpreted the future in secret were often accepted as sufficient proof of high treason and an attempt to usurp power. Indeed, whenever a particular occupation entailed great hazards and daily risks to one's life, there was in antiquity a very strong tendency to try to find out in advance what the next day would bring. Soldiers and brigands were alike in this respect. It would seem that their behaviour has not changed over the centuries: the Greek minister, Sotiropoulos, who was held captive by a gang in the Peloponnese for over a month in 1866, noted that the robbers told their fortunes from the shoulder-blades of each animal they slaughtered, and that every morning they discussed their dreams of the previous night.[62]

This shows perhaps how significant it is that Eunus received news of the future from the gods, that Salvius was skilled in divination

[62] Gustav Meyer *Essays und Studien* II (Strassburg 1893), 184ff. and particularly 204f. (on banditry in the Balkan peninsula).

and that Athenion was an astrologer (Diod. 34, 2.5; 36, 4.4; 5.1). Spartacus' wife was able to tell fortunes, since she understood the significance of the snake which wound itself around his head while he was asleep during his fateful journey into slavery, and interpreted it as an omen of a great and terrifying power which was to bring misfortune to its possessor (Plut. *Crassus* 8, 4). The slaves near Enna only dared to open hostilities after Eunus had informed them of the gods' agreement (Diod. 34, 2.10).

We can gauge, to some extent, what an important role ancient indigenous cults played in the Sicilian revolt from the very incomplete accounts that survive. After the praetor at Syracuse had ordered them to return to their masters, the slaves gathered at the sanctuary of the Palici to organize their revolt. Salvius dedicated a purple mantle to the same gods in thanksgiving for his first successes (Diod. 36, 3.3; 7.1). These divine brothers were the demons of the volcanic springs that rise in the Lago dei Palici not far from Catania; they were the chthonic deities worshipped by the native Sicels with whom slaves on the run found refuge, underworld powers who watched over the sanctity of oaths.[63] In turning to the Palici, the insurgents professed themselves to be a sworn community bound to the soil of Sicily for good or ill. It seems that during the first war the slaves wanted to associate themselves with Zeus Aetnaeus, the god who was worshipped at Catania when it was recolonized and given the new name Aetne, and whose cult probably continued at the new settlement of Aetne-Inessa after the inhabitants had been expelled. The god also had shrines at other places in Sicily.[64] Posidonius reports that as a result of one of the Sibylline prophecies, the Roman Senate sent a delegation to Sicily with orders to make sacrifices at all the altars of Zeus Aetnaeus, and that the ambassadors put up barriers around the god's shrines to keep away all visitors except those who had to perform the customary sacrifices on behalf of their municipalities (Diod. 34, 10). This may well have been intended to prevent the insurgents from obtaining the god's blessing.[65] It is

[63] Ziegler *RE* XVIII, 3, 100ff.; B. Pace *Arte e civiltà della Sicilia antica* III, 520ff.; J. H. Croon 'The Palici—an Autochthonous Cult in Ancient Sicily' *Mnemosyne* IV, 5 (1952), 116ff.; L. Bello 'Ricerche sui Palici' *Kokalos* 6 (1960), 71ff. On the Sicel nature of the cult see Diod. 11, 88.6; on rights of asylum for slaves, Diod. 11, 89.6ff. For the reference to the *Palici* in the *Aetnaeae* of Aeschylus, see M. Pohlenz *Die griechische Tragödie* II² (Göttingen 1954), 198ff.

[64] E. Ciaceri *Culti e miti nella storia dell'antica Sicilia* (Catania 1911), 34f., 145f.; A. B. Cook *Zeus* II (Cambridge 1925), 908ff.; Pace *op. cit.* III, 539f.

[65] A. Holm *Geschichte Siciliens im Altertum* III (Leipzig 1898), 111. The reason

certainly fair to assume that Demeter, who was honoured throughout Sicily, was invoked by the slaves in both wars. Cicero (*Verr.* 2, 4.112) expressly states that Eunus' slaves did not dare to touch the shrine of the goddess at Enna. And the fact that after the murder of Tiberius Gracchus a delegation of priests was sent to Enna because of a Sibylline oracle *Cererem antiquissimam placari oportere* (*Verr.* 2, 4.108) shows that during the first revolt the Romans too tried hard to win the favour of the goddess. At Catania, and presumably in other places in Sicily as well, there was an image of the goddess which only women were allowed to see; perhaps it was at the secret rituals of one of these shrines that Salvius served as a flute-player at performances for women (Diod. 36, 4.4). The story of the people who were punished by the goddess during the first war for having eaten her sacred fish remains unexplained.[66]

The Syrian goddess Atargatis played an even more powerful role than did the native deities; because of her and her prophet Eunus, the first revolt almost took on the character of a religious war at its onset. At the command of the gods, the magician and miracle-worker Eunus predicted the future first on the basis of dreams and then of visions, and he finally declared that the Syrian goddess was appearing to him and promising him that he would become king (Diod. 34, 2.5–7). In other words, he appealed to a deity whom we know to have had particular associations with slaves, admittedly not from any evidence about her original Syrian shrine at Hierapolis (in spite of what Lucian writes and in spite of the excavations that have been carried out there),[67] but rather from Delos. The inscriptions found on Delos show clearly that Atargatis, generally called 'Holy Aphrodite' (Ἁγνὴ Ἀφροδίτη) had a much higher status than her consort Hadad, and that, as the 'Deity who listens' (ἐπήκοος θεός), she intervened directly in the lives of her devotees, who dedicated their offerings in obedience to her

for the Roman embassy was an eruption of Etna, which can be dated to 135 B.C. on the testimony of Obsequens 26 and Orosius 5, 6.2.

[66] Diod. 34, 9. On the sacred fish in the cult of Atargatis (Lucian *De Syria Dea* 45ff.), see F. Cumont *Les religions orientales dans le paganisme romain*[4] (Paris 1929), 108f. [= *The Oriental Religions in Roman Paganism* (New York 1956), 117.]. H. Stocks 'Studien zu Lukians De Syria dea' *Berytus* 4 (1937), 6; Goossens *op. cit.* 61ff.

[67] On this pamphlet of Lucian's, see C. Clemen *Lukians Schrift über die Syrische Göttin* (*Der Alte Orient* 37, 3/4: 1938); on Hierapolis, apart from the above-mentioned works by Stocks and Goossens, there are the brief notes by F. Cumont in *Études Syriennes* (Paris 1917), 35ff.

commands (κατὰ πρόσταγμα).[68] Theogenes, one of the many slaves who took part in her cult, set up an inscription which bears impressive witness to the support the goddess gave slaves and to the comradeship of the faithful in her cult. Theogenes implored the help of Helios and the Holy Goddess, ritually cursing his mistress, who had deprived him of some money he had entrusted to her (apparently for the purpose of buying himself free), and perhaps also of his manumission itself. 'May she not escape the power of the Goddess! I request and beg all the faithful to speak ill of her continually.'[69] In other words, the whole community of her devotees (θεραπευταί) had to support Theogenes by cursing his perjured mistress 'hourly' (καθ' ὥραν), that is, without intermission.

Syrian slaves must surely have played the same prominent part as at Delos when they introduced the worship of their native goddess to Sicily. Eunus of Apamea claimed her authority for his most important prophecy, and had learnt how to exhale sparks and flames from his mouth to prove that his prophecies were the result of divine possession (ἐνθουσιασμός). We have a description of Eunus' trick, which consisted of injecting a glowing substance into a nut which had holes bored into it at either end, and then exhaling flames by breathing through it. But that does not mean that from the start Eunus was consciously a fraud like Alexander of Abonuteichos, the false prophet described by Lucian (Ἀλέξανδρος ἢ ψευδομάντις 8: 11ff.), who, when people were terrified by his sermons on fear and hope and asked him for information about the future (πρόγνωσις), made them rave with divine inspiration by pretending to be in ecstasy, having discovered how to make himself foam at the mouth. According to the view generally held in antiquity, flames which appear mysteriously could accompany intuitive prophecy—they certainly recall Dionysus' habit

[68] Roussel *op. cit.* 261ff.

[69] μὴ ἐκφύγοι τὸ κ[ρά]τος τῆς θεᾶς, ἀξιῶ δὲ καὶ δέομαι πάντας τοὺς θερ[α]πευτὰς βλασφημεῖν αὐτὴν καθ' ὥραν *BCH* 6 (1882), 500, no. 24 (Hauvette) and *BCH* 28 (1904), 151f. (Durrbach); cf. Roussel *op. cit.* 266ff. In his study of the *Syria Dea*, Bömer (III, 93) questions the assumption that Theogenes was in fact a slave. Admittedly the relevant words that would have followed his name have been lost, but Theogenes' complaint against the woman runs: αὐτὴ δὲ λαβοῦσα παρα[κα]ταθήκην εἰς ἐλευθερίαν ἀπεστέρησε. This can hardly be interpreted in any other way than as the accusation of a slave who has been tricked out of his manumission. Bömer's interpretation of the uprisings of Eunus and Aristonicus (III, 96ff., 154ff.) is extremely interesting, but I cannot agree that religious motivations were of as little importance in these movements as he suggests.

of breathing out flames (πυρίπνοος).[70] In the ancient Near East, as in the Old Testament, God's tongue was visualized as a devastating flame. In a text as late as the Apocalypse of Ezra, the Messiah appears in battle working miracles; he exhales a flaming and fiery breath from his mouth and his lips, and raging sparks fly from his tongue to consume his enemies.[71] Eunus also breathed out flames when he prophesied, and at the assault on Enna he advanced at the head of his band of followers spewing out flames (Diod. 34, 2.11). I am sure that he believed himself to be divinely inspired as a prophet and warrior, and was accepted as such by his followers; it was, after all, precisely his ability to perform miracles which led to his being chosen as king. If he was also a priest of the Syrian goddess—which is not, of course, certain—then, like his counterpart John Hyrcanus, the son of Simon the Maccabee, he combined in his person three extremely important attributes—political leadership, the priesthood and the power of prophecy.[72] We cannot say whether it was with Eunus himself or only in the judgement of his enemies that this enthusiastic faith became a mere pretence. Many of our reports about the events that led up to the Jewish War show how a war of liberation, which broke down traditional restraints and awakened a consciousness that was willing to be inspired, also provided the opportunity for wizards (γόητες) and impostors (πλάνοι): 'cheats and deceivers appeared who, on the pretence of being divinely inspired, schemed to bring about revolutionary disturbances and goaded the mob to act with such madness that they went out into the desert to witness divine signs of their coming liberation'.[73]

We ought, indeed, to consider to what extent the general character of Eunus' uprising was influenced by the Maccabean war of liberation. Slaves who came from Syria will have known how a small nation with divinely inspired leadership had thrown off the yoke of kings who still

[70] Hopfner *RE* XIV, 1261ff. On breathing connected with divine inspiration, and sometimes with the appearance of fire, see H. Kleinknecht's article 'Pneuma' *Theologisches Wörterbuch zum Neuen Testament* VI, 333ff.

[71] IV *Ezra* 13, 9ff.; cf. Eisler *op. cit.* II, 723, 2, and also 718, 1 and 725, 6.

[72] Josephus *BJ*. 1, 2.8: τρία γοῦν τὰ κρατιστεύοντα μόνος εἶχε, τήν τε ἀρχὴν τοῦ ἔθνους καὶ τὴν ἀρχιερωσύνην καὶ προφητείαν: ὡμίλει γὰρ αὐτῷ τὸ δαιμόνιον ὡς μηδὲν τῶν μελλόντων ἀγνοεῖν.

[73] Josephus *BJ* 2, 259; also P. Volz *Die Eschatologie der jüdischen Gemeinde im neutestamentlichen Zeitalter*[2] (Tübingen 1934), 183f.; further evidence can be found in J. Pickl *Messiaskönig Jesus in der Auffassung seiner Zeitgenossen*[2] (Munich 1935), 30ff.

claimed to be world-rulers. Religious and nationalistic motivations were inextricably intertwined in this struggle—the Maccabees were often looked upon as kings who would bring in the era of salvation,[74] yet the result of their achievement was the creation of an independent national state. It has been suggested that Diodorus' statement that Eunus became the 'Lord of All' (κύριος τῶν ὅλων) and called his followers Syrians (Diod. 34, 2.15 and 24) means that he was declared to be a universal ruler in the sense customary in the ancient Near East, and that his ultimate aim was to spread the revolt throughout the whole of the world and to unite all the oppressed into a single Syrian nation.[75] But the text actually says something different: immediately after the account of his election, τῶν ὅλων δὲ τοῖς ἀποστάταις καταστὰς κύριος can only mean that he was given supreme authority over the Sicilian insurgents. Once we have seen Eunus as a new Antiochus treading in the footsteps of the Seleucids, we can interpret this designation of his followers as Syrians as the collective term for a subject population that was customary at the time of the later Seleucids, so that according to the formulation of the period, his rule would have been a βασιλεία τῶν Σύρων.[76] This claim will then mean nothing more than that in the struggle against Rome the nation of 'Syrians' that was constituted by the king's decision would win its freedom under his leadership. It was, after all, during these same years that the Jews in Palestine were transformed from a group of rebels into a national community. While Antiochus IV's general Lysias had his messages to the rebels addressed τῷ πλήθει τῶν Ἰουδαίων, the Roman ambassadors in the same year (165/4) wrote τῷ δήμῳ τῶν Ἰουδαίων, thereby recognizing the Jews as a political community, a *Demos*.[77] Thirty years later, John Hyrcanus, whom we compared to Eunus in his role as a ruler, priest and prophet, took over the leadership of the people and sundered the last ties between his community and the Seleucid empire, putting

[74] H. Windisch *Der messianische Krieg und das Urchristentum* (Tübingen 1909), 3ff.; Volz *op. cit.* 173ff.; M. Hengel *Die Zeloten* (*Arbeiten zur Geschichte des Spätjudentums und des Urchristentums* 1: Leiden-Cologne 1961), 277ff.

[75] Eisler *op. cit.* II, 724ff.

[76] Bikerman *Institutions des Séleucides* 4f.; M. Launey *Recherches sur les armées hellénistiques* (*Bibliothèque des écoles françaises d'Athènes et de Rome* 169, 1/2), I (1949/50), 536.

[77] II *Macc.* 11, 16 and 34; cf. E. Meyer *Ursprung und Anfänge des Christentums* II (Stuttgart-Berlin 1921), 213; E. Bickermann *Der Gott der Makkabäer* (Berlin 1937), 83, 180 [= *The Maccabees*, tr. M. Hadas (New York 1947), 40 (the appendices do not appear in this translation)].

his own name on coins and describing himself as head of the commonwealth of the Jews.[78] This was the most spectacular example possible of how a people could rise from the level of a religious community to that of an independent state. It seems that this event made such an impression that a Sibylline Oracle was spread about in the Orient which was aimed against Rome this time: Asia would take manifold revenge for the wealth Rome had stolen and the people from Asia she had enslaved.[79] Many Syrian slaves must have been animated by such ideas of revenging themselves on the Romans. If we suppose that Eunus' originally religious enterprise began to take on the character of a struggle for national freedom, it becomes quite understandable why the Sicilian townships preferred to stay aloof from what would have been a movement aiming at foreign domination.

Of the remaining slave-leaders, only Aristonicus, as far as we know, had a similar religious and political plan. But the brief reference to the fact that he called his following of poor people and slaves *Heliopolitai*, leaves so much unanswered that we can discuss the meaning of this name with only a limited degree of certainty. There is a widely held view, recently repeated, that Aristonicus' City of the Sun is a reference to the community inhabiting that Island of the Sun lying in the Ocean which according to Diodorus (2, 55–60) was described by Iambulus in an imaginative political romance. They were a happy people who lived together in complete concord in a classless society without slaves, private property or marriage, and took their name from the highest of the gods, Helios.[80] But the date of Iambulus' work is still uncertain, despite the attempts to pinpoint the philosophical and religious influences on his political ideal and the historical experiences behind his utopian scheme.[81] In the circumstances of the ancient world,

[78] Meyer *op. cit.* II, 275; M. Noth *Geschichte Israels* (Göttingen 1950), 326f. [= *The History of Israel*, revised trans. P. R. Ackroyd (London 1960), 387]; G. Ricciotti *Storia d'Israele* II (Turin 1938), 337 [= German trans. *Geschichte Israels* II (Vienna 1955), 369].

[79] *Or. Sib.* 3, 350ff., also Rzach *RE* II A, 2128; H. Fuchs *Der geistige Widerstand gegen Rom in der antiken Welt* (Berlin 1938), 7ff., 30.

[80] On Iambulus see W. W. Tarn *Alexander the Great and the Unity of Mankind* (London 1933), 9; id. *Alexander the Great* II (Cambridge 1950), 411ff.; F. Altheim *Römische Religionsgeschichte* II (Baden-Baden 1953), 37ff.; F. Altheim and R. Stiehl *Die Araber in der alten Welt* I (Berlin 1964), 80ff.

[81] R. Andreotti 'Per una critica dell'ideologia di Alessandro Magno' *Historia* 5 (1956), 295f., justifiably leaves the date open. Others expressing doubts about the

it would have been extraordinary for a proletarian community in the process of being formed to have been given a name which might just have been comprehensible to those with a literary education. A more credible interpretation would be that in using this name, Aristonicus was thinking of the Syrian city of Heliopolis, whose chief god, called Ζεὺς Ἡλιοπολίτης in the Hellenistic world, represented the 'union of a Semitic god of the weather, sky and fertility, such as Hadad or Baal-Shamen, with a sun-god, Helios',[82] and who was to become particularly closely associated with the lower classes when his cult spread westwards. Astarte and Adonis (= Aphrodite and Hermes) were linked with this deity to form a trinity; the cult of Aphrodite included communal marriage and prostitution.[83] It may, of course, be that none of these reasons explain why Aristonicus chose this particular name. There is the added objection that the city of Heliopolis and its cult are only attested at a fairly late date in the ancient world, not before Pompey's appearance in Syria, and that we know as little about the earlier stages of the cult in Syria as about the earlier buildings which must have preceded those from the late Hellenistic and Imperial periods. So the most likely theory remains that Aristonicus meant his *Heliopolis* to be a newly founded community to be ruled over by Helios, who in Hellenistic eyes and according to the beliefs of various Asiatic nations was the god of justice and protector of the oppressed. We may compare this to the city of Uranopolis which Alexarchus, a brother of Cassander, established on the peninsula of Mount Athos,[84] a particularly apt comparison in view of the fact that Alexarchus, a disciple of the god-man Menecrates Zeus, gave himself the name Helios. It is possible that Aristonicus also wanted to be a *Helios*[85] to the citizens of his new commonwealth, and, as such, wanted to embody

connections between Aristonicus and Iambulus are D. Magie *op. cit.* II, 1041, n. 18, Vavřínek *op. cit.* 43 and Bömer III, 165ff.

[82] O. Eissfeldt *Tempel und Kulte syrischer Städte in hellenistisch-römischer Zeit* (*Der Alte Orient* 40: 1941), 46ff. It is with reference to this god that H. Bolkestein *Wohltätigkeit und Armenpflege im vorchristlichen Altertum* (Utrecht 1939), 325, would explain the origins of Aristonicus' *Heliopolitai*.

[83] Euseb. *Theophania Syr.* 2, 14 (p. 85 in Gressmann's edition); Socr. *Hist. Eccles.* 1, 18. On the abolition of prostitution by the Emperor Constantine, see Honigmann *RE* Suppl. IV, 719f. and also O. Eissfeldt *Reallexikon für Antike und Christentum* I, 1115; F. Vittinghoff *Rh. Mus.* 96 (1953), 361.

[84] The evidence is collected by H. Berve in *Das Alexanderreich* II (Munich 1926), 21, n. 41; cf. Tarn *Alexander the Great* II, 429ff.

[85] This suggestion is made by O. Weinreich *Menekrates Zeus und Salmoneus* (*Tübinger Beiträge zur Altertumswissenschaft* 18: 1933), 15.

true justice like other kings who took the ritual titles Δικαιοσύνη or Δίκαιος.[86] Not long before the time of Aristonicus, Heliocles, the last king of Bactria, who favoured the native element among the population of his country, called himself *Dikaios* on his coins, thereby uniting in his personal name and his title the idea of the just sun-god.[87] Membership of a Sun-city in this sense would have represented the highest level of citizenship for Aristonicus' followers—higher even than that offered to the Jews by the Seleucid monarchs when they proposed to have them enrolled as citizens of Antioch or even to give them the same rank as the Athenians.[88]

The people who wanted to join the Pergamene prince must have been of very diverse national origins; but because his state only lasted for such a short time, we are not told how the Phrygians and Mysians, Lydians and Carians got on together. During Spartacus' uprising on the other hand, national differences played an important and even fatal part. This was because of the strongly nationalist stamp of his best soldiers, coupled with the largely military nature of the revolt. The military organization of the Hellenistic as of the Roman world-empires was, after all, one of the factors which tended to strengthen the individuality of each country, whereas the cosmopolitan trends of the intellectual world tended to obscure national differences in supranational states. Macedonians, Greek mercenaries and barbarian auxiliaries retained their own peculiarities of armour and tactics for a long time in the armies of the kings, thereby preserving their national identity. When levies were raised, Thracians and Illyrians, Cretans and Galatians formed units of their own; and the Macedonians, Persians and Mysians remained in their own groups even in the military settlements and districts of Egypt, Syria and Asia Minor.[89] Similarly, the Romans used foreign auxiliaries such as the Iberians, Balearians and Numidians, armed in their own characteristic ways and with their individuality untouched. We can see how varied these Roman levies

[86] Rostovtzeff *Social and Economic History of the Ancient World* III, 1523f.

[87] W. W. Tarn *The Greeks in Bactria and India* (Cambridge 1938), 270ff., 447. On the Pythagorean doctrine that because the king shared the power of the sun, he was the νόμος ἔμψυχος of his kingdom, see E. R. Goodenough 'The political philosophy of Hellenistic Kingship' *YCS* 1 (1928), 82.

[88] II *Macc.* 4, 9; 9, 15; also Meyer *op. cit.* II, 145, 460f.

[89] Launey has collected and interpreted a large amount of material about the formation of ethnic groups in the first volume of his work; see also P. Heichelheim 'Die auswärtige Bevölkerung im Ptolemäerreich' *Klio* Beiheft 18 (1925), 39f., 76ff. and Bikerman *Institutions des Séleucides* 57ff.

could be from the fact that the army deployed against Salvius consisted of Romans, Italians, Bithynians, Thessalians, Acarnanians and Lucanians (Diod. 36, 8.1). The same national groups existed among gladiators as among soldiers, in that prisoners of war were originally made to fight with the weapons of their own peoples. This meant that, although there were, of course, changes in the types of weapon and in the way they fought, Samnites, Gauls and Thracians fought one another as different classes of gladiators; these distinctions were preserved with particular tenacity, because military discipline was enforced in their barracks, and they were allowed to form their own clubs.[90] Contests between Gauls and Thracians were particularly popular. It so happened that from the very beginning Thracians and Gauls constituted the nucleus of Spartacus' supporters; his subordinate commanders Crixus and Oenomaus were Celts. However great the number of slaves who joined him from all parts of Italy, there always remained differences and even contrasts between the Thracian and the Celtic or Germanic sections of his army. It almost seems as if in the course of a war against a common enemy, professional rivalry between groups of gladiators played an important part in creating serious tensions, which not even Spartacus was able to overcome. Those of Celtic and Germanic origin wanted to fight a pitched battle and then march on Rome itself, whereas Spartacus' plan was to lead the slaves back to their homelands in Thrace or Gaul.[91] Is it possible that the Gauls may have been influenced by the idea of capturing the Roman Capitol in emulation of Brennus, or was it just desire for adventure that made them an over-confident horde unwilling to take the undefended road towards the Alps after the battle of Mutina?

In the context of the history of national groups in antiquity, Spartacus' wish to repatriate the slaves (the greatest proportion of whom were originally prisoners of war) deserves to be given a more positive evaluation than it has had so far. The Greeks and Romans took it for granted that exiles and political refugees should have no other wish than to return to their own country. Whole peoples who had been deported—like the Jews at Babylon—aimed at and succeeded in

[90] K. Schneider *RE* Suppl. III, 773ff.; and in particular L. Robert *Les gladiateurs dans l'Orient grec* (Paris 1940) with supplementary material in *Hellenica* III (1946), 112ff., V (1948), 77ff., VII (1949), 126ff., VIII (1950), 39ff.

[91] Plut. *Crass.* 9, 9. Pareti's suggestion (*Storia di Roma* III, 694f., 697f.) that Spartacus' raids through Italy and the division of his army were not intended to achieve the ultimate aim of a return home for the rebels, but rather to incite the rest of Italy to revolt, is not supported by the literary sources.

returning to their country of origin. But there seem to be no strong indications of this wish to go back home in these disturbances among slaves. Only in the case of the revolt in Latium of 198 B.C., in which aristocratic Carthaginian hostages were involved, could a return home have been an ultimate aim. But we may wonder what would have happened if the praetor Nerva had freed whole groups of slaves of the same nationality at Syracuse, as he had been instructed to do. These persons would then have had to be repatriated, though now as free men. The fact that Spartacus wanted to guarantee slaves their freedom in their own country marks him out as a man who, although he had seen military service with the Roman army, and had been captured and had lived for a time as a gladiator, still retained a conscious feeling of solidarity with other members of his own tribe. Probably he would have found it impossible to lead his followers outside the orbit of Roman power even in Thrace or Gaul. Nevertheless, his underestimation of the range of a world-empire should not detract from the magnitude of his vision.

The Organization of Warfare and Brigandage

After they had united to form larger groups, those rebels who wanted to assert their freedom, either by setting up a new state, or by returning to their old homes, had to fight to defend themselves against the existing powers—the civic police forces, the provincial garrisons and finally the levies which the Roman government sent out against them in regular war. In warfare, just as in constitutional matters, the slaves were dealing with completely unfamiliar things. There may well have been many among them who had been captured in war, but these would generally have forgotten their skills. They had insufficient arms, money and material; everything had to be improvised. Our sources enable us to follow at least some aspects of the rebels' peculiar conduct of war, and also to see how they applied their own new methods of warfare side by side with indiscriminate imitations.

The problem of who was to hold the military command did not arise in the case of Aristonicus, who was both ruler and general. Spartacus had two additional leaders with him, and this meant that he was sometimes forced to intervene to assert his own personal authority on the question of the supreme command. In the two Sicilian wars, as we have seen, the king was supported by a *strategos* as his subordinate;

this division of duties was fairly widespread in contemporary Hellenistic states, and it also enabled Cleon and Athenion, who were at first the leaders of separate bands, to be given influential positions immediately under the king. The ruler's *synedrion* occasionally functioned as a council-of-war, and it could happen that it would accept the advice of the *strategos* rather than that of the king (Diod. 36, 8.2). Because of the large number of slaves who flocked to join the insurrection, there was no need to raise any special levies, but it was all the more necessary to pick out those men who would be most suited for military service. We are told of special measures of this kind taken by Athenion (Diod. 36, 5.2) and Spartacus (Sall. *Hist.* 3, fr. 98B; cf. Appian *Bell. Civ.* 1, 545). Military exercises are expressly attested in the case of Salvius (Diod. 36, 4.5). Clothing and provisions in plenty were to be found on the farms whose masters had been killed and in the townships and enemy camps that had been overrun and captured, but the supply of weapons presented some difficulties. Eunus set the captive citizens of Enna to work producing arms, but initially his troops were equipped in a very makeshift way, with axes, slings, sickles and spits; for some time the slaves were no better armed as they faced the regular troops than were sixteenth-century German peasants during their insurrections. Their main source of weapons was what they captured from the enemy, for whatever arms factories there were in the towns of Sicily and Italy (the description of the island in Cicero's *Verrines* does not give us any information as far as Sicily is concerned) were working for the government. A large number of lead sling-stones has been unearthed near Enna; many of them bear the name of the consul L. Piso, showing that they date from the siege of the town in 133 B.C. A club and a dagger were scratched on one of these missiles, apparently to denote the primitive weapons of the besieged.[92] Spartacus' excellent military judgement is exemplified by the references, in the surviving accounts of his activity, to the systematic capture of weapons, the production of spears and shields and the provision of iron and metal ores.[93] As for the two Sicilian wars, horses and riders are only mentioned occasionally in connection with Salvius and Athenion, but the raising and proper use of cavalry was a key element in Spartacus' tactics.[94]

[92] Liebenam *RE* VII, 1378f.; Pace *Arte e civiltà* I, 287.1.

[93] Sall. *Hist.* 3, fr. 96, 101–3; Appian *Bell. Civ.* 1, 540, 542, 547; Plut. *Crass.* 8–11; Flor. 2, 8.6.

[94] Diod. 36, 4, 5; 8.3; Sall. *Hist.* 3, fr. 101; Appian *Bell. Civ.* 1, 553 and 556; Flor. 2, 8.7.

Generally speaking, it would seem that only Aristonicus and Spartacus had properly equipped troops under their command.

Nor is it particularly meaningful to say that the leaders of the Sicilian slaves had a 'strategy' of any kind. When Salvius avoided the towns and ordered his followers to march through the countryside in three divisions (Diod. 36, 4.4), he was making a virtue of necessity, for the towns had barred their gates against him. His strategy, and also perhaps that of Eunus, could be described as one of guerrilla warfare, in that he terrorized the unprotected countryside. When it came to fighting Roman troops, the slaves had a good idea of how to gain the greatest advantage from the terrain; their successes are often ascribed to their selection of positions on sloping hillsides (Diod. 36, 2.6; 3.5; 4.3; 4.7). But we are never told whether they had any particular order of battle or attempted to outflank the enemy or to use any other kind of manoeuvre; when the slaves were victorious, it was generally owing to their numerical superiority and the bravery of individual contingents in their armies. The city-walls set a limit to their power. During the first war, Enna was captured by night in a surprise attack, and it remained the rebels' main stronghold until the end. The few other towns that fell into the slaves' hands—in particular Catania and Taorminium—were probably also captured by surprise.[95] Salvius laid siege to Morgantine without success; and Athenion nearly met with disaster before the walls of Lilybaeum, although they successfully defended themselves in Triokala (Diod. 36, 4.5; 4.8; 5.3f.; 8.4f.). Taorminium was held by the slaves in spite of extreme hunger which made them turn to cannibalism, and the Romans were only able to recapture it through treachery (Diod. 34, 2.20f.). The slaves who worked in the mines at Laureum were able to occupy the fortress of Sunium in the course of their second rebellion, and this gave them a base for their pillaging expeditions through Attica (Posid. fr. 35 Jacoby *F. Gr. Hist.* = Athenaeus 6, 272e–f).

Aristonicus pursued the twin policies of conquering the Greek cities along the coast and bringing the countryside over to his side by calling on the slaves to support him. While he was only partially successful in attaining the former of these aims, he achieved the second to a very

[95] Strabo 6, 2.6: Καταναῖοι καὶ Ταυρομενῖται καὶ ἄλλοι πλείους. For the almost successful attack on Messana, see Dio 27, fr. 93.4 (Boissevain I, 337). The events at Mamertium in Orosius 5, 9.7 remain unexplained; cf. Ziegler *RE* XIV, 952. Pareti (*Storia di Roma* III, 302) concludes on the basis of Diod. 34, 11 that the rebels did capture Morgantine, without sufficient reason.

great extent. He always had mercenaries at his disposal, and for a certain period levies from some of the Greek cities as well; these various forces gave him a large degree of manoeuvrability.[96] Spartacus' strategy was quite remarkable, for he at all times stood by his plan to break out of Italy—first during his advance to the Po valley, then when he tried to reach Sicily, and finally during the retreat in the direction of Brundisium. The tactical measures he took were intended to serve this long-term aim; he led his troops into the rural areas, which were rich in booty and militarily less dangerous, he abandoned his baggage-train on occasion, and gave up the idea of marching on Rome 'as he did not yet consider himself sufficiently prepared for a pitched battle and his forces were not yet properly armed for war'.[97] His operations included a wide variety of stratagems, from the time when he led his men down from their encircled positions on the heights of Vesuvius to the secret evacuation of his camp by night and the occasion when he bridged Crassus' great ditch.[98] If someone like Spartacus had been able to persevere in his aim of holding his ground in Italy or Sicily for a considerable time, his military intellect would surely have enabled him to discover the techniques of guerrilla warfare in town and countryside which alone would have ensured long-term success for the oppressed class.

Characteristic of the slaves' struggles in every theatre of operations were the systematic attempts to recruit supporters, to incite those slaves who were still in their masters' service to join them, and to demoralize the enemy army. In a struggle which shook the structure of society to its very foundations and recognized no clearly defined limits to the field of military operations, propaganda became a matter of far greater importance than it had been in regular wars between states. We do not know what appeals were used to tempt slaves to join the movements for their liberation, but we are told that when Eunus was besieging a city he not only hurled insults at the Romans, as was normal between two rival camps, but also had mimes, presumably of the traditional Sicilian type, performed in the sight of the townsfolk, which celebrated the slaves' revolt and abused their masters for their cruelty.[99] When Salvius laid siege to Morgantine, he called on the

[96] Vavřínek *op. cit.* 32ff, 45ff.

[97] Sall. *Hist.* 3, fr. 98B, 100; Appian *Bell. Civ.* 1, 545 and 547.

[98] Plut. *Crass.* 9f.; Sall. *Hist.* 3, fr. 96B; Frontinus *Strat.* 1, 5.22.

[99] Diod. 34, 2.46. The text suggests that Eunus laid siege to the town. Another example of this custom is that of Xenarchus, a composer of mimes, who

slaves living in the town to assert their freedom; and before the battle in front of the city, he issued a proclamation that his men should not kill those enemy soldiers who threw away their arms, by which he broke the fighting spirit of his opponents (Diod. 36, 4.7). These forms of psychological warfare were, of course, countered by the enemy, and occasionally it happened that urban slaves preferred to be promised their freedom by their own masters than by the rebels. In times when slave conspiracies threatened, their oppressors had traditionally made use of the well-tried method of making slaves inform and betray each other by offering massive rewards. The Romans achieved some success when they applied these methods in Sicily. Rupilius captured Taorminium and Enna by treachery, Lucullus was able to bribe Vettius' general, and Nerva conquered an enemy stronghold through bribery and betrayal (Diod. 34, 2.21; 36, 2.6; 3.5). There were no traitors among Spartacus' men: if he thought it necessary on one occasion in the critical last months of his enterprise to have a Roman prisoner crucified in the space between the two armies as an extreme example to his followers of the kind of treatment they could expect if they were defeated, this was to goad them on to fight for their lives rather than to discourage them from deserting (Appian *Bell. Civ.* 1, 553).

Among the revolutionary freedom-fighters there were always many who realized that as runaway slaves, rebels and brigands, they could expect no mercy from the Romans, and it was these resolute warriors who gave the struggle that ugly element of stubbornness and defiance that so often appears in our sources. Cleon and Athenion were killed in battle, Spartacus and before him the obstinate chieftains Crixus, Castus and Gannicus went bravely to their deaths at the head of their troops. Those survivors who realized the hopelessness of their position killed themselves with the desperation shown by so many of Rome's enemies—Eunus' bodyguards decapitated each other while their master and his servants sought a last refuge in the caves; Vettius killed himself; Varius' men threw themselves over a precipice; Comanus committed suicide by suffocating himself while he was being interrogated at Enna; Satyrus and his followers, condemned to fight wild beasts at Rome, slaughtered each other at the altars in the arena.[100] It is characteristic of a primitive type of military valour that at the height

wrote a play at the instigation of the tyrant Dionysius in which the people of Rhegium were ridiculed as cowards (Suidas, s.v. Ῥηγίνους τοὺς δειλούς); on this subject see K. F. Stroheker *Dionysius I.* (Wiesbaden 1958), 100; 216, 81.

[100] Diod. 34, 3.6; 10.3: Val. Max. 9, 12 ext. 1.

of a battle the chieftains should challenge enemy commanders to single combat: Athenion was killed by the bravery of M'. Aquillius, and Spartacus met his death when he tried to attack Crassus (Diod. 36, 10.1; Plut. *Crassus* 11, 9). The heroic deaths of these men determined what picture future generations formed of them, so that people were able to tolerate Athenion as a champion of the two Sicilian uprisings, while Spartacus, however much he was detested as a rebel leader, was nevertheless honoured for the manner of his death.[101]

It was in the nature of these insurrections that they should turn into wars aiming at the utter destruction of the other side. Only through revolt, rioting and the use of violence could the slaves organize themselves as a fighting force, while the Romans considered escapees and guerrillas of this kind to be rebels and bandits, just as they later described and treated the Jewish partisans in the hills of Palestine as robbers.[102] There was no need to declare war on such people; it was a matter of fighting them until they were wiped out. *Hostes hi sunt, qui nobis aut quibus nos publice bellum decrevimus; ceteri latrones aut praedones sunt* was how a jurist formulated the legal distinction between regular warfare and police actions against robbers.[103] And, in fact, men who had previously been robbers like Cleon and Spartacus came to lead the insurgents and imposed some of their own modes of thinking and living as robbers on the course of the war.

The robber-bands of antiquity had their own peculiar codes of conduct, codes which survived among such gangs for centuries in the mountains of the Balkan peninsula, Asia Minor, Syria and Sicily, particularly in situations where the struggle for national freedom was associated with banditry. The bandit's *nomos* covers not only the technicalities and methods of applying force, but also the art of capturing the greatest amount of booty with the least possible bloodshed. Such a society is founded on trust and loyalty as well as on

[101] On Athenion see Cic. *Verr.* 2, 2.136; 3.66 and 125; *Har. Resp.* 26; cf. *Att.* 2, 12.2 and Appian *Mithr.* 59. These authors agree in giving Spartacus credit for his courageous death. There is a Pompeian mural which depicts a combat between two horsemen; one of these is identified as Spartacus by an accompanying inscription (A. Maiuri *Notizie degli Scavi* 3 (1927), 21f., fig. 5). Mischulin's suggestion (*op. cit.* 83f.) that this picture and an adjoining one of two men fighting on foot might in some way be connected with the death of Spartacus does not seem to me to be absolutely certain. Similar doubts are expressed by Brisson (*Spartacus* 277f.), who reproduces the mural on p. 239.

[102] Pickl *Messiaskönig Jesus* 22ff.; Hengel *op. cit.* 25ff.

[103] Pomponius *Dig.* 50, 16, 118; also Hengel *op. cit.* 31f.

fear; this means that its members must have an equal share in the dangers that have to be faced and the rewards that are to be won, and that they must be rigidly subordinated to their leader. These aspects of banditry were not the inventions of the rhetorical schools, nor of the novels of Hellenistic and Roman times which immortalized the figure of the noble bandit.[104] The fact that bands of robbers had this form of organization must, instead, be gleaned from numerous descriptions in historical and political writings dating from the classical period of the Greek city-states onwards. In his discussion of the early history of Greece (1, 5), Thucydides recognizes that the hierarchical form of robber societies was a primitive social structure which still survived in some districts.[105] The Sophists, and many later philosophers of various schools of thought, including the Christian Fathers, recognized that banditry was a limiting case of human existence, and cited the concord and order that robbers established between themselves in order to prove the indispensability of concord and justice among men, or, alternatively, concluded that founding a state by means of military conquest was nothing more than banditry on a large scale. At one point, Cicero argues that justice is required by nature, by referring to the *leges latronum* (*De Officiis* 2, 40), and elsewhere, in his discussion of the nature of justice in the *Republic*, he makes Carneades' disciple Philus defend the view that the state is based just as much on injustice as is any gang of robbers. To illustrate his point, he tells the story of the pirate who was captured by Alexander the Great and was asked to state by what outrages he had dared to make the seas unsafe. He answered: 'The same as those by which you make the world unsafe' (*Rep*. 3, 24).[106]

Organized banditry existed at all times in the ancient world. Sometimes it was pushed back into the peripheries of the major empires, only to reappear in the areas of greatest civilization. It was always and everywhere one of the forms of resistance against the plutocracy of the citizen-body, and a symptom of that basic human demand for equality which forced itself upon a society founded on slavery.

The personality of the slave leader and robber chief Drimacus from

[104] E. Rohde *Der griechische Roman*[3] (Leipzig 1914), 383f.; L. Radermacher 'Lukians πλοῖον ἢ εὐχαί' *Wiener Studien* 33 (1911), 228.

[105] H.-J. Diesner *Wirtschaft und Gesellschaft bei Thukydides* (Halle 1956), 33ff.

[106] These ideas were taken up by St. Augustine *Civ. Dei*. 4, 4, and elsewhere. Cf. H. Fuchs *Augustin und der antike Friedensgedanke* (*Neue Philologische Untersuchungen* 3: Berlin 1926), 19ff., 111ff., 140f.; F. G. Maier *Augustin und das antike Rom* (*Tübinger Beiträge zur Altertumswissenschaft* 39: 1955), 118f.

Chios, a notorious ancient centre of slavery, has come down to us, and from it we can see how civic society and robber society complemented one another. This figure is worth mention in connection with ancient slave wars. Athenaeus (6, 265c–266e) found this story in Nymphodorus of Syracuse's *Periplus Asiae*, which dates to the end of the third century B.C.[107] Drimacus was the leader of some runaway slaves from the city of Chios who were living in the mountains, from which they raided the Chians' property. The citizens of Chios mounted repeated campaigns against them without success. At Drimacus' suggestion, the city and the robber chief thereupon came to an arrangement by which he would carefully measure the weight and quantity of the booty he took from the Chians and then shut the barns and storehouses again with his own seal. In exchange, he was conceded the right to examine the case of every slave who was henceforth to come over to him from the city and either keep the slave with him or send him back to his master, according to the reasons for which he had run away. The result of this agreement between the legal and illegal communities of Chios was that there were fewer fugitives from the city, and that there was some measure of discipline among the bandits. Later the Chians put a reward on Drimacus' head after all, but the chieftain persuaded his lover to kill him and send in his head. After this, banditry of the old kind returned. Nevertheless, in memory of his justice, the Chians put up a shrine to Drimacus, at which both citizens and fugitive slaves were to offer sacrifices in later years.

There have been attempts to find both factual and theoretical contradictions in this story which might suggest that two entirely different tales had been confused in some way. But the minor inconsistencies that do occur can all be explained by the fact that the story as we have it is only a summary.[108] If we consider the incident as a whole, it makes

[107] Jacoby *F. Gr. Hist.* 572 F 4 comments on this; also Laqueur in *RE* XVII, 1625.

[108] Laqueur *op. cit.* 1627f. thinks that a war against a slave-leader with a price on his head who later lets himself be killed by his lover (whose date is given as μικρὸν πρὸ ἡμῶν in 265d) cannot be made consistent with the idealistic situation established by Drimacus through his organization, and upheld after his death by means of his authority as an *Heros* (ἔτι καὶ νῦν 266d). He sees formal evidence of two different levels in the story in the fact that the man's position as leader is at one point described as 'like a king' (265d) and at another as 'like a *strategos*' (266a). But these objections are unfounded. The two dates do not require us to assume that they were separated by a long period of time, and the use of the word βασιλεύς side by side with στρατηγός also occurs in Lucian's story of Samippus,

excellent sense. Drimacus brought about a just *modus vivendi* which overcame the differences between the state of the free citizens who ill-treated their slaves and the community of fugitives who robbed without restraint. He did this by taking only what was absolutely essential for himself and his men, by guaranteeing to protect the storehouses and by scrutinizing the complaints of each individual fugitive, with the result that fewer slaves ran away from their masters. On the other hand, both sides had to institute penalties to preserve this state of order, which explains why the city ultimately decided to kill the brigand after all. But by sacrificing himself, Drimacus turned the whole affair to good account, and thereby continued to exist in a generally beneficial way as a 'kindly hero' (ἥρως εὐμενής). In other words, the basis for the achievements of this robber and peacemaker, law-giver and judge, was that he brought about a *modus vivendi* between the claims of citizens and of slaves and won legal recognition for lawlessness—slavery would remain, there would also still be fugitive slaves who obtained their livelihood at the citizens' expense, but both of these were to conduct themselves according to agreed rules. Thus, whatever the historical reality behind it, this story is an admission that slavery and brigandage complement each other.

The leaders of the Sicilian and Italian rebels did not intend to come to any agreement with the state against which they were fighting; the only means that remained open to them were robbery and violence. But even in the circumstances of a war to the bitter end, they still held to the principles of just revenge—Eunus' slaves killed Damophilus and Megallis, a proud and cruel pair, but they brought their daughter, who had treated slaves well, to a place of safety without touching her. Eunus himself saved from death those who had previously behaved

who similarly rose from the level of a brigand to that of a king (πλοῖον ἢ εὐχαί 28f.), where the two terms ἄρχων and δυναστεία also occur. The question why a reward could be offered for this man if there was such an excellent understanding between the city and him can be answered by the statement that there continued to be attempts to deal with him, against which he in his turn had to defend himself (τιμωρεῖσθαι refers to indisciplined slaves, but also expressly to attempts on his life, clearly organized by the owners of the slaves—266ab). The fact that his death was voluntary explains why his beneficial influence could continue to be felt after his death. Thus Laqueur's conclusions seem to me wrong. A rather more remarkable point in this story is the fact that Drimacus' attitude ranges him on the side of the slave-owners; he is concerned about unnecessary losses on the part of the Chians (265d) and he wants to ensure his lover happiness as a free man, i.e. as a member of the world of the free citizens (266c). This shows how strong the influence exerted by the categories of the *polis* remained.

kindly towards him (Diod. 34, 2.39 and 41). Eunus and Spartacus did occasionally make an example of someone by treating a prisoner in the same way as he had previously treated his slaves—Eunus fettered the prisoners he forced to work in the arms factories, while Spartacus made hundreds of Roman captives fight each other in single combat at Crixus' funeral.[109] The way in which Cleon, Athenion and Spartacus collected bands of followers, and then had themselves chosen as their leaders on the grounds of their strength and bravery, is strongly reminiscent of the customs and rules of brigandage. A few years before Spartacus, Zenicetes had founded a robber-state in Lycia, whose king he remained until he was defeated by P. Servilius Isauricus.[110] In earlier times there had been the case of Drimacus, who is depicted by Athenaeus as a commander and a king. Later it was considered the pinnacle of good fortune for a robber leader to become king, as Lucian shows in the person of Samippus, who had started off with a band of thirty and intended to increase its size to a thousand, ten thousand, ultimately fifty thousand hoplites and five thousand cavalry, and then be elected king: 'First a bandit, then from bandit to king; and because king by his own grace, therefore higher than all the potentates of the earth.'[111] Among historical brigand chiefs, the *famosi latrones*, we repeatedly find those who see themselves as the foils of those in power and as the means whereby compensatory justice is to be won. Felix Bulla, who terrorized Italy with a band of six hundred brigands at the beginning of the third century, sent slave-owners a message that they should treat their slaves better so that they would not be forced to take up banditry. When he was captured and interrogated by the Praetorian Prefect, he answered the question 'Why are you a robber?' with 'Why are you Prefect?'[112] In more recent times, the brigand Giuliano won fame throughout Sicily for setting himself up as the leader of the exploited and the island's saviour. He could say of himself: 'All I am doing is protecting myself against this government, which hunts me down like a wild beast because I am a living symbol of my people's aspirations to freedom.' Giuliano once appeared

[109] Diod. 34, 2.15; Flor. 2, 8.9; Orosius 5, 24.3; Appian *Bell. Civ.* 1, 545.

[110] Strabo 14, 5.7; O. Benndorf *Festschrift zu O. Hirschfelds 60. Geburtstag* (Berlin 1903), 81ff.; Ormerod *Piracy* 216f.; E. Ziebarth *Beiträge zur Geschichte des Seeraubs und Seehandels im alten Griechenland* (Hamburg 1929), 34f.

[111] Lucian πλοῖον ἢ εὐχαί 28f.; the quotation is from Radermacher *Wiener Studien* 33 (1911), 226.

[112] Dio 77, 10; also L. Friedländer *Sittengeschichte Roms* I[10] (1922), 356. [= I, 297 of the English edition.]

at carnival-time as a king, with a crown over his black curls and his beard in plaits according to the ancient fashion, and with his queen Giannina at his side with a band around her forehead.[113] Thus the rebel who seeks justice and plays with the idea of monarchy can also be found in a society where, not indeed slavery, but other harsh forms of oppression exist.

A Worldwide Proletarian Movement?

If we survey the large variety of factors behind the slave wars from Eunus to Spartacus, and their divergent and even mutually contradictory aims, it is surprising how easily one school of modern scholarship has accepted the reduction of these movements to the common denominator of ancient socialism or communism. K. Bücher did indeed realize in his study of the topic[114] that there were some important respects in which individual insurrections differed, but he nevertheless believed that he had discovered that 'there was a wind of change at that time which moved men's hearts in every region, from the Capitol and the cliffs at Enna to the Taurus Mountains' (p. 114), and he describes 'the widespread proletarian movement of the thirties of the second century, the sudden emergence of socialism, which has unmistakable similarities to a phenomenon of the contemporary world, even if its demands have to conform to the dominant economic circumstances' (pp. 115f.). A. Rosenberg goes one step further;[115] for no particular reason he associates the attempted revolution of the Gracchi with the 'diffusion of Greek socialist ideas in Italy', and Aristonicus' state with 'the connections of the "Red International" of the ancient world' (pp. 58ff.). Later ancient history was modernized in a totally uncritical way by U. Kahrstedt.[116] Out of the dissolution of the political and social system which he describes so excellently he sees 'a consciously proletarian movement spanning the entire world' arising in the second and first centuries B.C. (p. 99). He talks in terms of Bolshevism in Sicily (p. 125) and ascribes to Spartacus 'a complete

[113] W. Helwig *Der Brigant Giuliano* (Frankfurt a.M. 1953), 20f., 29.

[114] *Der Aufstand der unfreien Arbeiter 143–129 v. Chr.* (Frankfurt a.M. 1874).

[115] *Geschichte der römischen Republik* (*Aus Natur und Geisteswelt*, Leipzig 1921).

[116] *Göttingische gelehrte Anzeigen* 188 (1926), 97ff. (Review of R. v. Pöhlmann's *Geschichte der sozialen Frage und des Sozialismus in der antiken Welt*[3] ed. F. Oertel (Munich 1925).)

proletarian communist state in Bruttium' (p. 127). He uses these terms again elsewhere,[117] and in spite of the well-founded objections of F. Oertel[118] and M. Rostovtzeff,[119] he finally[120] goes so far as to write of 'a united front of the proletariat against Capitalism and the bourgeoisie' in the first Sicilian revolt (p. 259), 'the classless state of the proletariat' with Aristonicus (p. 261), 'the socialization of land and of all the means of production' and 'the dictatorship of the proletariat' in the second Sicilian uprising (p. 274). The descriptions of G. Walter and B. Farrington[121] seem moderate in comparison with statements like these. They consider the slave revolts to have been preparatory steps towards communism, and talk about the dream of an international alliance of all the oppressed, and of a blueprint for a new form of society. Those scholars who have recently concerned themselves with the slaves in the mines at Laureum, H. Wilsdorf and S. Lauffer,[122] have shown greater restraint in speaking in terms of a 'latent' or 'potential International'. Soviet historiography, which has put the social movements of the ancient world in the forefront of its study, has done more justice to the individuality of the various slave rebellions by its precise analysis of the sources, than the kind of historicism which appears from time to time in the West, which is forever trying to find connections between events. A. W. Mischulin[123] only goes so far as to say that the peasants sympathized with the struggle against the great slave-owners in Sicily, and he fails to find any common element in the behaviour of slaves and peasants (pp. 38, 48). Although he over-emphasizes the participation of the impoverished peasantry in Spartacus' revolt and believes that he can see a 'struggle for the abolition of slavery and slave-holding property as such' (p. 73), he has to accept S. L. Uttschenko's correction that Spartacus' free

[117] 'Das Zeitalter des antiken Sozialismus und Kommunismus' *Hellas-Jahrbuch* 1929, 105ff.

[118] 'Die soziale Frage im Altertum' *Neue Jahrbücher für Wissenschaft und Jugendbildung* 3 (1927), 1ff.; *Klassenkampf, Sozialismus und organischer Staat im alten Griechenland* (Bonn 1942).

[119] *Social and Economic History of the Hellenistic World* III, 1367f.

[120] *Geschichte des griechisch-römischen Altertums* (Munich 1948).

[121] G. Walter *Histoire du communisme* I: *Les Origines* (Paris 1931), 529ff.; B. Farrington *Head and Hand in Ancient Greece* (London 1947), 73ff.

[122] H. Wilsdorf *Bergleute und Hüttenmänner im Altertum* (*Freiberger Forschungshefte* D 1: Berlin 1952), 145f. and Lauffer II, 242.

[123] *Spartacus, Abriss der Geschichte des grossen Sklavenaufstandes* (German edn. edited and with an introduction by S. L. Uttschenko, Berlin 1952).

supporters, numerically insignificant, 'could have had no great influence on the programme or on the aims of the movement' (p. 10). S. I. Kovaljov[124] and N. A. Maschkin[125] are able, by their clear picture of the structure of ancient society, to distinguish between the slave rebellions and the struggles of the free proletariat; they conclude that the rebellious slaves did not achieve anything that was fundamentally new.

It is the fact that the major uprisings were concentrated in a period of only a few decades, and that several uprisings occurred simultaneously, in different areas, that has made it possible for the slave revolts to be interpreted as a united, international proletarian movement. The basic explanation for these phenomena lies in the revolutionary climate of the whole of this period, which was discussed at the beginning of this chapter. But there is the additional factor that there were immediate personal contacts between the different areas of unrest and that news and propaganda were vigorously disseminated. The troubles began in Sicily in the year 135 B.C. at the latest.[126] As soon as the news of the initial successes of the Sicilian rebels had been received (Diod. 34, 2.19) there were uprisings at Rome, in the mines at Laureum in Attica and at Delos, the hub of the slave trade; the great slave-gangs at Minturnae and Sinuessa were also affected. The annalistic tradition which in its final form is preserved by Orosius (5, 9.4) uses

[124] *Storia di Roma* (Rome 1953), 335ff.

[125] *Römische Geschichte* (German edn. Berlin 1953), 251ff.; ibid. *Zwischen Republik und Kaiserreich* (German edn. Leipzig 1954), 289ff.

[126] The exact date of the beginning of the war is not certain from the historical tradition. Livy dates the beginning of the *bellum* to 134, but several praetors had to deal with the disturbances in Sicily before the consul of that year, C. Fulvius Flaccus (cf. Rathke *De Romanorum bellis servilibus* (dissertation, Berlin), 25ff.; T. R. S. Broughton *The Magistrates of the Roman Republic* (*Philological Monographs of the American Philological Association* 15), I, 483, 490; Pareti *Storia di Roma* III, 298ff.; and in particular Lauffer II, 231ff.). In his article on the chronology of the first Sicilian slave revolt (*VDI* 1940, 3/4, 62ff.), A. P. Djakonov would put the beginning of the uprising even earlier; cf. also Vavřínek *op. cit.* 23, note 60. E. Ciaceri *Roma e le guerre servili in Sicilia* (see p. 41, n. 9 above), 70ff., bases his suggestion that the movement may have begun in Italy on Obsequens' statement (27, 86): 'fugitivorum *bellum* in Sicilia exortum, coniuratione servorum in Italia oppressa'. But if we take the word *bellum* to refer to this new phase of the conflict that developed during Flaccus' consulship, previous actions in Sicily are not necessarily to be excluded, nor, therefore, the possibility that the unrest in Sicily had reciprocal effects on Italy. The *coniuratio* mentioned by Obsequens does not need to have been identical with the occurrences at Rome, Minturnae and Sinuessa.

the obvious and appropriate metaphor of sparks that travelled to Italy and the East from the Sicilian conflagration. In Aristonicus' case, there is a strong probability that this struggle was from the beginning not unconnected with what was going on in the West, and at a later stage there is proof of this in the person of Blossius. The second revolt in Sicily was preceded by the uprisings at Nuceria and Capua and Vettius' attempted seizure of power (Diod. 36, 2.1), and itself led to a second major rebellion on the part of the slaves at Laureum.[127] Although Spartacus' attempt to cross over to Sicily with the aid of the pirates came to nothing, he did succeed in bringing about unrest on the island.

We can assume that there was a certain amount of collusion between the rebels in Italy and Sicily during the whole of this period. The person referred to in an inscription from Polla[128] had, while praetor in Sicily, sent back to their Italian masters 917 slaves who had fled to the island; this occurred either before the middle of the century or in 135 B.C., which shows that Sicily was one of the places to which runaway slaves fled. On the other hand, Spartacus was able to organize effective agitation in Sicily from his base in Bruttium, as Cicero is forced to admit, albeit grudgingly. At the beginning of his final oration against Verres (*Verr.* 2, 5), he deals with Verres' supposed military achievements, and in particular with his claim to have prevented the disturbances among Italian slaves from spreading to Sicily. At first Cicero denies that there had been any such contact across the straits (5ff.), but then he has to explain away conspiracies among Sicilian slaves, which he claims that Verres had invented in order to be

[127] Posidonius Fr. 35 Jacoby *F. Gr. Hist.* (= Athenaeus 6, 272ef.). A detailed study of this uprising is in Lauffer II, 236ff.

[128] The author of the eulogy discovered at Polla in Bruttium (*CIL* I^2, 638 = *ILS* 23) claims that among other achievements he had tracked down runaway slaves belonging to Italians when he had been praetor in Sicily and had had 917 of them returned to their masters. The assumption, widespread since Mommsen, that this refers to P. Popillius Laenas, whose praetorship has been dated to 135 or shortly before (Broughton *Magistrates* I, 483, 490), has recently been questioned (V. Bracco 'L'Elogium di Polla' *Rendiconti Acc. arch., lett. e belle arti di Napoli* 29 (1955), *Estratto*.). The author of the inscription may have been T. Annius Luscus, consul in 153. In that case the operations against runaway slaves which it refers to would have taken place some years before 153. But it has not been indubitably proved that P. Popillius Laenas was not responsible for the inscription (cf. Tibiletti 'Lo sviluppo del latifondo' (see p. 43, n. 15 above), 255, 1). If it was, in fact, he who returned the fugitive slaves to Italy about 135 B.C., then this still does not prove that the disturbances originated in Italy.

better able to oppress the Sicilians (9ff.). But fabrications of this kind could only have made an impression on people who were already willing to assume that there was some connection between the unrest in Sicily and that in Italy. This also applies to Verres' claim that Gavius of Consa, a Roman citizen, had been sent to Sicily by the slave-leaders as a spy (*speculandi causa in Siciliam a ducibus fugitivorum esse missum*, 161). It seems that Spartacus did send spies and agents across the straits, but that Verres prevented these rebels from setting foot on the other side, just as he prevented the outbreak of a large-scale slave revolt on the island.[129]

Cicero also shows us how many and how varied were the contacts between Sicily and the eastern Mediterranean. He relates how Verres plundered ships that came to Syracuse from the whole of the rest of the world, on the pretext that they were sailing in aid of the rebel Sertorius. These ships came from Asia, Syria, Tyre and Alexandria, and to prove that they did not come from Sertorius' province of Spain, their captains laid out their wares: purple from Tyre, incense, perfumes, linen cloth, precious stones and pearls, Greek wines and Asiatic slaves (*Verr.* 2, 5.145f.). This shows that the ports of Sicily were the transit depots for trade between Italy and the East, and it goes without saying that along with merchandise, there was a constant traffic in news and political ideas. Because piracy was so well organized, channels of trade, news and propaganda all tended to be prejudiced against Rome, and, indeed, against regular governments generally. The pirates were involved in the wars with Mithridates, Spartacus and Sertorius, and the fight against piracy could of itself lead to an increase in revolutionary agitation. Cicero says that when Verres captured a pirate ship, he gave his Sicilian and Roman friends those of the prisoners who were young and had been taught a skill or a trade (*Verr.* 2, 5.63f.). No doubt the activity of the pirates in the western Mediterranean would have been less widespread thirty to fifty years previously, but their commercial interests were at all times bound up with the slave trade.[130] Asia was the exporter in this traffic, Delos the depot, Athens, Syracuse and Rome the insatiable consumers. The international character of this trade necessarily led to mutual contacts not only between dealers but also between their victims in all areas with large slave populations. It is not surprising that Attica was affected by

[129] The evidence for this is in E. Maróti *Acta Antiqua* 4 (1956), 197ff. and 9 (1961), 41ff.

[130] Ormerod *Piracy* 207; Ziebarth *Beiträge* 33f., 40f.

the first rebellion in Sicily, nor that it was precisely those slaves who had just been brought onto the market who rose at Delos, an island which did not employ exceptionally large numbers of slaves in its own economy.[131] Even if the length of time they were held on Delos was extremely short (and the market was proverbial for its speed), contact between men from East and West could not be avoided.[132] It seems probable that the rebels of Laureum who gained control of Sunium in 104/3 B.C. were in contact with Cilician pirates as well as with Sicily.[133]

One other factor must be taken into account if we are to understand the connections between the various areas in which slave revolts occurred, a factor which played a very important role in the public life of ancient society, based as it was on slavery: the news media of the Greeks and Romans depended to a great extent on the use of slaves. Runners and messengers, both public and private, were generally slaves or freedmen who were able to read and write and could find their way about. Occasionally slaves had to perform this arduous duty as a punishment, having to run forty or more miles in a day.[134] Surely it is obvious that on the crowded routes taken by the news services between Rome and Sicily, or Rome and Athens and Asia, these messengers would have spread the news that concerned their own class over land and sea like walking newspapers. Large gatherings of people at festivals, athletic contests and fairs would have helped to carry the news to the workshops and mines and onto the agricultural estates. The danger of slaves congregating in the countryside at harvest-time in midsummer was another of the things expressly pointed out by Cicero: the slaves could see how many they were, their work was particularly oppressive, there were large supplies of corn to tempt them and the weather was fine—a whole host of factors which favoured unrest (*Verr.* 2, 5.29).

If we consider these numerous ways of transmitting and receiving news, the way the rebellion spread will explain itself without our having to postulate a 'Red International'. Indeed, seen against this background, the degree of solidarity shown by slaves during this period of rebellions was remarkably small. There were always geographical gaps between the various areas in which rebellions occurred;

[131] J. A. O. Larsen *Economic Survey of Ancient Rome* IV, 416.

[132] On Strabo 14, 5.2 see Larsen *op. cit.* 351.

[133] Lauffer II, 239.

[134] W. Riepl *Das Nachrichtenwesen des Altertums* (Leipzig 1913), 139ff., 248; Schroff *RE* IV A, 1844ff.

while the Sicilian slaves were up in arms, those in Etruria and Apulia stayed quiet; and the miners of Laureum clearly received no assistance from the urban slaves at Athens. Even in Sicily there was no unity among the slave-class. Many preferred to have their freedom promised them by their present masters, rather than by the rebel leaders, and there was no lack of traitors when their situation became difficult. There was never any demand that the institution of slavery as such should be abolished. What tendencies there were towards a new social and economic system aimed at sharing property out anew rather than at the abolition of private ownership of the means of production—to use Oertel's terms, it was socialism based on sharing rather than on communal ownership.[135] The free proletariat never seriously supported the rebellious slaves. It is quite true that its impoverishment was, to a great extent, due to the same causes as the misery suffered by the slaves and there can be no doubt as to its revolutionary frame of mind at this time. But the free proletariat itself did not constitute a unity; it was composed of poor peasants and hungry townsmen, and not even the traditional slogans about the redistribution of land or the abolition of debts could mould it into a body able to act, except when an aristocrat like Catiline put himself at its head. Although Aristonicus appealed to all the poor for their support, and Spartacus was given a good deal of assistance by peasants, the cities of Asia, Sicily and Italy themselves stood aside during the troubles. The lack of unity displayed by the free workers is underlined by the unrestrained pillaging they indulged in,[136] for which there is ample evidence in both Sicilian uprisings. The doctrines of philosophers and of the mystery-religions, concerning the unity of mankind and the equality of all mortals before the divine, fell far short of creating a proletarian philosophy to unite all the oppressed in opposition to the dominant form of society. It was, and it remained the general opinion, even among those citizens who were revolutionary-minded, that slaves were absolutely essential. In their isolation, slaves had no alternative but to strike down their masters, take over their estates and fight forcibly for the freedom denied them by everyone else.

So we should not really be surprised that during their long struggle for freedom, the rebels evolved different political and social concepts

[135] *Neue Jahrbücher für Wissenschaft und Jugendbildung* 3 (1927), 1ff.; *Klassenkampf, Sozialismus und organischer Staat* 5, 41ff.

[136] I cannot accept Pareti's views on this matter when he speaks in terms of concerted action on the part of the impoverished peasantry and the slaves (*Storia di Roma* III, 295f., 482, 694f.).

at different times and in different places, nor that these concepts were often not, militarily, in their best interests, and that to a considerable extent they were borrowed from the stock of ideas of the citizen-classes and the old dynasties. In the first Sicilian uprising, what passed for a constitution was a none-too-convincing copy of a Hellenistic monarchy with its court, council and officials and with a subject population that had been inverted, with the lowest layer on top. Our scanty sources do not tell us how Aristonicus intended to reconcile his original position as a pretender of doubtful legality with the creation of a state based on justice. A monarchical form of society appeared again in the second Sicilian war, but this time with western symbols of kingship. The intention to make land communal property did not survive for long. In the end Spartacus, overcome by the huge problem of fighting a war, did not advance beyond the elementary forms of military communism. A greater degree of independence is indicated where what the slaves did was based upon religious beliefs. We certainly cannot assume that Eunus intended to establish an ecumenical priestly community comprising all the adherents of the Syrian goddess. But if it is true that the religious wars of independence of the Maccabees inspired him (and perhaps also Aristonicus), then these would have been the first steps along a road that might have led beyond the Hellenistic concept of sovereignty and the Roman claims to world rule. Spartacus' plan to bring about the repatriation of slaves points in a similar direction; it was an idea that struck at the very roots of the alliance between imperialism and the slave-system.

We can, however, discern some originality in the methods of warfare applied by the rebels. As far as their battle order in open country, siege warfare and the defence of fortified towns were concerned, they naturally borrowed a great deal from conventional methods, but with regard to equipment and organization they had to improvise. They were conversant with the peculiarities of partisan fighting and made some use of the potentialities of psychological warfare. If these novel methods did not in the long run bring them any success, this was owing to the undeniable fact that everyone, including those who served as slaves in the urban households of Asia, Sicily and Italy, accepted slavery without question as an institution, so that as the war dragged on, they came to consider the freedom fighters as mere brigands. The movement's leaders failed to win acceptance for robber states based on their own principles of justice as counterparts to the dominant system based on exploitation.

The brave undertaking of the slaves has about it a touch of the tragedy of any attempt to achieve the impossible. We feel this all the more deeply when we see the inadequacies of the ruling classes and the victors. To be sure, these revolts came upon Rome at a time when she was in a very difficult position because of major wars elsewhere—in Spain, against the Cimbri, against Sertorius and against Mithridates. Yet the record leaves no doubt that, for a long time, the slave revolts, even that of Spartacus, were not considered particularly serious threats. For too long people had been used to thinking of disobedience or flight on the part of slaves and violence from robber-bands as everyday occurrences. So, at first, they took only the normal steps such as offering rewards for information about conspiracies, and hoped that one of the rebels might betray his fellows or that discord would split their ranks. When large-scale military operations became unavoidable, they found themselves in the novel situation of having to fight against several groups of rebels and fortified outposts covering a wide area, which meant that a pitched battle would provide no solution. For years the incompetence, greed and venality of the military leadership impeded the actions of a government which was itself insecure. Only very late in the day were commanders appointed whose harsh measures could restore discipline among their own soldiers; the consuls Piso and Rupilius in Sicily and Crassus in Italy were three such leaders—men who knew how to deal by unorthodox means with the novel problems they faced, as when Crassus hemmed in the rebels' line of retreat with a moat and rampart in order to force them to fight. It should be noted that in the course of these desperate struggles against the outlaws, methods of warfare were applied which were frowned upon by what we may call public opinion, if not actually forbidden by international law. An example of this was the poisoning of wells in those parts of Asia where the last pockets of resistance remained (Florus 1.35, 7). In a world in which slavery was, as a matter of principle, the fate allotted to prisoners of war, rebellious slaves could not expect to be allowed to return to their previous state of slavery if they were recaptured. The six thousand crosses lining the Via Appia showed all the oppressed that those who fought for their freedom would obtain the punishment meted out to brigands. After the fighting had reached an end, those countries which had been affected by the disturbances were given a government which secured Roman rule and the interests of the ruling classes, whilst doing nothing about slavery. It is not even certain that, after the bitter experience of the Sicilian uprisings, there were any serious attempts at least to reduce the number of slaves. At any rate, the Lex Rupilia of 131 B.C. did not prevent the island from being disturbed by a second insurrection a few decades later. It was the reorganization of the province of Asia that provoked Mithridates' attack, and the defeat of Spartacus did not save Italy from Catiline's rebellion. During the age of Caesar and Augustus, slaves played a considerable role in power-politics as organized gangs in the hands of individual party-leaders. Nevertheless, there were no further organized slave revolts after Spartacus had been overthrown. The government, steadily becoming a military autocracy, was once more able to overcome the weaknesses of its leadership and partially to stop the decline in the vitality of the bourgeoisie, thereby temporarily at least putting an end to any tendency towards social unrest. But this only lasted for a time, until the 'external proletariat', the barbarians from beyond the borders, broke into the Empire.

IV

Pergamum and Aristonicus

Aristonicus' rising after the death of the last king of Pergamum is generally included in the series of major slave revolts that shook the ancient world during the period from 140 to 70 B.C. While the fragments of Posidonius' history enable us to follow the course of the two Sicilian slave wars, and Sallust, Appian and Plutarch tell us about Spartacus' undertaking, the surviving literary sources dealing with Aristonicus consist of no more than the scanty references of the annalistic historians and a brief but valuable summary in Strabo. Fortunately, these are to some extent supplemented by several inscriptions from Greek cities in Asia Minor; and the modern interpretations of the uprising by M. Rostovtzeff,[1] E. V. Hansen[2] and particularly D. Magie,[3] are based primarily on epigraphical evidence. I would like to consider just two inscriptions from Pergamum, a resolution of the *demos* (*Inschriften von Pergamon* 249 = *OGIS* 338 = *IGR* IV, 289) and the *senatusconsultum* proposed by Popillius (*OGIS* 435 = *IGR* IV, 301). Both these texts have been discussed on several occasions and been given various interpretations since their detailed

This chapter is a revised version of an article first published in *Atti del terzo congresso internazionale di epigrafia greca e romana* (*L'Erma di Bretschneider*, Rome 1959), 45–54.

[1] *Social and Economic History of the Hellenistic World* II, 807f., III, 1521ff.

[2] *The Attalids of Pergamon* (New York 1947), 140ff.

[3] *Roman Rule in Asia Minor* (Princeton 1950), I, 30ff., II, 1033ff.

examination by P. Foucart[4] and G. Cardinali.[5] Although these resolutions do not mention Aristonicus by name, I believe that a thorough analysis of the text can lead us to important conclusions about the beginnings of the revolt as well as about Aristonicus' aims and his role in history. I am pleased to see that my interpretation agrees in several respects with that given to these inscriptions at the same time as mine by V. Vavřínek in his excellent discussion of the revolt of Aristonicus.[6]

The resolution passed by the *demos* of Pergamum soon after the death of King Attalus III in the spring of 133 B.C. begins by saying that in his will—which still had to be ratified by the Romans—the king has given the city where he resided its freedom and a part of the royal estates (l. 5f.). Making immediate use of its autonomy, the assembly decides (l. 10ff.) upon a series of concessions to the lower classes who do not possess citizen-rights, namely the granting of citizenship to the *paroikoi*, to soldiers who have settled there, to Macedonian and Mysian military colonists, to troops of the garrison, to mercenaries from Mastya and to the guards and watchmen; and, furthermore, the assembly decides to grant the rights of *paroikoi* to the descendants of freedmen, to the royal slaves (with the exception of those who had been acquired during the reigns of the last two kings and those belonging to private estates that had come into the king's hands) and finally to the public slaves. After this (l. 26ff.), all inhabitants are informed that those who have left or are going to leave the city and its territory are to be outlawed and their property is to be forfeit to the city. The inscription then breaks off.

The individual clauses raise many problems; there has recently been a good commentary on them by G. Niedermayer[7] which explains them in the light of the political and social structure of the Attalid kingdom. Earlier commentators had already referred the grant of new rights and the prohibition on emigration to developments outside the city itself which favoured the slaves—whether they had in mind Aristonicus, as did Wilcken (*RE* II, 963) and Foucart (*op. cit.* 322), or whether they assumed that a slave revolt had been going on for

[4] 'La formation de la province romaine d'Asie' *Mémoires de l'Académie des Inscriptions et Belles-Lettres* 37 (1904), 297ff.

[5] 'La morte di Attalo III e la rivolta di Aristonico' *Saggi di Storia antica e di archeologia* (*a Giulio Beloch*) (Rome 1910), 269ff.

[6] V. Vavřínek *La révolte d'Aristonicos* (*Rozpravy Československé Akademie VĚD* 67: 1957), particularly 16ff.

[7] In a dissertation written under H. Bengtson, *Fünf Testamente hellenistischer Herrscher zugunsten der Römer* (typewritten dissertation, Munich 1954), 31ff.

some time without the participation of Aristonicus, as did Cardinali (*op. cit.* 280). Aristonicus, who laid claim to the throne as an illegitimate son of Eumenes after the death of Attalus and the publication of his will, would initially have collected supporters in those parts of the kingdom near the Greek cities. Magie has recently suggested that the decree of Pergamum may have been a measure intended to protect the town against Aristonicus; there is no reason to suppose that there was a slave rising in the inland areas, and the granting of rights to *paroikoi* and slaves looks like a prophylactic measure against a possible attack, and corresponds to the usual reaction of a *polis* when faced with such a crisis.[8] M. Segre[9] goes even further when he suggests that the intention of the Pergamum decree favouring the lower classes was to protect the inhabitants of the χώρα against potential encroachments by the Romans by giving them a place in the legal framework of the city-state. I do not believe that these last explanations take sufficient account of the general position suggested by the text of the resolution.

It is obvious (and it is accepted by all commentators) that Pergamum was in a desperate situation. There were threats to general security (l.8 ἕνεκα τῆς κοινῆς ἀσ[φ]αλείας); it was absolutely essential to have the lower classes included in the citizen-body (l. 7f. [ἀναγκαῖ]ον or [ἐπιτήδει]ον), since they had shown their good will towards the city (l. 9f.). Ever since the death of the king, people had been trying to leave both the town and the rural districts, and evidently this applied to free and slave alike (l. 26ff.). The emergency, therefore, by no means concerned the χώρα alone, and the resolution of the people of Pergamum was founded not on any desire for the welfare of the lower classes but only on a concern for security. That is why there is so much consideration for soldiers, military colonists, guards and watchmen. Greek cities certainly fell back on the support of their slaves often enough when in military danger. Magie cites a resolution of the people of Ephesus (*SIG*³, 742), passed at the very moment the town left Mithridates' side and returned to the Roman camp. In this Ephesian resolution inhabitants with lesser rights were declared free, the *paroikoi* were granted full citizenship if they took up arms (l. 44ff.), and the municipal slaves were to become *paroikoi* if they too took up arms (l. 48ff.). A comparison of these two decrees reveals one essential difference: at Pergamum the new rights were granted without any previous action being required on the part of the *paroikoi*, soldiers or slaves. This is

[8] *Op. cit.* I, 148, II, 1036, 8 and 1040, 17.

[9] *Athenaeum* 16 (1938), 123f.

certainly not the way a Greek city-state would normally have acted. This entirely exceptional resolution suggests directly that the rights being granted by Pergamum had already been promised to the groups in question by someone else. This is the only explanation for why people were leaving the town and country districts; and this also helps us to understand why there must still have been some supporters of Aristonicus in Pergamum even after this resolution had been passed by the city, as the honorary decree to Diodorus Pasparus shows (*IGR* IV, 292 l. 11ff.). So the people of Pergamum were not induced to grant these rights by the danger of the general situation alone; the step was virtually forced upon them by something that Aristonicus had done.[10]

It seems extremely probable, therefore, that Aristonicus put forward his claim to the throne immediately after the king's death, while organizing and equipping his supporters. The interregnum between the king's death and the confirmation of his will by the Romans gave the claimant his opportunity. For it can be assumed that the king's will corresponded to what the Romans wanted or had even been drawn up in consultation with them, as certainly happened in the case of Ptolemy Euergetes II and Cyrene.[11] Similarly, it was to be supposed that the citizens of the Greek cities would rally to the side of the Romans, who for a long time had successfully understood how to play off the city-states against the monarchies. Nevertheless Aristonicus dared to seize the crown: *velut paternum regnum Asiam invasit* says Justin (36, 4.6); *Asiam occupavit* is what we read in Livy (*per.* 59); and I would understand *regiam occupavit* from Horace (*Odes* 2, 18):

neque Attali
ignotus heres regiam occupavi.

For it is obvious that the poet does not wish to suggest that Rome was unjustified in taking over the legacy,[12] and it is clearly not the Romans whom he is describing as usurpers with 'the unmistakably critical

[10] In the original version of this article I referred to an inscription containing what was supposed by H. v. Prott and W. Kolbe (*Ath. Mitt.* 27 (1902), 106ff.) to be a list of new citizens of Pergamum. But this is, in fact, a list of *epheboi*, of no relevance to the matter under discussion here; cf. W. Kolbe *Ath. Mitt.* 32 (1907), 145ff. This correction is noted by L. Robert *Rev. ét. gr.* 73 (1960), 'Bull. épigr.' 191f., no. 339.

[11] W. Otto 'Zur Geschichte der Zeit des 6. Ptolemäers' *Abhandlungen der Bayerischen Akademie* 1934, 11, 97ff.

[12] So Foucart *op. cit.* 298f.

phrases *ignotus heres* and *occupavi*'.[13] In his polemic against luxury, Horace is only reminding us of something that every Roman was familiar with, how Aristonicus, an heir of low origins, had seized power. So Aristonicus must have passed himself off as king immediately after Attalus' death, hoping to receive the support of the Greek cities by cunning or by force, and of the lower classes in the towns and in the countryside by making some sensational promises to them, just as King Mithridates, some forty-eight years later, declared the Greek cities independent, remitted debts and granted citizenship to metics and freedom to slaves (Appian *Mithr.* 48). Aristonicus was not very successful with the towns; only Phocaea joined him of her own free will; Pergamum slipped from his grasp because of prompt action on her part, and was therefore free to become the base for the Roman counter-offensive.

We know that immediately after its publication Attalus' will was an important issue in Roman domestic politics. Tiberius Gracchus demanded that the royal treasure be used to finance his policy of colonization, and the serious domestic strife that ensued seems to have prevented a quick decision being reached on the question of Pergamum. Yet although no one could have doubted for one moment that the legacy would be accepted, and there was already news of Aristonicus' uprising, Rome was in no position to send troops to Asia, for the siege of Numantia and the slave war in Sicily claimed all available forces. In any case Rome often reacted astonishingly slowly to developments in the East—for example, the appearance of Andriscus in Macedonia was not taken particularly seriously for some time; it was only after the pretender's resounding initial successes that they sent out, not indeed an army, but the single legate P. Cornelius Scipio Nasica Corculum, who in 150 B.C. collected together a force from the Greek allies, put himself in command and began the war against Andriscus.[14] The reaction to the Attalid disturbances was very similar. After the death of Tiberius Gracchus in the summer of 133 B.C. the Senate seriously considered the question of Pergamum and decided to send out P. Cornelius Scipio Nasica Serapio, who was a son of Nasica Corculum and had made himself unpopular with the Roman populace because of the violence he had used against Tiberius Gracchus. The majority of our sources say only that he was sent to Asia, without giving any details of his commission, and only mention the matter at all in the context of

[13] So A. Kiessling, R. Heinze *Oden und Epoden*[10] (Berlin 1960), 235, 5.

[14] Zonaras 9, 28.4; Livy *Per.* 50.

Roman domestic politics.[15] On the other hand, Strabo, referring to the events in Asia, tells of the arrival from Rome of a commission of five (14, 1.38), which has been correctly identified as Scipio Nasica's embassy.[16]

The chronology of Strabo's excursus on Aristonicus' revolt is not as open to criticism as Magie is inclined to suppose.[17] Strabo first gives the course of Aristonicus' actions from his initial appearance through the defeat in the naval battle off Cyme up to his retreat inland, where he 'quickly gathered about him a crowd of poor people and slaves who had been invited to win their freedom';[18] then he gives us—again in chronological order—the actions of his opponents: how the cities began to levy troops and the kings of Bithynia and Cappadocia sent support, how the arrival of the five ambassadors from Rome was followed by the landing of an army under the consul P. Crassus, and how, finally, the arrival of M. Perperna brought about the capture of Aristonicus who was then sent to Rome. Crassus did not arrive until the year 131 B.C. Until that time the Greek cities and Asiatic client-rulers had to fend for themselves, and this they were quite willing to do, since the revolt stirred up among the lower classes by Aristonicus threatened the vital interests of these cities and potentates. It was the task of the Senate's five-man commission (which probably arrived in 132 B.C.) to represent Roman interests by delivering messages from Rome and to conduct diplomatic negotiations with the various cities and rulers. In particularly critical situations Roman legates did act on their own initiative, whether they had been invested with special powers or not, and they became emissaries and even military commanders, like Scipio Nasica Corculum in Greece in 150 B.C. (see above), Sulla in Cilicia in 92 B.C. and the embassies to Asia of M'. Aquillius the younger in 90 B.C. and Q. Oppius in 88 B.C. There is some evidence to show that Sulla was sent to Cilicia *pro praetore*; and we know that Aquillius and Oppius commanded troops side by side with the governor, C. Cassius.[19] Oppius is called a *legatus* by Licinianus (p. 27), στρατηγός in Appian (*Mithr.* 17 and 20) and *proconsul* in Livy (*per.* 78). When we consider this combination of diplomatic and military duties, we should

[15] Plutarch *Tib. Gracch.* 21; Val. Max. 5, 3.2; *vir. ill.* 64, 9.

[16] Münzer *RE* IV, 1504.

[17] *Op. cit.* II, 1037, 11.

[18] κατακεκλημένων clearly describes what has taken place in the past, and therefore refers to a declaration of freedom that must have occurred at the beginning of the revolt.

[19] Evidence in Magie *op. cit.* II, 1163ff.

not be surprised that Appian simultaneously or interchangeably uses the terms στρατηγοί and πρέσβεις (*Mithr.* 11f., 56).

This ought to make it clear that the decision to send out the embassy of five led by Nasica Serapio towards the end of 133 B.C. was not so minor a matter as some have thought, and does not justify the conclusion that no news of the disturbances in Asia had reached Rome by that time.[20] In the absence of strong arguments to the contrary, we may interpret the Pergamene inscription *OGIS* 435 = *IGR* IV, 301 to refer to Nasica's embassy. This document contains an extract from a *senatusconsultum* about the despatch of an embassy to Asia. Admittedly, the text of this inscription, which has been widely discussed,[21] does not provide any certain indications of its precise date. The man named as the official who summoned the Senate (l. 3) is [Γ]άϊος Ποπίλλιος Γαίου υἱὸς σ[τρατηγός]. We have no evidence regarding a praetor called C. Popillius C. filius during the years in question, but there is no reason why one should not assume that a person of this name was praetor in 133 B.C. and presided over a meeting of the Senate in the absence of both the consuls.[22] All that is preserved of the date is (l. 4f.) πρὸ ἡμ[ερῶν . . .] εμβρίων, which gives us the months September, November or December. The purpose of the *relatio* (l. 5ff.) was to discuss matters relating to Pergamum, or to be more precise the commission [τοῖς εἰς 'Α]σίαν πορευομένοις στρατηγοῖς, and in particular the question 'whether whatever was instituted, granted, remitted and inflicted by the Kings up to the death of Attalus should be recognized as binding'. This restricts us to the years 133 to 129 B.C., the period between the king's death and the date when Asia was established as a province. As P. Crassus was sent out to Asia as consul in 131, as also were M. Perperna and M'. Aquillius in 130 and 129 respectively, while our text refers to στρατηγοί being sent out, these years must be excluded. This designation also rules out the Board of Ten sent to join Aquillius in 129. So we are left with the years 133 and 132, and it is most probable that this important question of whether the king's arrangements in Asia were to remain in force was put to the

[20] Magie *op. cit.* II, 1033, i; also Vavřínek *op. cit.* 22.

[21] Among others by Foucart *op. cit.* 311ff.; Cardinali *op. cit.* 93ff.; Magie *op. cit.* II, 1033, 1; A. Passerini *Athenaeum* 15 (1937), 280ff.; M. Segre *Athenaeum* 16 (1938), 124. Thanks to the kindness of G. Klaffenbach, I was able to have at my disposal a squeeze of the inscription from the collection of *Inscriptiones Graecae* of the German Academy of Sciences at Berlin.

[22] T. R. S. Broughton *The Magistrates of the Roman Republic* I (New York 1951), 492, 496f.

Senate for deliberation and a final decision as early as the last months of the year 133.[23]

This is more or less the same date as has been established for Nasica Serapio's mission. The reference to the agents as οἱ εἰς Ἀσίαν πορευόμενοι στρατηγοί in any case poses problems, whatever date or embassy we relate the text to. The plural στρατηγοί rules out any reference to a single praetor or consul; furthermore, the form of words prevents us from thinking of the various governors going out to Asia year by year in the future, but rather suggests an embassy about to leave at that time. This description can best be explained if we assume that it refers to legates with extraordinary powers, to commissioners who, like Nasica Corculum, Sulla, Oppius and Aquillius the younger, were to act on their own initiative in the affairs of allied states and where appropriate even to intervene militarily. After all, Roman law recognized that 'in a case where there is at first no magistrate with *imperium* at or after the outbreak of a war, there can under certain conditions be a temporary *imperium*' to be held by a *legatus*.[24] The Latin form for the *imperium* held by these legates would have been *pro praetore* and they would have been referred to as *legati pro praetore*. The Greek translation simplified this to στρατηγοί, which in the language of the inscriptions renders both propraetors and proconsuls,[25] while historians and other writers, as we have seen, occasionally used these expressions to refer to extraordinary legates. There was an obvious reason for an extraordinary embassy of this kind at the end of 133, when Rome had to intervene in the confused situation in Asia.

The second section of the inscription records the Senate's decree that the decisions made by Attalus and the other kings were to remain valid, and that the legates were to leave them in force. This decision also recognized Attalus' testament and in particular the decision in his will to declare his residence a free city. Popillius' *senatusconsultum* secured the status of Pergamum and was, therefore, inscribed on stone

[23] Cardinali *op. cit.* 93f.; Passerini *op. cit.* 280; Broughton *op. cit.* 496 and Vavřínek *op. cit.* 22, who do not accept the date assigned to the *senatusconsultum* by Magie.

[24] Mommsen *Römisches Staatsrecht* II³, 690. In his remarks about the *senatusconsultum* on Pergamum (*Ath. Mitt.* 24 (1899), 190ff. = *Gesammelte Schriften* IV. 63ff.), Mommsen did not take this exceptional case into account, and this led him to reject the view that it had any bearing on Nasica's commission of five.

[25] D. Magie *De Romanorum iuris publici sacrique vocabulis sollemnibus in Graecum sermonem conversis* (Leipzig 1905), 84; M. Holleaux Στρατηγὸς ὕπατος (*Bibliothèque des écoles françaises d'Athènes et de Rome* 113: 1918), 41ff.

together with a letter of P. Servilius Isauricus, proconsul in 48 B.C. referring to the city's constitution.[26] On the other hand, it remained an open question after the Senate's decision whether Rome would recognize the grants made by the people of Pergamum to the lower classes. Inscriptions from Smyrna show that there were soon disputes between Pergamum and the *publicani* about the χώρα of Pergamum.[27] It is of relevance to our investigation, which we have restricted to the beginning of the Asian uprising, that the scope of the royal decisions whose validity is in question is described in greater detail in the formulation of the *senatusconsultum* than in the *relatio* that introduces it. This states ὅ[σα ἐν 'Ασίᾳ ἕω]ς τῆς 'Αττάλου τελευτῆς ὑπὸ τῶν [βασιλέων δι]ωρθώθη ἐδωρήθη ἀφέθη ἐζημιώ[θη] while the *senatusconsultum* says ὅσα βασιλεὺς Ἄτταλος οἵτε λο[ιποὶ βασιλεῖς] διώρθωσαν ἐζημίωσαν ἢ [ἀφῆκαν ἐδωρήσαντο, ὅ]σα τούτων ἐγένετο πρὸ μιᾶς [ἡμέρας ἢ Ἄττ]αλον τελευτῆσαι. To eliminate any uncertainty, the Senate was not satisfied with the general statement 'up to the death of Attalus', but gave a precise definition: 'up to the last day before the death of Attalus'. So, strictly speaking, any decree passed only on the day of his death would no longer have been covered by the Romans' recognition of the will. It is quite conceivable that during his last hours decrees were falsely issued in the king's name, and that Aristonicus—who, as we may conclude from Horace's words, *regiam occupavit*—published a royal document which promised him the succession. In this case the Senate would have excluded such last-minute regulations and maintained a discreet silence about the name of the claimant to the throne.[28]

To sum up, I would hold that the inscriptions and the literary testimony make it probable that Aristonicus made his presence felt immediately on the death of King Attalus. After he had laid claim to the throne, this illegitimate member of the royal family did not hesitate to stir up the lower classes because of the difficult circumstances in which he found himself as a result of the king's perfidious will. During the subsequent course of the rising he proved himself a capable

[26] As Foucart *op. cit.* 317f. already pointed out.

[27] In particular *IGR* IV, 262; cf. A. Passerini *Athenaeum* 15 (1937), 252ff.; M. Segre *Athenaeum* 16 (1938), 119ff.

[28] The interpretation of the different dates suggested here is a possible but by no means necessary one. For in a similar case to this, as Samuel Schmid pointed out to me, the language of Roman political institutions uses the phrase *quo die pugnatum est* side by side with *pridie quam pugnatum est* without any clear distinction in meaning (Livy 37, 56); compare also *OGIS* 436, line 10: εἰς ἐσχάτην ἡμέραν. On this subject see Bikerman *Rev. ét. gr.* 50 (1937), 225f.

organizer both as a military leader and as a politician. We can appreciate why Tiberius Gracchus' friend the philosopher C. Blossius should have preferred to carry on his struggle against Rome with Aristonicus in Asia than with Eunus in Sicily. But we do not know for certain what Aristonicus' *Heliopolis* represented, and this is not the place for yet more conjecture.

V

Human Relationships in Ancient Slavery

Slavery was an essential element in the social structure of antiquity, and has for a long time been the subject of detailed investigation; for such study began in connection with the anti-slavery movement of modern times. The first comprehensive monograph on the subject by Henri Wallon[1] was the result of an entry for a prize awarded in 1837 by the *Académie des sciences morales et politiques* of Paris. As the quantity of source-material continued to increase, there were more detailed investigations of individual aspects of ancient society and economics during the course of the following decades. W. L. Westermann's study of the institution[2] threw light on its many different aspects and transformations. But there is still no straightforward account of the functions of slavery in ancient society, no objective analysis of the role it played in the creation, development and decline of this civilization. The Marxist approach to history pays particular attention to slavery, but because it can only approach the subject in terms of material production and the creation of a class structure, the lively interest in social history shown in Communist countries often falls prey to a fatal tendency to

This chapter is a revised form of an address delivered on my installation as Rector of the University of Tübingen (*Rektoratsrede: Universität Tübingen* 47, published by J. C. B. Mohr (Paul Siebeck), Tübingen 1958). It is dedicated to Hermann Bengtson and Karl Friedrich Stroheker.

[1] H. Wallon *Histoire de l'esclavage dans l'antiquité*[2] (Paris 1879).

[2] W. L. Westermann, article on 'Sklaverei' *RE* Suppl. VI (1935), 894ff. and *Slave Systems*.

over-schematization.[3] Under these circumstances I feel that our immediate task should be to look at slavery in ancient society in the context of the various legal frameworks of the master/servant relationship; to describe as precisely as we can the part it played in the system of production and the development of culture in as many respects as possible; and to investigate in greater depth the attitude of both the citizen-classes and the slaves to this institution. Through the Academy of Science and Literature at Mainz I have found colleagues to help me in this task. To give but a few examples: there has been an investigation into the vast subject of the connections of ancient religious cults with slavery; a monograph has been published on the slaves who worked in the mines at Laureum, and the evidence on the mass enslavement of the inhabitants of conquered cities has been examined. I myself have tried to show how ill-founded have been the attempts to bring Hellenism and slavery into harmony with one another, and have rejected the hypothesis that some kind of 'Communist International' existed in antiquity, in an examination of the structure of slave wars in the ancient world.[4] Contributions are expected from younger members of the group on the portrayal of the unfree person in Greek and Roman literature, on the use of slaves in warfare, and on the changes that affected the institution as a whole in late antiquity. Once these and other questions have been clarified, it will perhaps be possible to judge to what extent and in which respects ancient civilization was based on slavery.

I wish here to say something about a number of surprising features, which constitute only minor details in the context of the phenomenon as a whole, but which do show us that certain groups of slaves had particularly close relationships with free men. Of course, no one would suggest that the institution of slavery in itself encouraged humane tendencies. When we consider that Plato would have had no objections to the buying and selling of human-beings like mules, as property in the market-place, and that Vedius Pollio, a friend of the Emperor Augustus, was allowed to punish his slaves by throwing them into his fishpond as food for his lampreys with complete impunity, it should be clear that the whole system blatantly contradicted everything that we understand by the term humane. Greek Sophists declared this openly, and pointed to the fact that Nature had made no man a slave. Stoic philosophy gave everyone some share in the sum total of Reason

[3] See below p. 184f.

[4] See Chapters I and III and the references given on p. 2, note 4.

in the universe, and developed from this belief ideals of humanity and of a universal state. And, without being specifically bound to any one of the major schools of thought, the 'idea that those who are not free in law are nevertheless endowed with the ability to make moral decisions' won some acceptance.[5] Although these precepts failed to put an end to slavery over the centuries, they were able to mitigate its harshness. But I do not wish to consider here those high values of classical thought, *philanthropia* and *humanitas*; I intend rather to show how in Greek, and even more in Roman society, slaves had certain tasks to perform at crucial times, looking after their masters when they were most vulnerable, as babies, children and patients, and how, without reference to any theoretical ideals, these relationships could result in intimacy, trust and friendship—one might almost go so far as to say an involuntary relationship on the human level. The nurses, tutors and physicians of the aristocracy are worth our attention, not because of any desire to look at the ancient world from the servant's point of view, but because here we can see that an extreme system can only survive by self-restraint at those points at which it is most vulnerable. One could, of course, apply these observations to the other occupations of domestic slaves, such as secretaries, valets or cooks. But let us consider only the long-lasting and well-attested institutions that served as protection against dangers to life itself.

The aged Euryclea was the first of the long line of nurses who, as enslaved servants suckled and cared for the children of Greek and Roman families. There were, of course, always mothers who reared their own children themselves; but in the cities, at least, it was customary to give unweaned babies to a wet-nurse (τίτθη) and subsequently (generally after the age of two) to a nanny (τροφός)—in other words, they were entrusted to slave-women, who were often even of foreign origin. This does not mean that these duties were considered unimportant—after all, the myths related that the offspring of the gods received their first nourishment and care at the hands of the nymphs themselves. Werner Jaeger has shown in a broader context how, when in the age of the Sophists Greek thought applied itself to the task of ordering life according to reason, an educational system was planned, which began with care for the unweaned baby, subsequently arranged his play-time, and then, in the child's seventh year, sent him to school to be educated.

[5] On this see W. Richter 'Seneca und die Sklaven' *Gymnasium* 65 (1958), 196ff.

In the fifth book of the *Republic* and the seventh book of the *Laws*, Plato deals with education during the successive stages of nursing (τροφή) and schooling (παιδεία), and suggests that the task of moulding a person through his upbringing has to begin when the child is still in the womb, and is of crucial importance in early childhood, when the infant must be moulded like wax while still malleable.[6] Precepts about the role of the nurse held an important place in the theories on the upbringing of children which developed as a special science in Hellenistic schools of philosophy. The last phases of these theories can be seen in Quintilian and Tacitus, Favorinus and Plutarch, and in Soranus' textbook on gynaecology. In these works it is emphasized that the natural person to feed a child is its mother, for she alone can dedicate herself to the task with genuine concern; all this has been instituted by Providence. Some writers even go so far as to argue, on physiological grounds, that a child's character is inherited through his mother's milk, and in consequence they demand an end to all wet-nursing. Physicians whose attitude is more realistic give precise advice as to how a nurse ought to be selected: Soranus requires her to be Greek, while Oribasius prefers women of Thracian or Egyptian origin.

This ought to make it clear that the question was always considered extremely important. But we can also be quite certain that there was a continual conflict between educational theory and practice—a state of affairs that is clearly necessary for the development of educational theory. Women of the aristocracy or the 'haute bourgeoisie' never put themselves to the trouble of wet-nursing their children. There are Hellenistic papyri that contain contracts concerning the employment of slaves and impoverished women of the citizen-class as nurses. This custom also became widespread in the Roman world when it became Hellenized. Certainly the good old practice by which a son was brought up 'not in the room of a nurse who has been bought, but in his mother's lap and at her breast', lasted until quite late; a Roman mother had a higher status and greater influence than her Greek counterpart. But here also education and affluence paved the way for the nurse and the governess, and it goes without saying that the *Graecula ancilla* was accepted in a bilingual society.[7]

[6] Plato *Laws* 7, 789a–e and following.

[7] Tacitus *Dial.* 28f. Apart from the ancient handbooks, there is a lot of information about nurses in Greece and Rome in W. Schubart's 'Die Amme im alten Alexandrien' *Jahrbuch für Kinderheilkunde* 70 (1909), 82ff.; W. Braams *Zur Geschichte des Ammenwesens im klassischen Altertum* (*Jenaer medizin-historische

So it was to slave-women, in the ancient world, that heroes and kings, poets and philosophers were entrusted in childhood. They were the ones who wrapped these infants against the cold and rocked them to sleep, who protected them against bad luck with spells and amulets, who entertained them with fables and stories and what we would call nursery-tales, and whose influence is recognized by Plato when he speaks of 'those who will not believe the tales which they have heard as babes and sucklings from their mothers and nurses, repeated by them both in jest and earnest, like charms'.[8] It was such women who brought to life for children the toys which we can see in paintings and handle as terracotta models. They were called barbarians at the time; we would consider them simple, natural creatures. Throughout a person's tender years, when life was simply a game (παιδία), they continued to fulfil this single role. To the philosophers of antiquity, the idea that a child should be allowed to develop freely was quite foreign—if, in spite of everything, a person's childhood was happy, this was generally due to his nanny or wet-nurse.

We can only partially assess the effect that this nursing by slaves had on the adult lives of their charges, and the significance it held for culture in general. Favorinus says that a mother who gives away her child excludes it from maternal feelings and takes the first step towards forgetting about it, so that the child will direct all its love towards its nurse.[9] The same would have been true of the governess. Slave-women accepted the challenge of the tasks they had been set, and created a spiritual bond between themselves and their charges that often lasted for the rest of their lives. There is considerable evidence for this. A faithful governess was pained to see her boy grow up, because then she had to entrust him to the gymnasium and the Forum.[10] She could console herself with the thought that she might now be freed and provided for at home as a trusted servant (in which role we see her in a pseudo-Demosthenic oration, loyal to the family even

Beiträge 5: 1913); G. Herzog-Hauser's article 'Nutrix' *RE* XVII, 1491ff. (1937). Basic to the history of education in general, and in particular for developments and changes in the precepts about nursing, are W. Schick *Favorin* περὶ παίδων τροφῆς *und die antike Erziehungslehre* (Leipzig 1912) and F. Glaeser *De Pseudo-Plutarchi libro* περὶ παίδων ἀγωγῆς (*Diss. Philol. Vindobon.* XII, 2: 1918); also of interest is the appendix in *Plutarch, Kinderzucht* (published by Ernst Heimeran, Munich 1947).

[8] Plato *Laws* 10, 887d.

[9] In Gellius *Noct. Att.* 12, 1.21ff.

[10] *M. Cornelii Frontonis Epistulae* ed. M. P. J. van den Hout (Leiden 1954), 95f.

in a crisis).[11] And it was expected of an educated person that he should show kindness to those who had seen him through childhood and should even provide for them if necessary; Cicero knew this and it is confirmed by Pliny the younger, who rewarded his nurse for her long and faithful service with the gift of a small estate.[12] It was on the basis of this real-life experience that nurses and nannies were made the foster-mothers of their charges and the confidantes of their mistresses in drama, and particularly in classical Greek tragedy. In Aeschylus' *Choephori* (734ff.), Orestes' nurse speaks when she hears the news of his death; in her grief, she combines a lament for the death of the one she loves with reminiscences of how troublesome and full of unpleasant surprises it had been to look after him as a child; and we may take her as representative of the many who remained silent. Here a slave mourns while a mother rejoices at the news of her son's death. This belongs to the nature of the tragedy; but it still tends to suggest something more general, considering how rare it was in the classical period for a Greek mother 'to look after the uncomprehending creature as a pet' (*Choephori* 753f.). Of course, this soliloquy does not rise above the level of a straightforward speech by a nurse; for, in tragedy, a confidante of slave status cannot participate fully in the action, even if she may be entrusted with a secret. Affected by the emotions and weaknesses of the ordinary person, she stands outside the realm of tragedy and has no share in either responsibility or misfortune.[13] But the very fact that this loyalty existed in small things and was described by poets was something very valuable in a world so often ruled by gross egoism. This affection is shown by many charming vase-paintings and terracottas, and in particular by the monuments that gave nurses and governesses some immortality through the cult of the dead. Whether they are grave-stones with reliefs or simply inscriptions with the name of 'the excellent nurse', these votive-offerings give slave-women a place in the family circle.[14] Whatever literature may have had to say about

[11] [Demosth.] 47, 55ff.

[12] Cicero *De amicitia* 74; Pliny *Ep.* 6, 3. On humanitarian tendencies among educated people in the Empire see A. M. Duff *Freedmen in the Early Roman Empire* (Oxford 1928), 99f.

[13] See above p. 18f. On the literary figure see H. Ahlers *Die Vertrautenrolle in der griechischen Tragödie* (dissertation, Giessen 1911).

[14] There are some examples in A. T. Klein *Child Life in Greek Art* (New York 1932), 2 and the plates. A study of the beautiful material contained in A. Conze *Attische Grabreliefs*, F. Winter *Die antiken Terrakotten* and similar collections might be rewarding. Cf. the interpretation of the funerary stele from Athens of the

the old woman who was dirty, drunk and talkative, these inscriptions show such a warm regard on the part of so many people (for instance, the important official who rose as high as the consulate, *nutrici et mammulae bene merenti*[15]) that we can be in no doubt as to which was the voice of real life. It is relevant to compare this figure of ancient society with another from a different century and a different continent —the 'black mammy', the old nurse who occurs in the black slave-society of America as a respected member of the master's household, and whose influence in real life, as in literature, has continued after emancipation right down to the present day.[16] But, however productive this comparison might be, we must restrict ourselves here to the ancient world. Standing apart from considerations of clan or faction, state or school of thought, which occupied the ambitions of others, these nurses show something of the truth in the Spanish proverb that 'the hand that rocks the cradle rocks the world'.

Tutors are often mentioned in the same context as nurses. They had an even deeper effect on public life, because they moulded the characters of young men. A sentence of Plato's shows what, precisely, was intended by this task: 'Neither a flock of sheep nor a herd of any other kind ought to live without a herdsman, nor boys without tutors or slaves without masters. And a boy is the most difficult of all creatures to manage.'[17] As Plato goes on to say, this difficult task was entrusted to the tutor, who had to restrain the folly of the child when he was no longer in the hands of his mother or nurse. It would have been difficult to find a free Greek willing to take on such a job, for he would have wanted to be his own master instead of serving someone else as an employee and for low wages. So people fell back on their slaves, choosing someone who had been loyal to the family, quite often a slave whose age made him unsuitable for work of any other kind. We are again

τίττη (*sic*) χρηστή Pyraichme given by S. Karouzos *Hellenika* 15 (1957), 311ff., to which my attention was drawn by Friedrich Matz.

[15] *ILS* 8532.

[16] I am grateful to my colleague R. Haas for drawing my attention to J. W. Parkhurst's 'The Role of the Black Mamij in the Plantation Household' *Journal of Negro History* 23 (1938), 349ff., and A. W. Calhoun *A Social History of the American Family from Colonial Times to the Present* II (New York 1945), 282f. Dilsey, the negro maid in William Faulkner's *The Sound and the Fury* (1929), is well known; she represents standards of decency which her white contemporaries fail to live up to.

[17] Plato *Laws* 7, 808d.

reminded of the negro slave in the American south who often became a child's intimate friend, and has been immortalized in literature in the character of 'Uncle Remus'.[18] Educational philosophers naturally enough objected to this use of worthless slaves of barbarian background, and their criticisms can be heard from the time of Plato and the Peripatetic Hieronymus right down to that of Plutarch.[19] But here again philosophy proved to be ineffective. Even in the leading households, slaves were used as supervisors to accompany and look after boys when they began to attend school in their seventh year. Even Pericles, when he saw a slave fall out of a tree and break his leg, is supposed to have said 'he has just been made into a tutor'.[20] One can see how conscientiously these tutors carried out their duties in the charming scene at the end of the Platonic dialogue *Lysis* (223). The tutors arrive in order to escort their charges home in good time; Socrates has been having far too long a discussion in the *palaestra*, and the tutors scold him so vehemently in their broken Greek that Socrates has to admit himself beaten and dismisses the gathering. Thus the barbarian servants bring the reader back from his journey through the heavens to the very necessary realities of life on earth. Tutors also often appear on vase-paintings and minor sculpture, grumbling in much the same good-natured way as portrayed by Plato. They are bald-headed foreign types with stubbly beards and long staffs—almost everyday versions of Socrates.[21]

The Romans, too, employed slaves for this purpose. In earlier centuries, of course, while the old Italian way of life persisted, a father himself looked after his son, and introduced him to the traditional customs and life of the community when his mother had seen him through childhood. But with the expansion of Rome, politics and education became so specialized that the *paterfamilias* had to look for support and relief from someone else. By a happy coincidence, Greeks were, at this time, beginning to be imported as prisoners of war and could be acquired as domestic slaves. These Greek slaves—as also free Greeks—were entrusted with every stage of a young person's

[18] J. Chandler Harris *Uncle Remus, His Songs and Sayings* (1881); cf. also Calhoun *op. cit.* 281ff., 311.

[19] Plato *Alcib. I* 121cff.; Hieronymus apud Stobaeus *Eclogia* 2, 233 (ed. Wachsmuth); Plutarch *De lib. educ.* 4ab. There are some remarks about the ancient objections to using slaves as tutors in R. H. Barrow *Slavery in the Roman Empire* London 1928), 39ff.

[20] Stobaeus *op. cit.*

[21] A. Klein *op. cit.* 28ff. and the collections referred to on p. 108, note 14 above.

education, and in particular with giving the individual tuition which supplemented schoolwork. A Greek-speaking attendant (*custos*) now became a member of every Roman household; in comedy, *servi paedagogi* occur so frequently that we may assume that this office and the words used to describe it had already been adopted in the third century. Later we find the word *monitor*, which shows clearly what was the main purpose of looking after boys. A young man's instructor, on the other hand, was called a *comes* or *rector*, and it was not unusual for a *monitor* who had proved his worth to be given his freedom and to advance to the higher rank of a *comes*; individual tutors even rose from the level of slaves to become professors of higher education (*litterator*, *grammaticus*, *rhetor*). And, because women had a recognized position in Roman society despite its decidedly masculine character, girls had a greater share of education and upbringing than among the Greeks; so there were also more tutors for girls than there had been in Greece, and we even come across the *paedagoga*.[22]

The duties and position of a tutor were fundamentally the same in Greece and in Rome. He would accompany the boy to school, carry his school-things, watch over him in the street—which in antiquity would have been as dangerous for boys as for girls—and teach him good manners and morals. The tutor would not have had anything to do with the actual lessons, except perhaps that occasionally he would have supervised homework and, in this capacity, would have gone through the work again with the boy. Although, at first sight, this task seems so simple, there was a clear educative function behind it, for it was expected that the boy's personality would be moulded not by his academic knowledge but by his associations with other people, as we can see from the well-known heroic example of the friendship between Achilles and Phoenix. So we can understand why people should have found less fault with a tutor who was ignorant than with one who was half-educated,[23] and that writers who theorized on the subject looked above all for a dependable character. There was no attempt to discover a method of education suited to children; on

[22] Evidence for the position of the tutor can be found in E. Schuppe's article 'Paidagogos' *RE* XVIII (1942), 237ff.; on the conditions in Rome see Barrow *op. cit.* 38ff. and R. Boulogne *De plaats van de paedagogus in de romeinse cultuur* (dissertation, Utrecht 1951). See also the descriptions of Greek and Roman education by P. Girard, A. Gwynn and in particular H.-I. Marrou *Histoire de l'éducation dans l'antiquité*[6] (Paris 1965) [= *A History of Education in Antiquity* tr. G. Lamb (London 1956)].

[23] Quintilian *Inst. Orat.* 1, 1.8f.

the contrary, writers often approved of the fact that these tutors were generally elderly men. But the danger that could result from the use of slaves, and especially foreign slaves, was repeatedly stressed by those who considered the matter: 'it is a bad thing that a free man should be ruled by a slave' says Socrates in Plato's *Lysis* (208c), and in the pseudo-Platonic *Alcibiades I* (121c–122n) he severely criticises the negligence of the Athenian educational system compared to the well-thought-out upbringing and instruction of princes at the Persian court. A story told about the philosopher Aristippus illustrates the risk run in giving a member of the despised lower classes the duty of educating children. Asked how much he would want to be paid to educate someone's son, the philosopher named the sum of a thousand drachmae. When the frugal father pointed out that he could buy a slave for that amount, Aristippus replied, 'in that case you will find yourself with two slaves instead of one'.[24] The lowering influence of slaves as educators was also feared by Romans who considered its long-term effects, only here this was reinforced by their conceited disdain for *Graeculi* (cf. Tacitus *Dialogus* 29). Above all, the imbalance of this unequal educational team must have led people to wonder how authority and obedience, trust and devotion could be inculcated at all. 'Are you my slave or am I yours?' the young master in Plautus retorts to his tutor's admonitions.[25] This was a dilemma that could not, indeed, be resolved by the rod.

And yet, if we consider the evidence as a whole, these slave tutors accepted the challenge and performed their task well, as teachers of morals to Greek and Roman youth. However difficult their position may have been, they did have the advantage of taking over their charges at such an early age that the differences in social rank did not preclude a close personal relationship right from the start. There was little competition from parents, and this gave tutors a position similar to nurses. In the stammering speech of childhood, they were affectionately nicknamed *tata* and *tatula*, *papas* and *nonnus* by their charges, and often retained this tender mode of being addressed for the rest of their lives.[26] Another indication of this close human relationship is the part

[24] Ps.-Plutarch *De lib. educ.* 4f.

[25] Plautus *Bacch.* 162. Cf. also P. P. Spranger *Historische Untersuchungen zu den Sklavenfiguren des Plautus und Terenz* (*Ak. d. Wiss. u. d. Lit.* 1960, 8).

[26] K. Zacher 'Zu den Juvenalscholien' *Rh. Mus.* 45 (1890), 537ff.; W. Heraeus *Kleine Schriften* (*Indogermanische Bibliothek* III, 17: 1937), 158ff.: Boulogne *op. cit.* 56.

tutors play as the confidants of heroes in tragedy, and of their young masters in comedy. The loyal servant, full of experience and kindness, has a more important role in the plot than the nurse, even though in the last resort there is still an unbridgeable gap between him and his master. Of course, there were also those who described their tutors as uncouth and incompetent teachers, but the prevailing view was that, although it might be inconvenient, the job they did deserved gratitude. A young man could breathe freely again when he got rid of his supervisor: *tandem custode remoto*,[27] but if he was honest with himself, he would have to admit that it was precisely because of the restrictions that were put upon him that his own character was able to develop. The poet Martial may be representing the opinions of many when he says (11, 39):

> It was you, Charidemus, who used to rock my cradle and watch over me as a boy and be my constant companion. Now the clippings from my beard make my towel quite black and my girl-friend complains about the sting of my lips. But in your eyes I have not grown up; my bailiff and my manager dread you, the house itself trembles. You will not let me gamble, you will not let me love; you will not let me do anything, but want to be allowed to do everything yourself—you chide and admonish and grumble and sigh, and in your anger can hardly be restrained from snatching up the rod. When I put on Tyrian ornaments or oil my hair, you shout, 'Your father would never have done that.' With knotted brow you count the glasses I empty as if the bottles came from your own store. Leave off! I cannot stand a freedman who thinks he is Cato. My girl-friend can tell you that I am now a man.

The old pedagogue had to give way, of course, as soon as a girl came on the scene; but, in spite of everything, it was a parting full of mutual respect, which surely indicates that this did not bring their friendship to an end. Among educated people it was generally accepted that, apart from one's parents, nurses and tutors also deserved love and respect for what they had done to further one's education.[28] It became the rule in the biographical tradition to give the names of the tutors of great men, so that along with Themistocles, Alcibiades and Alexander, Cato of Utica and Augustus, their slave educators also found a place

[27] Horace *Ars Poetica* 161.

[28] Cicero *De amicitia* 74; Seneca *Ep.* 60, 1; Pliny *Ep.* 5, 16.3. Cf. Cicero *Brutus* 210.

in history. When Augustus, already in a position of great power, honoured his tutor with a state funeral, this was at the same time a symbol of his gratitude for what he owed to him, and a public recognition of the work slaves were doing for the state.[29] Ordinary people are represented by the many funerary inscriptions that were set up for tutors by their pupils, and sometimes even for the latter by their former tutors. 'To her tutor and teacher', *paedagogo suo* καὶ καθηγητῇ says Claudia,[30] and thereby gives expression to an experience that cannot have been exceptional. For language itself, the history of the word *paedagogus*, continued to stress the achievements of the boy's companion without debasing the word. Whenever Seneca wants to describe the kind of exemplary teacher of philosophy to whom the disciple should feel himself under an obligation, he uses the word *paedagogus*, and when he outlines the philosopher's task of educating mankind, he calls him *paedagogus generis humani*. It is in a similar sense that the Law of the Old Testament is interpreted in Christian teaching as a tutor who brings mankind up to come of age in Christ.[31] But this does not mean that in later antiquity the consciousness that the word designated a slave had disappeared. On the contrary, it is precisely the servant's understanding, the loyalty of the uneducated man, the foreigner's strictness, that endowed the concept with this power of obligation. The Emperor Julian, one of the last of the ancient Greeks, assures us that it was to his tutor Mardonius, who had originally come from Scythia as a slave and only later studied literature and philosophy, that he owed the somewhat rough, blunt and ascetic virtues that he claimed for his own.[32] So the historical role of slaves as educators can be seen in the way that they were able to inject some natural vitality into an over-sophisticated society, and apply it to forming the character of young people. This is also true of most of the Greek-speaking tutors of the Roman world; but these had an additional contribution to make in helping their charges to learn Greek, and thereby facilitating the creation of a single cultural and intellectual community.

Finally, we have slaves as physicians. This is a particularly interesting subject, yet, as it concerns only Rome and the Roman world, it can be

[29] Dio Cassius 48, 33.1. [30] *ILS* 4999.

[31] Seneca *Ep*. 11, 9; 25, 6; 89, 13. Cf. also St. Paul's *Letter to the Galatians* 3, 24 and Bertram *Theologisches Wörterbuch zum Neuen Testament* V, 619f.

[32] Julian *Misopogon* 351f.; on this see J. Bidez *La vie de l'Empereur Julien* (Paris 1930), 17f. and note 6 on p. 360.

dealt with more briefly. The Greeks had, since earliest times, had a skilled healing profession, and had also treated their sick in religious shrines. The development of scientific medicine, the art of healing based upon precise observation of nature and rational diagnosis, was one of their achievements. This science and skill—which from the classical period onwards was closely linked to philosophical speculation —remained restricted to free citizens, and it was understood that physicians also had a duty to supervise the treatment of sick slaves. Plato describes the possibility in some ideal future society that physicians might initiate their slaves into the art of healing and use them to treat such of their patients as were slaves.[33] But, as the literary evidence and the numerous inscriptions testify, even in Hellenistic times there were practically no slave-physicians in the Greek world; and wherever one is mentioned, he was invariably the assistant of a free physician.[34]

The development of medicine at Rome tended in a completely different direction. The idealized society of early Rome was satisfied with the sort of domestic medicine whose household remedies were still being recommended by Cato the Elder. Scientific methods of healing, like science and, indeed, literature in general, were introduced to Rome by prisoners of war from the Hellenistic East. Distinguished Romans were prepared to pay a good price for slaves with medical training, or to have one of the more talented slaves in their own household trained as a doctor. The *servus medicus* was a physician who belonged to the household, and would accompany his master when he travelled to one of the provinces or went on a campaign. Deserving slave-physicians were given their freedom, and thus the chance to set up a practice of their own. From at least 200 B.C. free Greeks also came to the West as physicians, particularly when, from the time of Sulla, the city of Rome became the centre of all cultural and scientific activity. The teaching and practice of Greek doctors in Rome from now on constitutes the major part of the history of Greek medicine. These foreign physicians were granted citizenship by Caesar and Augustus, and the rights of *immunitas* (freedom from taxation) and of forming a corporation by Vespasian. In this way a medical profession came into being at Rome, whose most eminent representatives appeared as personal physicians at the Imperial court; it was a profession which also had valuable tasks to perform in the Roman

[33] Plato *Laws* 4, 720a–e and 9, 857cd. Cf. p. 15 above.

[34] L. Cohn-Haft 'The Public Physicians of Ancient Greece' *Smith College Studies in History* 42 (1956), 3, 14f., to which I was referred by Hans Diller.

army, in the theatre and arena, and in the guilds and municipalities.[35] Yet, in the course of the centuries, we meet only a few physicians of Roman birth. The medical profession was certainly considered an acceptable means of earning one's living for citizens who were not senators or *equites*, and even members of the upper classes were allowed to accept remuneration for any medical advice they may have given so long as they did not demand it. Imperial policy was explicitly aimed at keeping the medical and teaching professions open to free men. But the physician's art was, nevertheless, left to free Greek immigrants and apart from them to slaves and freedmen, who were overwhelmingly of Eastern origins. In the Imperial period, this is known to have been true not only of Rome but also of the provinces, as is shown by the hundreds of inscriptions mentioning doctors who had been slaves, men whose work had made them wealthy and famous.[36]

There were, of course, deep-seated reasons why Romans should generally have avoided medicine in this way. The scientific character of the art of healing did not seem very attractive to a people among whose abilities that of methodical and systematic abstract thought was not particularly well developed. They would have been put off by the fact that, in this profession, technical skill could easily lead to seeming dependence on the patient. Then there were the unfortunate circumstances under which the art of scientific healing had first come to Rome—purveyed in an imperious and obscurantist way by those same Greeks who had been subjected politically but were still intellectually

[35] There have been several studies of the history of medicine at Rome, for instance by M. Albert *Les médecins grecs à Rome* (Paris 1894), who does not generally give any references to his sources; T. Meyer *Geschichte des römischen Ärztestandes* (thesis, Jena 1907); T. Clifford Allbutt *Greek Medicine in Rome* (London 1921), rather heavy going. The best summary is in P. Diepgen *Geschichte der Medizin* I (Berlin 1949). There is a wide-ranging collection of the evidence in A. Gervais 'Que pensait-on des médecins dans l'ancienne Rome' *Bulletin Association Budé* (1964), 197ff.

[36] On the status of the medical profession see Cicero *De Off.* 1, 150f. On the legal and social position of physicians see Duff *op. cit.* 119f.; R. Herzog 'Urkunden zur Hochschulpolitik der römischen Kaiser' *Sitzungsberichte der Preussischen Akademie der Wissenschaften* (1935), 967ff.; K. H. Below *Der Arzt im römischen Recht* (*Münchener Beiträge zur Papyrusforschung und antiken Rechtsgeschichte* 37: 1953), particularly 57ff., and U. v. Lübtow *Gnomon* 29 (1957), 616ff. There is a good selection of prosopographical material in H. Gummerus *Der Ärztestand im römischen Reich nach den Inschriften* (*Soc. Scient. Fennica, Commentationes Humanarum Litterarum* III, 6: 1932).

superior. Cato's mistrust is notorious: he almost went so far as to ascribe a conspiracy against the Italian way of life as a whole to those perfidious Greeks whose only interest was in making money.[37] Yet two hundred years later can be found an even worse instance of Roman resentment, expressed by the elder Pliny.[38] He reiterates Cato's objections and emphatically supports Roman prejudices with the experiences people had had in the intervening period of court physicians and fashionable doctors: these people were using men's lives to make money, their trade was a dishonest one, they operated without being subject to supervision and were the only people who were allowed to murder a man with impunity. Modern scholars have been somewhat taken aback by this outburst of Pliny, who was usually such a trustworthy observer and collector of scientific facts. Doubtless, this is a further illustration of Roman limitations, but at the same time it gives us an insight into the harm done by a civilization which, in using slaves to provide so many essential services, ended by alienating men from themselves. At the end of his furious polemic, Pliny concludes (29, 1.19): 'This is just what we deserve, since no-one wants to learn what is necessary for his own well-being. We go out for a walk on other people's feet, we see things with other people's eyes, we greet with the help of other people's memories, we even stay alive through other people's help; the value of natural things has been destroyed, and so have the true reasons for living. We do not consider anything to be ours except pleasure.' So it is the fact that slaves took from them the natural functions of the body that excited Pliny so much: those who bore the litter did the work of the feet, the slave who recited what his master wanted to have read acted as his eyes, the slave who reminded him of the names of the people he met was his memory, and the physician took care of his health; Pliny's list could, indeed, have been much longer. This passage is a remarkable example of the extent of social criticism in antiquity; the way that man's self-alienation was seen as one of the results of slavery foreshadows the discovery of the same process in the institution of mechanical slavery in contemporary industrial society.

There seems to have been no opportunity for humanitarian ideals to spread in the uneasy situation in which medicine found itself in the Roman world. Slaves repeatedly allowed themselves to be involved in political crimes as personal physicians to Roman aristocrats and

[37] Cato *Ad Marcum Fil.* 1 (ed. Jordan p. 77).

[38] Pliny *Nat. Hist.* 29, 1.1–28.

emperors.[39] Others showed themselves so willing to do whatever their patients wanted, in contravention of all the rules of their profession, that the great physician Galen was moved to say indignantly: 'Whatever demands people may make of them, they obey in the manner of slaves, in contrast to those ancient disciples of Asclepius who are held in such esteem among doctors; for they wished to dominate their patients as generals their troops and kings their subjects, but did not obey and serve them in the fashion of those Getae or Tibians, Phrygians or Thracians whom one can buy.'[40] Nevertheless, the best representatives of the profession, whether slaves or freedmen, stood by Hippocrates' precept that the patient and the doctor had to face disease together,[41] and speak and act on a level of human equality. Cicero not only praises the knowledge, reliability and good will of the free physician Asclapon, but also laments the death of the slave Alexion, not so much because in him he had lost a good physician as because he had become the poorer through the loss of this man's respect, humanity and charm. And Seneca realizes that the debt we owe doctors or teachers cannot be paid off with money, because their professions involve them in friendships with us.[42] As a moralizer aiming to give practical advice, he puts forward a general maxim in his famous 47th letter to Lucilius, that master and slave are equal in nature and that a slave's value ought not to be judged by the kind of work he does but by his character. He knows that as an ethical being a slave can also become his master's benefactor, and that—and this is decisive—he is capable of being virtuous. For him the concept of *humanitas* has less to do with educational objectives than with practical philanthropy and social conviction.[43]

[39] Examples in Albert *op. cit.* 101ff.; for similar behaviour on the part of free physicians see R. Herzog 'Nikias und Xenophon von Kos' *Historische Zeitschrift* 29 (1922), 189ff.

[40] Galen *Meth. Med.* 1, 1 (X, 4 in Kühn's edition). Τίβιοι in the manuscripts should probably be emended to Θίβιοι; on this Pontic tribe, from whose territory we are told that slaves were exported, see Ziegler *RE* VI A, 272.

[41] Galen *In Hippocr. Epid. VI comm.* 4, 4.9 (XVII B, 147 in Kühn's edition); cf. J. Ilberg *Neue Jahrbücher für die klassische Altertumswissenschaft* 15 (1905), 310.

[42] Cicero *Ad Fam.* 13, 20; *Ad Att.* 15, 1.1; Seneca *De Beneficiis* 6, 16, *Ep.* 47; *De Beneficiis* 3, 18ff.

[43] J. Lichy *De servorum condicione quid senserit L. Annaeus Seneca* (dissertation, Münster 1927); G. J. ten Veldhuys *De misericordiae et clementiae apud Senecam philos. usu atque ratione* (dissertation, Utrecht 1935); M. Pohlenz *Die Stoa* I[3] (Göttingen 1964), 315f. In his detailed analysis mentioned on p. 105, n. 5 above,

It is evident that in this moral climate at Rome, a climate that was determined to such a great extent by the interactions of many nations and the fluidity of movement from one class to another, medical ethics came to acquire the character of a personal attitude. It has been shown that neither the Hippocratic Oath nor the Hippocratic writings of the fifth and fourth centuries recognize the moral duty to love other human beings,[44] and if one of the public physicians of Hellenistic times was praised for treating patients free of charge, this was obviously an exception.[45] Only in the time of the Roman Empire did Scribonius Largus state clearly in the preface to his textbook of pharmacology that a physician's skill is owed to all equally, and his heart ought to be full of forgiveness and humane feelings (*plenus misericordiae et humanitatis animus*).[46] This man had taken part in Claudius' campaign in Britain, and also knew what were the duties of a soldier and a good citizen (l. 34), so he was familiar with Roman modes of thought; but the evidence nevertheless suggests that he was a freedman, as was the influential patron to whom he dedicated his work, C. Julius Callistus, Claudius' secretary. It was also this emperor, considered by later generations to have been under the influence of his freedmen, who decreed that sick slaves abandoned by their masters on the *isola Tiberina* should be given their freedom.[47] I would suspect that in these cases ex-slaves played some part in bringing about the victory of humane ideas both in medical ethics and in imperial legislation. Later, the social role of the medical profession, whose existence had for so long been denied, won more and more recognition. The philosophical poem about the physician's duties reconstructed by Paul Maas from fragments of an Athenian inscription refers to an otherwise unknown second-century philosopher by the name of

W. Richter suggests that the views Seneca expresses on the subject of slavery in his 47th letter contain ideas which are not exclusively and perhaps not at all Stoic.

[44] K. Deichgräber 'Die ärztliche Standesethik des hippokratischen Eides' *Quellen und Studien zur Geschichte der Naturwissenschaften und der Medizin* 3 (1933), 35f.; L. Edelstein 'The Professional Ethics of the Greek Physician' *Bulletin for the History of Medicine* 30 (1956), 391ff.

[45] Cohn-Haft *op. cit.* 32ff.

[46] There is an edition of the preface with a commentary in K. Deichgräber *Professio Medici* (*Ak. d. Wiss. u. d. Lit.* 1950, 9); the quotation is from lines 29ff.

[47] Suetonius *Div. Claud.* 25, 2; Dio Cassius 60, 29.7. Cf. Duff *op. cit.* 34, 194; A. Momigliano *Claudius*[2] (Cambridge 1961), 71, 116 n. 61.

Serapion; here it is said that a physician has first of all to heal his own reason and help himself, and then, like a god, he will become the saviour both of slaves and the poor, and of the rich and the rulers, and will be like a brother to them all.[48] 'Doctors are the natural advocates of the poor', as Rudolf Virchow put it.[49] This idea had been prepared for in antiquity even before the arrival of Christianity.

This brings my survey to an end; of necessity it cannot do more than give a general outline of a field that is seldom touched on by historians, although it ought to be obvious that those major political events that tend to be the focus of our attention could not have occurred without the efficient working of everyday services and the smooth flow of the imperceptible currents of everyday life. The aristocrat of ancient civilization, who valued nothing more than independence and leisure, entrusted as much work as was practicable to slaves (particularly the gruelling work necessary in orchards, mines and factories, but laborious domestic chores as well) and accomplished his creative spiritual achievements in an exclusive society of which it was explicitly said that 'every slave is an enemy' (*quot servi, tot hostes*).[50] Hardly anywhere can the weaknesses of this social structure be seen more clearly than in the important part played by slaves in looking after and bringing up children and young people and caring for people's health. But it was here that the oppressed, because other human beings were entrusted to them, were elevated above slavery. The nurses, teachers and physicians rose to the tasks set them; they formed close relationships with their masters, thus overcoming class barriers at their most crucial points. Some of them achieved freedom in all formal respects, though without subsequently opposing the unshakeable slave system as free men. Others, although legally they remained slaves, in practice became the partners of free men in social life. One person who had risen from slave-status described his own experience with the words 'the slave who serves wisely has a share in his master's power.'[51] Above all, however, this suggests that on many occasions real humanity prevailed over the callousness of oppression.

[48] J. H. Oliver and P. L. Maas 'An Ancient Poem on the Duties of a Physician' *Bulletin for the History of Medicine* 1 (1939), 315ff.; Edelstein *op. cit.* 415.

[49] *Die medizinische Reform, Eine Wochenschrift* (Berlin 1848/9), 2.

[50] Festus 349, 23 (ed. Lindsay); Macrobius *Sat.* 1, 11.13.

[51] Publilius Syrus *Sententiae* 544 ed. Meyer = 596 in Duff's Loeb edition of the *Minor Latin Poets*.

From deep and indestructible human feelings, a sort of self-purification of the whole polluted system took place in some small but decisive respects, as a reminder of the eternal truth that man is something sacred to man:[52] *homo sacra res homini*.

[52] Seneca *Ep*. 95, 33.

VI

Slaves and the Liberal Arts in Ancient Rome

My contribution to the periodical *Vestnik Drevnei Istorii* in this anniversary year is intended as a sign of my gratitude for the many ideas it has given me in the course of my investigations into ancient slavery. It is to be welcomed that this problem is being studied with particular interest; for it seems to me that the scholar who looks closely at slavery as a substantial element in the structure of society is as it were trying to reach with X-rays the inner structure of ancient civilization.

The principle of robbing a particular section of the people of a state or society of their freedom and declaring them to be the tools of the rulers is so monstrous that it could never be consistently enforced in the Graeco-Roman world. People always had to make exceptions, both in situations when slaves were called upon to fight because of a serious threat to the survival of the state, and in domestic life when slaves were assigned duties which required a full measure of confidence and trust. Babies were given to slave nurses to be looked after and older boys and girls were committed to slave tutors. In the Roman world, a master who fell ill turned for help to his physician, generally a slave or freedman, and during the civil wars many political leaders who realized that they had been deserted by their whole retinue found their last faithful follower in the person of their slave. I have discussed these exceptional solutions to the problem, which often enabled humane

This chapter first appeared in a Russian translation in *VDI* 1967, 2, 98–103.

feelings to be experienced in a novel way, on more than one occasion.[1] But the extent to which slaves had freedom of action and were able to become influential in Roman society is much wider than this. It was not just looking after infants and caring for the sick that was left to slaves and freedmen; after a certain date they were also in the main entrusted with educating the young and teaching educational theory: the *artes liberales* became their domain.

Those branches of knowledge whose aim it was to lead free men to a state of ἀρετή had since the time of Plato and Aristotle been described as ἐλευθέριαι ἐπιστῆμαι or ἐλευθέρια μαθήματα. These fields of knowledge—in particular grammar and rhetoric—did not aim to provide a livelihood but were rather intended to educate a young man for his *Polis* and ensure that he had the independence of mind that was an essential requirement for the life of a free man. All of these subjects later came to be combined in the notion of an ἐγκύκλιος παιδεία, a general education.[2] From the third century B.C. the Romans took over the Hellenistic educational system in the form then current. This was part of that dynamic process by which Roman society was thoroughly penetrated by foreign cultural elements.[3] Roman nobles employed Greeks as their secretaries or readers and had their sons taught by Greeks; these men tended to be prisoners of war or slaves who had been bought in the market-place. When the idea of giving public instruction in schools became widespread, the teachers often came from among the slave class. Men who were imported from the East as slaves and who, when they arrived, still had chalkmarks on their feet to show that they were for sale, could be appointed to teach, and if they were lucky win their freedom and become famous, like Staberius Eros, who was said to have arrived on the same ship as Publilius Syrus, the composer of mimes, and the astrologer Manilius (Pliny *NH* 35, 199). Thus from this time on a certain section of the Roman intelligentsia was composed of slaves.[4] Numerous slaves and

[1] See Ch. V above and Ch. VII below.

[2] H.-I. Marrou *Histoire de l'éducation dans l'antiquité*[6] (Paris 1965), 266f. [= *A History of Education in Antiquity* tr. G. Lamb (London 1956), 176ff.]; H. Fuchs' article 'Enkyklios Paideia' *Reallexikon für Antike und Christentum* V (1962), 365ff.

[3] S. L. Uttschenko *Der weltanschaulich-politische Kampf in Rom am Vorabend des Sturzes der Republik* (Berlin 1956), 43ff.

[4] Cf. E. M. Shtajerman in her book on the hey-day of slavery in the Roman Republic (Moscow 1964), 9, 120ff., which has appeared in a German translation by M. Bräuer-Pospelova: E. M. Staerman *Die Blütezeit der Sklavenwirtschaft in der*

freedmen could be found at primary-school level; they also taught grammar, the knowledge of the Greek and Latin languages and literature, and opened the way to the higher levels of scholarship; and finally they taught rhetoric, which could serve as an introduction to the legal profession and generally to a political career. We are entitled to assume that the same was true for other disciplines about which we are not so well informed, indeed for all branches of knowledge which, following the Greek precedent, were described as *artes liberales*: *artes quae sunt libero dignae* (Cicero *De oratore* 1, 16.72). Varro combined nine different disciplines as part of a system which for centuries was to remain the basis of higher education: seven traditional subjects—grammar, dialectic, rhetoric, arithmetic, geometry, astronomy and music, together with the two specialized sciences, medicine and architecture.

The fact that over a long period the teachers of these educational subjects came from abroad and often began as slaves considerably diminished the prestige of these professions, even when men who came from the upper classes of Roman society began to develop an interest in grammar and appeared as instructors of the art of public speaking. The rhetorician Seneca the elder says that 'intra libertinos praeceptores pulcherrimae disciplinae continebantur, et minime probabili more turpe erat docere, quod honestum erat discere' (*Controversiae* 2, *praef.* 5). In his detailed discussion of the compatibility of economic gain with social status, Cicero says that medicine, architecture and instruction in respectable subjects (*doctrina rerum honestarum*) are professions worthy of free men, but he is here thinking of citizens who do not belong to the senatorial or equestrian class (*De officiis* I, 150f.). The younger Seneca labours the point that the money which is paid to a physician or *praeceptor bonarum artium* should not be seen as the price of the invaluable gifts they provide (health or knowledge of the liberal arts) but merely as payment for the trouble they have gone to (*mercedem non meriti sed occupationis suae*: *De beneficiis* 6, 14–16).[5] In spite of this high estimation of the *artes liberales*, of course, he considers that there is a deep gulf between these branches of knowledge and philosophy (*Epistulae Morales* 88). So even under the Empire,

römischen Republik (the second of the Mainz Academy's series of translations of foreign works on ancient slavery: Wiesbaden 1969), 5ff., 128ff.

[5] Cf. H. Siber 'Operae liberales' *Iherings Jahrbücher* N.F. 52 (1939), 161ff.; generally on remuneration for work in the liberal arts A. Bernard *La rémunération des professions libérales en droit romain* (Paris 1935).

intellectual professions, with the exception of the professorships which had been set up by the state, generally continued to be regarded with scant respect and to be poorly paid, even when they were exercised by free men. It is not without reason that Juvenal (*Satires* 7, 157) complains:

Nosse volunt omnes, mercedem solvere nemo.

It was under these conditions that the learned writer Suetonius, later to become Secretary of State at the court of Hadrian, wrote his *De viris illustribus*, a biographical survey of Roman achievements in poetry and prose, historiography, philosophy, and grammatical and rhetorical theory. The only part that is preserved in its entirety is that dealing with grammarians in conjunction with rhetoric (ed. R. P. Robinson, Paris 1925). The information which Suetonius gives about Roman philological and rhetorical studies, and the series of sketches of the lives of individual grammarians, were highly regarded in antiquity by St. Jerome and subsequent scholars, up to the composition of the Suda. Modern scholars too have found Suetonius a useful source for their attempts to compile a list of all Greek men of letters active in Rome[6] or to map out a history of Roman education in general.[7] Yet the remarkable fact that the great majority of the grammarians mentioned by Suetonius were slaves or freedmen has not so far been given the attention it deserves.[8] An important start has now been made by E. M. Shtajerman,[9] and in my opinion the results of her work should encourage us to examine the effects of the activity of slaves and freedmen on the *artes liberales* as a whole. It is over 150 years since the appearance of Daniel Theodor Gevers' *Disputatio historico-juridica de servilis conditionis hominibus artes, litteras et scientias Romae colentibus* (Lugdunum Batavorum/Leiden 1816). The book assembles valuable material, but it needs to be brought up to date and corrected in the

[6] A. Hillscher 'Hominum litteratorum Graecorum ante Tiberii mortem in urbe Roma commoratorum historia critica' *Neue Jahrbücher f. classische Philologie* Suppl. 19 (1892), 353–444.

[7] E. Jullien *Les professeurs de littérature dans l'ancienne Rome* (thesis, Paris 1885), 184f.; A. Gwynn *Roman Education from Cicero to Quintilian* (Oxford 1926), 31ff.; Marrou[6] *op. cit.* 356ff. [242ff. in the English edition].

[8] Cf. nevertheless R. H. Barrow *Slavery in the Roman Empire* (London 1928), 60ff. and A. M. Duff *Freedmen in the Roman Empire* (Cambridge 1958), 118ff.; and more recently also S. Treggiari *Roman Freedmen during the Late Republic* (Oxford 1969).

[9] *op. cit.* 120ff.

light of modern knowledge. In particular, we should now face the historical question whether the fact that these artists, scholars and writers came from a slave background affected their life and work to any appreciable extent. This question had already been formulated in antiquity—in the time of Hadrian, Hermippus of Berytus, according to the Suda ἔκδουλος ὢν γένος, wrote a book Περὶ τῶν διαπρεψάντων ἐν παιδείᾳ δούλων.[10]

The information given by Suetonius about grammar and rhetoric allows us to see how productive such a treatment within the context of the *liberales artes* as a whole would be. It cannot be doubted that freedmen came to dominate this aspect of cultural life and thereby became extremely influential in the education of Roman youth. In the time of Caesar, the first place is taken by Marcus Antonius Gnipho and Lucius Ateius Philologus; under Augustus, Marcus Verrius Flaccus and Gaius Julius Hyginus are of outstanding importance in philology, in antiquarian studies and also in geographical and historical writing. We would have to test the difficulties these men faced as well as the success with which they rose from the status of slaves to enter the cultural world of the dominant social class. We are told that Cornelius Epicadus completed and published the memoirs of his patron Sulla (Suetonius *De grammaticis* 12), that after Pompey's death one of his freedmen, Lenaeus, wrote a satire in which he defended him vigorously (Suetonius *De grammatics* 15), and that Ateius Philologus helped the historians Sallust and Asinius Pollio in their literary work (Suetonius *De grammaticis* 10). Other members of this 'intelligentsia', particularly those who originated from the Greek-speaking East, continued to be conscious of the fact that they were superior to the Romans by virtue of their education, and they came to share the conviction that a man who was intellectually gifted could not be enslaved at all.[11] Just occasionally the rivalry between these upstarts and the aristocracy seems to have led to a life-style that was ostentatious to the point of indecency and a pathologically excessive self-consciousness—as in the case of the notorious Quintus Remmius Palaemon, who considered himself a judge of all poets and poems and declared that the science of letters had been born with him and would die with him (Suetonius *De grammaticis* 23). As the son of a slave-woman, it was no doubt easier for a man like Palaemon than for many others to break with the old traditions of teaching, and introduce modern authors

[10] Hillscher *op. cit.* (note 6 above), 355, 1.

[11] E. M. Shtajerman *VDI* 1965, 1, 69, 78.

into his syllabus, as had Quintus Caecilius Epirota, another freedman, who was the first to discuss Vergil and other contemporary poets in his lectures (Suetonius *De grammaticis* 16).

In the other liberal arts, legal historians (particularly F. M. De Robertis and also J. Macqueron and D. Nörr) have recently made substantial contributions to our knowledge of the legal status of intellectual work. We also have prosopographical studies establishing the role played by slaves and freedmen in individual professions, such as physicians,[12] architects[13] and musicians.[14] Perhaps in the not too distant future there will be an examination of the question whether the experiences that these men underwent on the path from slavery to freedom left any traces on the practice or professional ethics of physicians and on artistic production. It would be wrong to assume that such a search is bound to be fruitless. For the experience of slavery has indeed left its mark on Roman poetry, particularly towards the end of the Republic and in the Early Empire. Like many other slaves at Rome, Publilius Syrus had been trained in the arts and sciences and had gained his freedom as a successful poet. In the surviving *Sententiae*, he gives advice on how to live an upright life that applies to both free and slave. It has quite rightly been said that his attitude is a strange mixture of the straightforward self-confidence of a working man and the obedient submissiveness of a dependent employee.[15] Here we find the line *qui invitus servit fit miser, servit tamen* (564 in G. Meyer's edition, Leipzig 1880 = 616 in J. W. and A. M. Duff's Loeb edition of the *Minor Latin Poets*, 1934) as well as *occidi est pulchrum, ignominiose ubi servias* (442 Meyer = 489 Duff). His language is particularly informative, since he uses the terminology of slave life to describe the conditions and express the precepts of all men, free men included. He warns against giving

[12] H. Gummerus *Der Ärztestand im römischen Reich nach den Inschriften* (*Soc. Scient. Fennica, Commentationes Humanarum Litterarum* III, 6: 1932); K. H. Below *Der Arzt im römischen Recht* (*Münchener Beiträge zur Papyrusforschung und antiken Rechtsgeschichte* 37: 1953). Cf. also A. Gervais 'Que pensait-on des médecins dans l'ancienne Rome' *Bulletin de l'Association Budé* 1964, 197ff.

[13] I. Calabi Limentani *Studi sulla società Romana: Il lavoro artistico* (Milan 1958).

[14] R. Benz *Unfreie Menschen als Musiker und Schauspieler in der römischen Welt* (typewritten dissertation, Tübingen 1961). Cf. also the two major works dealing with slaves and freedmen in the service of the emperors: G. Boulvert *Les esclaves et les affranchis impériaux sous le Haut-Empire romain* (dissertation, Aix-en-Provence 1964) and H. Chantraine *Freigelassene und Sklaven im Dienst der römischen Kaiser: Studien zu ihrer Nomenklatur* (*Forschungen zur antiken Sklaverei* 1: Wiesbaden 1967).

[15] E. M. Schtajerman *Die Krise der Sklavenhalterordnung im Westen des römischen Reiches* (Berlin 1964), 67f., 116f.

in too easily: *mansueta tutiora sunt, sed serviunt* (373 Meyer = 414 Duff); he mentions service for one's country: *populi est mancipium quisquis patriae est utilis* (471 Meyer = 519 Duff) and the bonds of morality: *pudorem habere servitus quodammodo est* (490 Meyer = 538 Duff). The task of reconstructing the language of slaves in the Latin-speaking world would be well worth while.

I will end with a reference to the fables of Phaedrus. From its very origins this genre of poetry allowed the unimportant man to have his say in reply to those in power; and there was a strong tendency to social criticism in these stories. The Greeks made Aesop the inventor of this kind of poetry and popular lore, and depicted him as a slave. All that we know for certain about Phaedrus is that he was the freedman of an emperor and that in his poetry he consciously tried to imitate the slave Aesop. I do not want to touch here on the disputed questions of when he lived, what particular writings can be attributed to him and what political allusions they may contain.[16] It is agreed that in his fables, which show some similarities to the lectures of popular philosophers, we are entitled to perceive the attitudes of the lower social classes: respect for manual skills and emphasis on the honesty of the poor man.[17] The poet declares openly that all literary fables originate in slavery and that this insight will allow everyone to attain independence of spirit. As we are told in the last poem of the second book, the Athenians erected a monument to Aesop on which the poet was explicitly referred to as a slave: *patere honoris scirent cuncti viam/ nec generi tribui sed virtuti gloriam* (2, 9.1–4 ed. Postgate, Oxford 1919). It is the same source of human experience that has produced the self-consciousness of a poet who in the prologue to the third book confesses that he has dedicated his life to the Muses and completely eradicated the desire for material wealth from his heart. In general terms he says here (33ff.) that it was the man who did not dare to say what he wished because of the insecurity of a slave's position who was led to express his personal feelings in the form of fables.

Thus the two slave-poets agree that education makes a man in a state of outward dependence free and superior—Phaedrus (4, 22.1): *homo doctus in se semper divitias habet*, and Publilius (544 Mayer = 596 Duff): *qui docte servit, partem dominatus tenet*. The scholar who studies the achievements of slaves and freedmen in the liberal arts should always keep these precepts in mind!

[16] On these points cf. L. Herrmann *Phèdre et ses fables* (Leiden 1950).

[17] Schtajerman *Die Krise* . . . 114ff.

VII

The Faithful Slave

'The Roman Empire was a slave state' said A. Piganiol at the beginning of the book in which he demonstrated humane tendencies in Imperial jurisdiction from the evidence of rescripts concerned with freedmen and slaves.[1] As a counterpart to this excellent study, which has lightened the dark picture presented by Roman slavery, I would like to show in what ways slaves themselves were able to enter the moral world which the dominant ideology reserved for free men alone.

In the sixth book of his *Facta et dicta memorabilia*, Valerius Maximus gives some examples of the key virtues of *gravitas*, *iustitia* and *fides*. *Fides* is portrayed under three headings: loyalty to the state, the faithfulness of wives to their husbands and the loyalty of slaves to their masters (6, 8). The place given in this classification to slaves is rather surprising. The author seems to have sensed this himself, for in his introduction he expressly states that the loyalty of a slave to his master deserves to be praised all the more, the less it is expected. The general opinion was, after all, that slaves were false and unco-operative, lying and treacherous, and always intending to run away. Slave-owners had found some harsh ways of protecting themselves against being deceived or threatened by their slaves; if they wanted to obtain the truth from a slave, they tortured him, and they grouped together slaves of different nationalities and languages to make conspiracy more

This chapter is dedicated to André Piganiol, and also appeared in *Mélanges d'archéologie et d'histoire offerts à André Piganiol* 3 (Paris 1966), 1499ff.

[1] A. Piganiol 'Les empereurs parlent aux esclaves' *Romanitas* 1 (1958), 7ff.

difficult. Ovid was of the opinion that Menander's characters would remain with us for ever—the false slave and harsh father, the shameless procuress and the flattering prostitute (*Amores* 1, 15.17ff.).

But there must also have been exceptions to the rule—for otherwise society could not have survived. Among domestic slaves in particular, there were many who reciprocated their master's good will and concern for them by industrious and dedicated work; there were always slaves who were dependable, as can be seen already in the poems of Homer, slaves to whom one could readily entrust one's property; and there were tutors and nurses who were deeply attached to those who had been put in their charge. The Greeks did not apply the term πιστός in the sense of 'loyal' or 'trustworthy' exclusively to partners in marriage or to friends, but also to messengers and watchmen, and often to slaves as well.[2] Classical tragedy was familiar with the character of the trusty slave who supports his master or mistress with advice and assistance, and in Euripides there even appears at the periphery of the tragic action the figure of the noble slave who lays claim to sentiments shared by free men. Admittedly, this idealistic picture and these isolated experiences nowhere lead to a demand for the abolition of slavery, not even in New Comedy. Menander says that a slave who is well disposed towards one is the best thing that one can own (Fr. 563 Körte: ὅταν τύχῃ τις εὐνοοῦντος οἰκέτου οὐκ ἔστιν οὐθὲν κτῆμα κάλλιον βίῳ), but the only opportunity he can see for the slave is internal moral freedom; he has no other chance to rise to the level of free society.

Roman society also made judgements of this kind, which found their way into literature, particularly during the period when the Romans were looking to Hellenistic literary traditions for inspiration.[3] There is a lot of evidence to suggest that the position of Roman slaves (who were traditionally members of the *familia*) was in many respects more favourable than in Greek society; this is certainly indicated by many investigations of the religious position of slaves.[4] Domestic slaves were given a far greater degree of freedom of movement in

[2] Bultmann, article 'πιστεύω κτλ' *Theologisches Wörterbuch zum Neuen Testament* VI, 175ff.

[3] For the way in which slaves were regarded in literature and philosophy see Chapter I above; also W. Richter 'Seneca und die Sklaven' *Gymnasium* 65 (1958), 206ff.; P. P. Spranger *Historische Untersuchungen zu den Sklavenfiguren des Plautus und Terenz* (*Ak. d. Wiss. u. d. Lit.*, 1960, 8), 18ff.

[4] Bömer I–IV; q.v., indices under 'Humanität' and 'Rom'.

Roman comedy than had ever been enjoyed by their Greek prototypes, both as the *servus callidus* who was the key figure of many plays, and as the *servus bonus* or *servus frugi* who often appeared as the counterpart to this cunning schemer. In several of his plays, Plautus puts into the mouth of the good slave a soliloquy in which the characteristics of the obedient servant are enumerated: he is more considerate of his master's affairs than of his own advantage, he wants to please his master even in his absence, and even in his sleep he wishes only to dream of his slavery.[5] Even if the motives for these sentiments appear to be fear of punishment or the hope that freedom may be granted, we are still left with the impression that this is an honourable and decent servant. Plautus gives such devoted slaves the epithets *fidus* and *fidelis*.[6] There are some outstanding characters among them who do good for its own sake, such as the self-sacrificing Tyndarus in Plautus' *Captivi*, or Geta in Terence's *Adelphi*, whose feelings correspond entirely to those of his master.[7] Educated Roman society was sufficiently open-minded in the second century B.C. to recognize that such devoted servants and assistants possessed that part of the moral personality embraced in the concept of *fides*, and which covered whatever was expressed by the terms trustworthiness, reliability and loyalty.[8] For this we have the significant evidence of the poet Lucilius, who testified to the faithfulness of his slave Metrophanes in an epitaph that was considered noteworthy even in antiquity (579f. Marx):

Servus neque infidus domino neque inutilis quanquam
Lucili columella hic situs Metrophanes.[9]

[5] In an essay the manuscript of which was very kindly made accessible to me by Karl Büchner, G. Lüdeke refers to the following soliloquies: *Aul.* 587ff., *Men.* 966ff., *Rud.* 920ff., *Pseud.* 1103ff.

[6] References in Jachmann's article 'fidelis' *Thesaurus Linguae Latinae* VI, 655ff.; Bauer, article 'fidus' *ibid.* 703ff.

[7] Spranger *op. cit.* 27, 29; on Geta, Donatus *Ad Ter. Ad.* v. 301 comments: *mira in servo fides.*

[8] E. Fraenkel, article 'fides' *Thesaurus Linguae Latinae* VI, 661ff.; R. Heinze *Vom Geist des Römertums* (Leipzig and Berlin 1939), 25ff.; L. Lombardi *Dalla 'fides' alla 'bona fides'* (Milan 1961), 4ff., 38ff.

[9] 'Here lies Lucilius' slave Metrophanes, at no time disloyal to his master, nor insignificant as a pillar of the household.' Bömer IV, 166ff. justifiably stresses the Roman elements in this attitude on the part of masters, whereas the Greek influence is overestimated by E. M. Shtajerman in her article on the position of slaves in the time of the late republic (*VDI* 1963, 2, 96ff.). It is interesting that Lucilius should express his approval of the slave by noting the absence of certain faults: *neque infidus neque inutilis.* Obviously the presence of these faults was

From this time on, we find epitaphs praising slaves both in Greek and, more frequently, in Latin. The fact that master and slave were often buried in a common grave is further evidence of the humanitarian attitude typical of Roman society in particular.

But, however valuable a possession a devoted slave might be, and however frequently his loyal services might be praised, these experiences were not sufficiently common for slaves to be glorified as examples of loyalty on the same level as wives, or for their actions to be included in anthologies of memorable and exemplary deeds. For this to happen, a situation first had to arise in which slaves stood the test of that devotion in circumstances there were out of the ordinary; they had to make a conscious decision in favour of their own master and against another power which claimed an overriding allegiance for itself. This, in fact, occurred during the century of the Roman civil wars, when, as the unity of the government disintegrated, the closed class-structure of society broke apart. Paul Jal has outlined the frightening examples of political self-annihilation, social dissolution and moral decay of the period from Sulla to Vespasian in his valuable book on the civil wars.[10] During these disorders, slaves were confronted with situations of extreme danger and, as the same time, great temptation. In remote areas rich landowners began raising bands of soldiers from among slaves, and carrying out large-scale robbery with their help. In the city of Rome, party bosses formed bodyguards of slaves and barbarians, and it was soon realized that as long as they were properly fed and efficiently officered, these gangs would be more effective in inverse proportion to their involvement in the political questions that were in dispute. The way in which these mobs of slaves were organized by political bosses and their agents (Milo and Clodius may serve as examples[11]), calls to mind the bodyguard of slaves and foreigners formed with great success by Dionysius of Syracuse, a typical Greek tyrant.[12] On the other hand, it also foreshadows the bodyguard of

accepted by many Romans as the rule. Thus the *vilicus*, whether a slave or a freedman, was often considered unreliable—cf. M. E. Sergeyenko's article on the *vilicus* in *VDI* 1956, 4, 50ff.

[10] P. Jal *La guerre civile à Rome, Étude littéraire et morale* (Paris 1963).

[11] M. Zeller *Die Rolle der unfreien Bevölkerung Roms in den politischen Kämpfen der Bürgerkriege* (typewritten dissertation, Tübingen 1962); E. M. Shtajerman in her article on slaves and freedmen in the social struggles of the late republic in *VDI* 1962, 1, 24ff. and particularly 36ff.

[12] Cic. *Tusc.* 5, 58: 'credebat eorum nemini, sed iis, quos ex familiis locupletium servos delegerat, quibus nomen servitutis ipse detraxerat, et quibusdam convenis

Germans constituted by the Julio-Claudian emperors, who were under obligation solely to themselves and remained slaves from the time of Augustus up to that of Caligula.[13] In later centuries, oriental despots in particular (e.g. the Ayyubids and Mamelukes in Egypt or the Ottoman dynasty in the Turkish empire) inculcated in their slave troops a blind loyalty to their masters and a genuine satisfaction with their lot as slaves by seeing that they had undisguised material advantages.

But it was not this exploitation of slaves' collective loyalty that provided *exempla* for the historians of the Roman civil wars or compilers of handbooks such as Valerius Maximus. The most serious trial of a slave's loyalty came when he was formally called upon to betray his master and was promised his freedom as a reward for disloyalty. To a limited extent this happened in the time of Marius and Sulla, and it was widespread under the Triumvirate in 43 B.C. All the bonds that held Roman families together were torn asunder in the proscriptions, and virtues such as *pietas* and *fides* were suppressed for reasons of state. Edicts were issued ordering wives and children, friends and clients, freedmen and slaves to inform against their masters and protectors, and to deliver them up under the threat of extreme penalties. It was now up to each individual to make up his mind where his loyalties lay. Contemporaries considered this to have been a reign of terror; many a household had its traitors and its martyrs, and the following generations remembered both the actions that shocked them and the examples of virtue. Many slaves turned traitor, many joined the side that offered them the greatest rewards; and yet there was a considerable number who remained loyal in spite of the temptation. When historians of the civil wars speak of these trials of *fides*, they mention the slaves of the proscribed as well as their wives and sons. Velleius (2, 67.2) summarizes his knowledge in a few words by saying that as regards their behaviour towards those who had been proscribed, the fidelity of wives was generally speaking outstanding, that of freedmen average, that of slaves moderate and that of sons non-existent (*id tamen notandum est fuisse in proscriptos uxorum fidem summam, libertorum mediam, servorum aliquam, filiorum nullam*). It became an established commonplace for

et feris barbaris corporis custodiam committebat.' Cf. K. F. Stroheker *Dionysios I.* (Wiesbaden 1958), 42f., 152f. On this trait of Greek tyranny in general, see H. Berve *Historische Zeitschrift* 177 (1954), 14f.

[13] The personal devotion and loyalty of foreigners is particularly stressed in the case of *Germani corporis custodes* by Josephus *Antiq.* 19, 149; Tac. *Ann.* 15, 58; Suet. *Galba* 12, 2.

historians, orators and poets to express the terrors of the civil wars by describing the reactions of free men and slaves without distinction of rank.[14] And the heroism of those who passed this test of character was recorded in the collections of famous examples—the topic *de fide servorum* was added to that *de fide uxorum*.

The earliest detailed description of the awful fate suffered by those proscribed in the year 43 B.C. is contained in Appian's *History of the Civil Wars* (4, 13.49–51.224). It has been shown that this account—as rich in its dramatic power as in its romantic embellishments—does not come from the historian's main source, but has been taken from elsewhere.[15] In his introduction, Appian vividly portrays the complete disintegration of the domestic community, which gave the victims more cause to fear their wives and children, freedmen and slaves, debtors and neighbours than the soldiers who were searching for them (4, 13.51). Members of the same family became enemies; almost everyone was disloyal enough to put his own advantage above compassion for others (4, 14.53f.).[16] This summary is followed by a description of the various actions taken in self-defence by those who were proscribed, how they went into hiding and as often as not were found, with grim results; only then (4, 15.59) does Appian mention the zeal and virtue of those wives and children, brothers and slaves who tried to save the outlaws. In these introductory sentences, the author draws our attention to what was unusual in these events compared with the time of Marius and Sulla, and restricts himself to reporting glorious or notorious deeds (τὰ λαμπρὰ καὶ τὰ χείρω γενόμενα); he intends to relate only those things that are the most astonishing and bear out what he has said before (4, 16.63). 'There is a great deal of material here, and many Romans have recorded it in their own way in many books. I only want to give a few examples of each individual kind so that everyone will be persuaded, and also for the satisfaction of the present age—but for reasons of length I will record only the most important cases' (4, 16.64). So there must have

[14] References in Jal *op. cit.* 412.

[15] E. Gabba *Appiano e la storia delle guerre civili* (Florence 1956), 223ff.

[16] In §§53 and 54 οἰκεῖος means a member of one's house in the sense of a near relative, as in 4, 17.66 and elsewhere generally. P. Jal *op. cit.* 413 is surely mistaken in translating οἰκεῖος as slave in §53 but as master in §54. Nor is it correct to take Appian 4, 29.126f. to mean that after the slaughter had ended the populace demanded that action be taken against all slaves who had betrayed their masters; only a single slave is referred to in this passage.

been Roman historians (Ῥωμαῖοι συνέγραψαν) who had dealt with these topics; and there must also have been precedents for the classification of events in terms of good and evil deeds, and therefore presumably for arranging anthologies of examples under various sub-headings.[17]

The limited amount of material to which Appian restricts himself nevertheless covers a wide and varied field. It is so ordered that we are first told of men who suffered ruin (4, 17.65–35.148) and then of individuals who were unexpectedly saved (4, 36.149–51.223). The large number of victims have been arranged so that cases in which sons, brothers and wives, respectively, played a major role are classed together,[18] although the good or evil done them by slaves is also mentioned. The loyalty or treachery of slaves is illustrated by a long series of examples, such as that of the slave who showed his respect for his master by striking down the centurion who had murdered him, and then killing himself (4, 26.108). In the introduction to the section, which gives examples of unexpected rescues, the good will shown by slaves towards their masters, described as beyond what nature would lead one to expect, is compared to the love of wives for their husbands or sons for their fathers (4, 36.154: εὔνοιαι . . . θεραπόντων ὑπὲρ φύσιν ἐς δεσπότας). There follows a long and continuous succession of tales about loyal slaves (4, 43.179–48.208). These are generally cases of slaves who kept their master's hiding place secret or helped him to escape, actions which involved a risk to their own lives; there was also the extreme test of loyalty, the willingness to give up one's life for one's master (4, 44.185f.). On considering the passage as a whole one comes to a more favourable verdict on the behaviour of slaves than Velleius' remarks might lead one to expect. While government was degenerating into tyranny, the ruling classes were tearing themselves apart and almost every family was suffering from severe internal strife, many slaves proved their loyalty in a heroic way. They contributed considerably to preserving in society a basis of decency and trust, and, at the same time, enabled their own class to achieve new positions of influence. Under subsequent rulers, no longer able to trust members of their own social class, there was to begin the long

[17] In his account of the proscriptions of 43 B.C., Dio Cassius (47, 9–13) also stresses the great variety of methods of slaughter and rescue, and then confines himself to recounting a few particularly memorable examples.

[18] Jal *op. cit.* 269f. notes the remarkable fact that in these passages the catchword occurs only at the end.

line of *servi Augusti* who rose to high rank in the Imperial household and in the government.

We may infer from what Appian says that the extraordinary personal tragedies of the year 43 B.C. had been described in histories and collections of anecdotes. Certainly, the comparable events of the civil war between Marius and Sulla and the equally notable occurrences of the Gracchan uprising had been similarly treated in literature. It should be noted that slaves were now thought capable of memorable deeds and sayings, and even their names were sometimes recorded in historical writings because of the important roles that some domestic slaves had played in this period of social change. It is certainly true that, in earlier times, individual slaves, who had endured pain or who had in another respect done something out of the ordinary, were remembered in annalistic writings or by a state cult; and sometimes even their names were preserved. But the unbroken series of impressive acts performed by slaves begins at the same point as do the histories of the civil wars, with the appearance of the Gracchi. Valerius Maximus' chapter *de fide servorum* (6, 8) is a surviving example of this new literary *genre*. It begins with the slave who proved himself 'devoted and brave' at the trial of the orator M. Antonius in 113 B.C. remaining steadfast in spite of terrible tortures. This is followed by the action, described as a 'saving sacrifice', of the slave who killed young Marius to save him from Sulla's terror. After this, the slaves of C. Gracchus and C. Cassius are mentioned by name; they were both famous for their loyalty, because when their masters, realizing the hopelessness of their own position, had asked to be killed, the slaves had obeyed and subsequently committed suicide. The three final examples portraying *fides* and *pietas* are taken from the dreadful year of the triumviral proscriptions. The slaves of C. Munatius Plancus let themselves be tortured until their master gave himself up; Urbinius Panapio's slave allowed himself to be killed in place of his master; Antius Restio's slave, although his master had previously put him in chains and branded him, now saved him by means of a macabre ruse—he killed an old beggar and threw him onto a pyre, telling the soldiers searching for his master that the latter was atoning in the fire for his past cruelty to his slaves. The actions of these last two heroes are mentioned again in Appian's history (4, 44.185, which does not give any names, and 4, 43.181–4), and they later recur in Seneca and Macrobius (see below), who use the examples in the course of philosophical argument. It has not been possible to pin-point precisely the source from which any of these authorities took his examples. Klotz has postulated that Valerius Maximus normally used an anthology of examples and a collection of biographies,[19] while Helm would claim that he followed the major historical narratives at first hand.[20] We ought to keep both possibilities open with respect to Valerius Maximus, as also with Appian. But the question of what sources were used is less important here than the way in which judgements of noteworthy actions, and estimations of the slave-class in general, differ from one authority to another.

As well as honouring the slaves of Gracchus and Cassius, Valerius Maximus severely censures their masters (6, 8.3f.): Gracchus had lost his presence of mind, or else he would have struck the mortal blow himself and not let his slave surpass him in the glory of his death. Cassius, on the other hand, deserved to be punished for having committed the dreadful offence of assassinating Caesar, and the divine Julius had personally avenged himself by robbing the traitor of his senses so as to make him turn for help to a man of the lowest kind (*sordidum auxilium*). Although this attack on Cassius may well be explained by the fact that Valerius Maximus dedicated his book to the Emperor Tiberius, it was nevertheless the general opinion that Gracchus and Cassius had forfeited a certain degree of dignity by accepting the help of slaves. This view can also be felt in Appian's account of Brutus' death (4, 131.551f.): Brutus asked his friend the orator Strato to kill him, but when the latter counselled further reflection, he summoned one of his slaves. Strato thereupon performed the deed himself, on the grounds that Brutus should rather have a friend than a slave to carry out his last wishes. This shows us how difficult it must have been for men of the ruling class to bring themselves to ask a slave to perform this last service for them. However, there are numerous examples of such a request for *sordidum auxilium*, particularly during this period of social disruption. Whether because there were still certain religious scruples against killing oneself or because a man in a state of exhaustion or despair did not have the requisite physical or mental faculities to plunge a sword into his

[19] A. Klotz 'Zur Literatur der Exempla und zur Epitoma Livii' *Hermes* 44 (1909), 198ff.; id. *Studien zu Valerius Maximus und den Exempla* (*Sitzungsberichte der Bayerischen Akademie, Phil.-Hist. Klasse* 1942, 5). Cf. also K. Alewell *Über das rhetorische Paradeigma* (dissertation, Kiel 1913), 44f.

[20] R. Helm 'Valerius Maximus, Seneca und die "Exemplasammlung"' *Hermes* 74 (1939), 130ff.; id., article 'Valerius Maximus' *RE* VIII A, 90ff.

own body,[21] individual generals and emperors, when in extreme danger and deserted by those of rank, were on several occasions helped to their deaths by slaves or freedmen—for example Flavius Fimbria,[22] M. Antonius,[23] the Emperor Nero[24] and several others. This shows that in such an extreme situation the coercion exerted by slavery gave way, and human beings could treat each other as human beings. Just as a baby was entrusted to a slave nurse or a child to a tutor, just as a sick man was glad to be able to put himself into the hands of a slave trained as a physician,[25] so the hero who had lost the will to live was ready to have a slave for his final benefactor. But, surely, it is the way one acts at the last that is the ultimate test of the honesty of an individual and of a society as a whole.

Not long after Valerius Maximus had honoured this *beneficium servi* (6, 8.3), Seneca wrote a detailed and thorough exposition of the relationship between masters and slaves—the only Roman author to do so. This can be found in eleven chapters of the third book of his *De beneficiis* (3, 18–28), probably written in about A.D. 60, and some time later in the famous 47th letter to Lucilius. With as much moralizing as literary skill, he advocates the doctrine that slaves are human beings, and draws the conclusion for slave-owners that their behaviour towards slaves should reflect this fact. An excellent recent interpretation of these statements of Seneca's[26] has shown, in particular, that his maxims are to be seen less as the result of Hellenistic philosophical theories than of the individual experiences and standards of enlightened Roman slave-owners. The arguments found in both passages are closely interconnected, but it will be enough for the examination of this motif of slave loyalty to examine the ideas contained in the treatise *De beneficiis*. Valerius Maximus had already called it a *beneficium* to show loyalty in an extreme crisis, but Seneca attempts to demonstrate in detail how it is that a slave could confer a favour on his master. He begins by countering the opinion then current that when a slave was kind to his owner, he was only doing what was his duty anyway (*ministerium*), with the philosophical conviction that being human in itself entails the faculty of doing good to others, and that it is possible to attain *virtus* whatever one's status: 'it is possible for a slave to be just,

[21] Cf. the informative comments by J. Bayet 'Le suicide mutuel dans la mentalité des Romains' *Année Sociologique* Sér. 3 (1951), 35ff., particularly 51f.

[22] Appian *Mithr.* 59f.; Plut. *Sulla* 25, 1–3.

[23] Plut. *Ant.* 76, 7f.

[24] Suet. *Nero* 49, 3.

[25] See chapter V, p. 103ff. above.

[26] W. Richter 'Seneca und die Sklaven' *Gymnasium* 65 (1958), 196ff.

brave, and magnanimous, and therefore it is also possible for him to confer a benefit, for this also is a part of virtue' (3, 18.4). He mentions the extraordinary feats of loyalty performed by a slave who had given up his life without considering his own advantage (*impendisse spiritum fidei*), and says: 'Consider, rather, whether in the case of slaves a manifestation of virtue is not more praiseworthy just because it is so rare' (3, 19.3f.). He then goes on to show that a slave's kindness lies precisely in the fact that as his mind is free and independent, his action would not be the result of obedience to a command but a free decision to go beyond what normal service required (3, 20–22). There follow some *beneficiorum exempla* (3, 23–27)—a practical application of the theme *de fide servorum* that had interested Valerius Maximus and other compilers of such examples. It cannot, however, have been Valerius who served as Seneca's source, for almost without exception the examples are different. For the first deed, Seneca gives a reference to the eighteenth book of Claudius Quadrigarius' *Annales*, although this quotation does not exclude the possibility that his method here was the same as in other works in which he introduces examples from Roman history, namely to use the books of examples at his disposal.[27] The list begins (3, 23) with the slaves of Grumentum in Lucania and the faithful companion of Vettius, the Italian leader, both examples belonging to the Social War; they are such convincing cases of greatness in action (*magnificentia*) that we find them again in Macrobius, the latest of our authorities (see below). Next, comes the slave of Domitius when Domitius was besieged in Corfinium by Caesar (3, 24), followed (3, 25) by the same victim of the proscriptions whose death on his master's behalf had been mentioned by Appian (4, 44.185); the master's name is not given here, although both Valerius Maximus (6, 8.6) and later Macrobius (1, 11.16) supply it as Urbinius Panapio. The list is brought to a close by *nostri saeculi exempla*, two good deeds done by slaves during the principates of Tiberius and Augustus (3, 26f.). At the end of this passage, Seneca justifies his view with the same arguments as he uses in the 47th letter, referring to the common origin of slaves and free men and to the fact that both are equally slaves to their passions.

It is not merely because he expanded the theme of loyalty on the part of slaves into the general idea that slaves are human beings and as such capable of any virtue, that Seneca is on a higher level than the

[27] F. J. Kühnen *Seneca und die römische Geschichte* (dissertation, Cologne 1962).

historians and compilers of *exempla.* He also realized how great and enduring was the historical importance of such magnanimous actions done by slaves. 'How much did willingness to die for one's master mean in an age when it was already a sign of unusual loyalty not to want one's master's death? To be found to be sympathetic in spite of universal terror, and loyal in the midst of treachery instigated by the government? To seek death as the reward for that loyalty when huge rewards had been offered for treachery?' (3, 25). These words wonderfully contrast the behaviour of those in power during the civil wars, who had no respect for trust and loyalty, with the edifying acts of slaves who behaved decently. But the last two of these examples show that *fides* continued to be endangered under the Principate.

This is not the place to trace the influence of Seneca's doctrine that slaves were human beings and that their masters had a duty to treat them humanely. It has recently been demonstrated, on the evidence of literature and epigraphy, that during a period when the institution of slavery was for several reasons going through a crisis, the Roman ruling classes tried to bind slaves, freedmen and clients ever more tightly to the family group, and that slaves and the poor proletariat, for their part, developed a certain degree of class consciousness, and a sense of commitment to virtues such as reliability and decency (*fides, pudor*).[28] Thus the inevitable realities of economic and social processes combined with philosophical and religious ideas to bring about a mitigation of slavery that can be seen in particular in Imperial legislation and the administration of justice. A generation before the Emperor Theodosius II issued his great code, there appeared the last advocate of humanitarianism to back up his philosophical arguments with historically attested *virtutes servorum.* In his *Saturnalia* (1, 11), Macrobius makes Praetextatus conclude his discussion of the origins of the Saturnalia by proving the humanity of slaves with a fine display of scholarship. After showing that Jupiter had on occasion intervened in favour of slaves (1, 11.3–5—his example is probably taken from the annalist Gn. Gellius[29]), he goes on to give his philosophical reasons (1, 11.6–15—basically following the same lines as Seneca). This is followed by a long series of historical illustrations of *fides, benignitas* and the other *virtutes* appertaining to slaves (1, 11.15–29). He goes on to infer

[28] E. M. Schtajerman *Die Krisis der Sklavenhalterordnung im Westen des römischen Reiches* (Berlin 1964), 112ff.

[29] E. Türk *Macrobius und die Quellen seiner Saturnalien* (typewritten dissertation, Freiburg 1961), 119f.

that slaves had been of value to the state, from the fact that they had been called upon to do military service (1, 11.30–34). He mentions female slaves (1, 11.35–40) and honours the *servi philosophi* (1, 11.41–45), coming to the conclusion (1, 11.46) 'that one ought not to disregard or belittle people because they are slaves; for Jupiter cares for slaves, and it is true to say that many of them have shown themselves faithful, prudent, brave and even philosophical' (*multos ex his fideles providos fortes philosophos etiam extitisse*). So once again loyalty heads the list of slave virtues.

If we restrict ourselves to the catalogue of historical examples, we will notice that here also most of the cases in this long list (which follows no chronological order) are taken from the period of the civil wars, although Macrobius does give some instances of loyalty during the Principate (1, 11.16–21)—but none after the Augustan period. This corresponds to the general prejudice of late antiquity in favour of the classical period of Roman history. His examples also reach back into history to the father of Scipio Africanus (1, 11.26), and in the final section we are reminded of some outstanding slaves of the Hellenistic period and the age of the Greek tyrants (1, 11.27–29). So Macrobius' material came from a very wide field, probably including both anthologies of examples and historical writings. He mentions the slaves of Grumentum and Vettius' slave (1, 11.23f.) in the same order as does Seneca, but his account of the story about Vettius diverges widely from Seneca's. So he cannot have consulted Seneca alone; perhaps they both made use of the same collection but selected different details.[30] The story of Antius Restio's slave (1, 11.19f.) agrees in all its essentials with Valerius Maximus' version (6, 8.7) but there are no verbal parallels to indicate that Macrobius was directly dependent on him. In any case, this eulogy on faithful slaves is a fine testimony both to the meticulous scholarship and to the humanitarian principles current among the last Roman pagans.

This constant glorification of the famous deeds of individual slaves must now be set against a new ethical, and, indeed, religious, evaluation of the *servus bonus* whom we have already met both as a figure in Greek and Roman literature and as a genuine phenomenon of Roman life. This transformation of the faithful slave into one who does nothing particularly heroic, but merely performs his duties with

[30] Cf. Kühnen *op. cit.* 29, 5. Ancient testimony for the individual occurrences mentioned by Macrobius can be found in the notes to the editions of Jan (Leipzig 1848) and Nissard (Paris 1883).

devotion, belongs not to pagan literature but to the writings of the early Christians. I shall restrict myself to the Gospels, fully realizing that nothing that can be found there will be entirely new to theologians. But perhaps theological interest has tended to overlook one point of a mundane nature: I refer to the δοῦλος ἀγαθὸς καὶ πιστός, the good and faithful servant of Matthew 25, 21. Translations of the Gospels into European languages have turned this slave into a 'servant', 'serviteur' or 'Knecht', adapting the state of dependence of a servingman to the social conditions of a more recent era; but they have thereby disguised the actual reference in the words of Jesus.

Many theologians, interpreting the parables and similes which involve slaves, talk of servants or inferiors being in a state similar to slavery, or even of bondsmen.[31] But the vocabulary of the Gospels does not leave any doubt that the word δοῦλος, just like the Hebrew *'ebed*, refers to a slave subject to the will of another person, a man who has no legal capacity of his own.[32] This records a social reality which can be seen particularly well in the Gospel parables. 'The parables taken together constitute a picture of life in the *petite bourgeoisie* and working classes of a Roman province to which there is scarcely a parallel in the whole literature of the period.'[33] In the parable of the vineyard (Matthew 20, 1–16), we find the master of the house (οἰκοδεσπότης) hiring workers and telling his bailiff (ἐπίτροπος) to pay them their wages. In the parable of the unfaithful vine-dressers (Matthew 21, 33–41; Mark 12, 1–9; Luke 20, 9–16), the master lets his land out to be farmed, but sends his own slaves to claim the revenues. The king who prepares a marriage-feast for his son (Matthew 22, 1–13; Luke 14, 16–24) sends out his slaves to summon those whom he has invited to the wedding. The householder and his slaves again appear in the parable of the tares (Matthew 13, 24–30). Such conditions of ownership and labour were perfectly familiar to those who heard these words; in Galilee there were principalities and estates on which slaves were employed as well as paid workers;[34] and the social unrest

[31] Even as excellent a judge of historical reality as J. Jeremias in *Jerusalem zur Zeit Jesu*[3] (Göttingen 1962) occasionally confuses slaves with serfs and at one point even goes so far as to interpret the servants who occur in those of Jesus' parables set in the countryside as hired workers (p. 125 n. 3). [= *Jerusalem in the Time of Jesus* tr. F. H. and C. H. Cave (London 1969), 110 n. 5.]

[32] Rengstorf, article 'δοῦλος' *Theologisches Wörterbuch zum Neuen Testament* II, 264, 268f., 274.

[33] C. H. Dodd *Gospel and Law* (Cambridge 1951), 53.

[34] F. C. Grant *The Economic Background of the Gospels* (Oxford 1926), 65f.;

that was widespread in the countryside is neatly portrayed in the story of how the unfaithful vine-dressers killed the landowner's son.[35] But slavery, and domestic slavery in particular, was an established institution at Jerusalem and in Judaea at this time. Jewish slaves had the privilege of being able to demand their freedom after six years, while gentile slaves were in the same position as anywhere else in the world, having no legal rights whatsoever. The word 'slave' was used as a term of abuse, and in rabbinical writings slaves are habitually idle, thieving and vicious.[36]

But in the parables of Jesus, the slave's condition of utter subjection to another's will comes to symbolize the relationship between man and God. Judaism had for many years expressed the absolute superiority of God by describing mankind, including even the rulers and prophets of Israel, as God's slaves.[37] Jesus grasps the full meaning of this metaphor; the kingdom of God has come, not in the sense that the people of Israel are now to exercise dominion over all nations, but in the novel sense that the devout who perform the Will of God are to be judged by the extent to which they do justice to their position as God's slaves. Because it is this message that the comparisons serve to put across, this picture—the imagery of the simile—is of the utmost importance. The slave's life is realistically portrayed in a way with which the audience would be familiar, so that it might be realized how inexorable is the service of God, the thing the image refers to.[38]

The good and faithful slave recurs in parable after parable, illustrating all the aspects of man's dependence upon God. We follow Matthew 6, 24 in saying that 'no man can serve two masters', but Luke has kept the more stringent formulation of the phrase which alone explains why dependence on God must exclude all else: 'no *slave* can serve two

J. Jeremias *Die Gleichnisse Jesu*[6] (Göttingen 1962), 19ff. [= *The Parables of Jesus* tr. S. H. Hooke (London 1963), 37f.]; A. N. Sherwin-White *Roman Society and Roman Law in the New Testament* (Oxford 1963), 132ff.

[35] C. H. Dodd *The Parables of the Kingdom*[2] (New York 1961), 97.

[36] J. Jeremias *Jerusalem zur Zeit Jesu* 347ff., 380ff. [= *Jerusalem in the Time of Jesus* 312ff., 345ff.]; H. Daniel-Rops *La vie quotidienne en Palestine au temps de Jésus* [= *Daily Life in Palestine at the time of Christ* tr. P. O'Brian (London 1962), 172ff.].

[37] Rengstorf *op. cit.* 270ff.; F. Grant *op. cit.* 67; C. H. Dodd *The Parables* 126f.

[38] E. Linnemann *Gleichnisse Jesu* (Göttingen 1961), 32ff.; E. Kamlah 'Die Parabel vom ungerechten Verwalter (Luk. 16, 1ff.) im Rahmen der Knechtsgleichnisse' in *Abraham unser Vater. Festschrift für O. Michel* (Leiden and Cologne 1963), 284ff.

masters' (16, 13: οὐδεὶς οἰκέτης δύναται δυσὶ κυρίοις δουλεύειν). One cannot claim any thanks or rewards for this service, as the comparison with the slave's reward shows: 'And you, when you have done all that was commanded of you, are to say "We are your slaves, and worthless (δοῦλοι ἀχρεῖοι); it was our duty to do what we have done"' (Luke 17, 10). The behaviour of the good and faithful slave in contrast to that of the bad one is described with reference to a whole series of tasks; the slave must be dependable during his master's absence and awake when he returns (Mark 13, 33–37; Luke 12, 35–38); and the slave who has been favoured by having had authority over others entrusted to him must be particularly reliable during his master's absence, as the parable of the faithful and the false slave shows (Matthew 24, 45–51; Luke 12, 42–48). The faithful and wise slave (ὁ πιστὸς δοῦλος καὶ φρόνιμος) looks after the household, the false slave (ὁ κακὸς δοῦλος) falls to beating his fellows, eating and drinking. The great test of a slave's behaviour comes when his master returns unexpectedly and says 'give an account of your stewardship' (ἀπόδος τὸν λόγον). This 'hour of reckoning' applies to the senior slaves in particular, as in the parable of the unmerciful debtor (Matthew 18, 21–35) who beats those slaves who owe him money,[39] and in that of the unjust steward, the οἰκονόμος who has been accused of mismanagement and is suddenly summoned before his master to give an account of himself, but is prudent enough to realize what the situation requires of him (Luke 16, 1–12); it is said of this inspection of accounts (with as much severity as comfort for slaves) that 'he who is trustworthy over a little sum, is trustworthy over a greater' (ὁ πιστὸς ἐν ἐλαχίστῳ καὶ ἐν πολλῷ πιστός ἐστιν).[40] The whole relationship is finally summed up in the parable of the talents (Matthew 25, 14–30; Luke 19, 11–27); the master's absence, his return and strict stock-taking, which results in a reward for the good slave and condemnation of the base and slothful one (πονηρὸς δοῦλος καὶ ὀκνηρός). The master's words have been given a new shade of meaning: 'Well done, my good and faithful slave; since you have been faithful over little things, I have great things to put into your keeping; come in to share the joy of your Lord.'

It is not my purpose to examine the origin or the handing-down of

[39] On this 'parable of the unmerciful servant', see Jeremias *Die Gleichnisse Jesu*[6] 207 ff. [= *The Parables of Jesus* 210ff.]

[40] Jeremias *Die Gleichnisse Jesu*[6] 180ff. [= *The Parables of Jesus* 181f.]; Kamlah *op. cit.* 276ff.

these similes and parables or to mention the theological implications they held for Jesus' disciples. All that matters here is to recognize how slaves had been ennobled merely by becoming the symbols of man's place in the kingdom of God. To this must be added the recognition, reward and blessing given to a slave who was faithful. Of course, it is true that this also entailed the acceptance of slavery as an institution, but in the sense that slavery was now applied to the service of God, the contrast between slave and master within the new Christian community could only be a relative one. Perhaps one could even go so far as to say that in the new era of salvation, slaves (and indeed all the underprivileged) were to have a particular calling if they remained faithful. A new kind of evaluation of property and power had appeared: 'the poor have the Gospel preached to them' (Matthew 11, 5); 'whoever has a mind to be great among you must be your servant, and whoever has a mind to be first among you, must be the slave of all' (Mark 10, 43f.).

VIII

Ecce Ancilla Domini: the Social Aspects of the Portrayal of the Virgin Mary in Antiquity

In the early morning, at noon and in the evening, throughout the Catholic world bells ring out for the prayer called the Angelus. It consists of three Hail Marys, each preceded by some of the words announcing the mystery of Salvation: 'The angel of the Lord declared unto Mary: and she conceived of the Holy Ghost', 'Behold the handmaid of the Lord: be it done unto me according to thy word' and finally 'And the Word was made flesh, and dwelt among us'. I would like here to consider in the light of ancient slavery the meaning which the crucial phrase by which Mary expresses her devotion has in St. Luke's Gospel and continued to have in Christian thought during the first few centuries: Luke 1, 38: ἰδοὺ ἡ δούλη κυρίου—*ecce ancilla Domini*. The traditional English translation of δούλη κυρίου and *ancilla domini* as 'handmaid of the Lord' can easily be misleading, particularly as the word 'maid' originally referred to an unmarried woman and only later came to mean a servant. The words 'handmaid' and 'servant', like *servante* in French, *ancella* in Italian and *Magd* in German, reflect types of dependence in societies in which slavery was no longer known except as a peripheral phenomenon. Just as the *servants*, *serviteurs*, *servi* or *Knechte* of modern translations into European languages have the effect of toning down the strict moral content of some of the

This chapter first appeared in *Vigiliae Christianae* 23 (1969), 241–63.

parables in which Jesus mentions slaves,[1] so also the phrase 'handmaid of the Lord' obscures the radical significance contained in the terms δούλη and *ancilla* in the world of Greek and Roman antiquity and in the Israel of this period. I would like to focus my considerations on this statement of Mary's to be a 'slave of the Lord', on her rejoicing that the Lord of Salvation 'has remembered his humble slave-girl' (Luke 1, 48: ὅτι ἐπέβλεψεν ἐπὶ τὴν ταπείνωσιν τῆς δούλης αὐτοῦ), and on the question of what exactly these words meant to Christians, Jews and pagans in the period from Luke to St. Jerome. I shall ignore the important questions about Mary that dominate theological speculation —conception from the divine pneuma, the theogamy, the immaculate virgin mother, the typological parallels between Mary and Eve and between Mary and the Church, the epithet 'theotokos', indeed questions of the development of dogma in general, and most of the history of the cult of the Virgin Mary. Large books have been devoted to these problems, and a special science called Mariology has developed; but the 'slave of the Lord' has almost been lost sight of, with her humility and her poverty and her association with slaves and the poor.[2]

The story of the Annunciation by the angel Gabriel, to which Mary listens as the 'slave of the Lord', and of her visit to Elisabeth, whose greeting Mary answers with the *Magnificat*, a hymn praising God and rejoicing in the fact that He has remembered His humble slave-girl, is to be found in St. Luke's account of the childhood of Christ, in the first two chapters of his Gospel. Scholarship has shown this narrative of the birth and childhood of the Lord to have originated in a Jewish-Christian community. The basic theme of the narrative is the beginning of Salvation for Israel, whose sons turn to the Lord. It accords well with such a Jewish attitude that the language and vocabulary of these two chapters are very similar to those of the Septuagint version of the Old Testament. The stories of the birth of Samuel (1 Samuel 1–3) and of Samson (Judges 13) might almost be considered the literary models on which the proto-Lucan account was based.[3]

[1] See p. 141ff. above.

[2] See for example the important work by C. Cecchelli *Mater Christi* (*Oriente e Occidente* 1, 1946; 2, 1948; 3–4, 1954), and the *Lexikon der Marienkunde* I (Regensburg 1967) under *ancilla domini*.

[3] Of the many studies of this subject I would like to mention G. Erdmann *Die Vorgeschichte des Lukas- und des Matthäus-Evangeliums und Vergils vierte Ekloge* (Göttingen 1932), 10ff.; S. Lösch *Deitas Jesu und antike Apotheose* (Rottenburg a.N. 1933), 81ff.; H. Sahlin *Der Messias und das Gottesvolk. Studien zur protolukanischen*

Samuel's mother Anna, in particular, is portrayed as an exemplary ideal woman when she begins her vow in the presence of the Lord with the words 'If you will remember your humble slave . . .' (1 Samuel 1.11: ἐὰν ἐπιβλέπων ἐπιβλέψῃς ἐπὶ τὴν ταπείνωσιν τῆς δούλης σου) and when, as a result of the priest's words of encouragement, she gives thanks with the words: 'your slave has found favour in your sight' (1 Samuel 1.18: εὗρεν ἡ δούλη σου χάριν ἐν ὀφθαλμοῖς σου). The prayer with which she gives praise to the Lord after presenting her son in the Temple is very similar to the *Magnificat*, both in general terms, in the expression of thanks for the favour which God has bestowed upon those who have acted according to His will, and particularly, in the glorification of the Lord's power to exalt and to humble. Anna states that 'the Lord makes men poor and wealthy, he humbles and exalts, raises the poor man up out of the dust and makes the beggar get up from his dung-hill to sit with those who are powerful, apportioning to them the seat of honour' (1 Samuel 2.7f.: κύριος πτωχίζει καὶ πλουτίζει, ταπεινοῖ καὶ ἀνυψοῖ, ἀνιστᾷ ἀπὸ γῆς πένητα καὶ ἀπὸ κοπρίας ἐγείρει πτωχὸν καθίσαι μετὰ δυναστῶν λαῶν καὶ θρόνον δόξης κατακληρανομῶν αὐτοῖς). Mary's words of praise sound almost like a response to this: 'He has done mighty deeds with His arm, scattering the proud in the conceit of their hearts; he has put down the mighty from their thrones and has exalted the humble; He has filled the hungry with good things and sent the rich away empty-handed' (Luke 1.51–53: ἐποίησεν κράτος ἐν βραχίονι αὐτοῦ, διεσκόρπισεν ὑπερηφάνους διανοίᾳ καρδίας αὐτῶν. καθεῖλεν δυνάστας ἀπὸ θρόνων καὶ ὕψωσεν ταπεινούς, πεινῶντας ἐνέπλησεν ἀγαθῶν καὶ πλουτοῦντας ἐξαπέστειλεν κενούς). In both of these songs, the 'slave of the Lord' who has found favour combines her thanks with the assurance that those who fear God, the pious, are under the Lord's protection, while their foes, the powerful, have been cast to the ground, and the humble and poor have been exalted. In eschatological thought religious and political hopes, the coming of God's grace and the reversal of the social order are inextricably linked.

Since we can see that the basic religious themes and literary motifs

Theologie (*Acta Sem. Neotest. Upsal.* 12: 1945); R. Laurentin 'Structure et théologie de Luc I–II' *Études Bibliques* 46 (1957), 9ff.; W. Grundmann *Das Evangelium nach Lukas*[2] (Berlin 1961), 53ff. On the attempt to ascribe the original version of the story of the *Magnificat* to Elizabeth rather than Mary (taken up again recently by Sahlin *op. cit.* 161ff. in particular) see S. Lyonnet 'Il racconto dell'annunciazione' *La Scuola Cattolica* 82 (1954), 415ff.

of Luke's account of the childhood of Christ reach back so clearly to the Old Testament, it would be reasonable to trace the concepts which we are interested in—slavery, poverty and humility—in the historical development from the old Israel to the new People of God. The Greek linguistic expressions used in the Septuagint are more significant for the connections between the two communities, the old and the new Israel, than the terminology found in Hebrew. In the Old Testament the group of words based on δοῦλος serve primarily to describe unfree servants, men in a state of slavery, called *'ebed* or *šifḥa* and *'amā* in Hebrew, although the free-born subject too throws himself to the ground at the feet of his king with the words 'Look, I am your slave' (2 Samuel 9.6: ἰδοὺ ὁ δοῦλός σου).[4] But subjection to the Lord, the service of Jahweh, also comes to be described as slavery in a metaphorical sense, whether it is the whole of the people of Israel or only a part of this people or an individual member of the community who is called the 'slave of the Lord'.[5] It is characteristic of the relationship between master and slave in Jewish religious thought that Jahweh is not conceived as a mere despot but also as the protector of the people and of the pious; master and slave appear in close human proximity—indeed, are inseparably united. This is particularly true of the many periods of Israel's suffering, and it is to the advantage of the oppressed and exploited sections of the population in particular. If we take the relationship between master and slave to refer to God's readiness to come to the help of His people, we will be able to understand how it was that the prophets could use the idea that there was a relationship of love between God and His people as well as the image of slavery to describe the bond between Israel and Jahweh. Again, in this image of Israel and Sion as the wife or bride of the Lord, it is often precisely the deserted and poor who are chosen. In the *Song of Songs*, with its wonderful mystical treatment of the bride-theme, it is the shepherdess from the wilderness who is decked out with jewels and goes forth wonderfully arrayed.[6]

[4] A similar phrase occurs in 2 Samuel 9, 8. Cf. Sahlin *op. cit.* 140; A. Schlatter *Das Evangelium des Lukas*[2] (Stuttgart 1960), 166.

[5] J. Hempel *Gott und Mensch im Alten Testament*[2] (*Beiträge zur Wissenschaft vom Alten und Neuen Testament* 3, 2: 1936), 178ff.; C. Lindhagen *The Servant Motif in the Old Testament* (dissertation, Uppsala 1950); also W. Brandt 'Dienst und Dienen im Neuen Testament' *Neutestamentliche Forschungen* 2, 5 (1931), 43ff.

[6] It will suffice to refer to A. Miller 'Die Brautmystik des Alten Testamentes' *Benediktinische Monatsschrift* 9 (1927), 260ff.; J. Ziegler 'Die Liebe Gottes bei den

The idea that Jahweh was closest to the poor and the oppressed came to be endowed with a new significance in the period of alien rule and of the Exile. In a situation where terrible enemies were invading the country and social contrasts were becoming ever more acute, men sought refuge with a Lord who was jealous of worldly power, who turned towards those in need, and who proclaimed salvation for the faithful poor: 'Stronghold thou art of the poor, stronghold of the helpless in their affliction, refuge from the storm, shade in the noonday sun' says Isaiah 25, 4. It was as a result of this faith in a Lord who set a high value on pious poverty and divinely ordained suffering that, in the post-exilic period, the idea of the slave of God developed into the exalted figure of the Saviour of Deutero-Isaiah, who takes upon himself the sins of the multitude and through his sufferings restores the covenant of Israel with God.[7] In the psalms, Jahweh is invoked as the God who exalts the lowly and brings down the proud; poverty becomes the basis of absolute trust in God, and the community of the poor is considered worthy of its divinely ordained mission. It is of some relevance to our understanding of the *Magnificat* that the word *anawim*, which is used in Hebrew to describe these poor people, is rendered in the Septuagint not only by πένης, πτωχός and ταπεινός, but also by the word πραΰς. This suggests that the poverty of the psalmist was not envisaged simply as material want, but as a pious acceptance of the need to put one's trust in God, just as the 'slave of God' experiences his total devotion to God precisely in his degradation (ταπείνωσις). The religious behaviour of the poor and lowly is turned into gentleness and humility, and in hellenistic Jewish thought the terms πτωχός and ταπεινός have come to be given a positive meaning—in complete contrast to the linguistic usage of the pagan hellenistic world; while the rich satisfy their own needs, the poor are in touch with God. This experience was felt again and again by Jewish holy men; as a result, the Essenes and the community at Qumran chose a life of voluntary poverty. Yet in spite of this spiritualization of poverty and lowliness, the idea that, as the lowest social class, the poor are called upon to take

Propheten' *Alttestamentliche Abhandlungen* 11, 3 (1930), 49ff.; and Schmid's article 'Brautschaft, heilige' in the *Reallexikon für Antike und Christentum* (Stuttgart 1950–) II, 543f.

[7] H. H. Rowley *The Servant of the Lord and other Essays in the Old Testament* (Oxford 1965), 1–90, surveys the different meanings attached to the 'Servant of God' and has a well-founded interpretation of his own. On Isaiah 25, 4 cf. J. Coste 'Le texte grec d'Isaïe XXV, 1–5' *Revue Biblique* 61 (1954), 36ff.

action—the notion that protest against existing injustice is associated with oppression—was never completely forgotten.[8]

So it is in the light of Jewish ideas about the service of the pious and the privileges of the poor that we can understand the mysterious words with which Mary welcomes the angel's message and with which she expresses her praise of God in the *Magnificat*. As the 'slave of the Lord', she professes her submission, obedience and devotion, in much the same way as the daughter of Sion had earlier bowed to the decrees of God. The fact that God has remembered His 'humble slave' signifies the beginning of the Last Days, in which the proud shall be scattered and despots overthrown, while the poor and holy are exalted. In Luke's narrative it is not forgotten that this pious devotion on the part of Our Lady was associated with actual poverty, for (in spite of her descent from the line of David) her sacrifice at the purification consists of a pair of pigeons (Luke 2, 24), the offering of the poor. Just as the favour of God is clearly shown in Luke's narrative of Jesus' childhood to be due to the virtues of obedience and humility, so on the other hand God emphatically repudiates pride, power and wealth. The description of the Nativity at Bethlehem also reveals the poverty of Mary (Luke 2, 7–20); indeed theological emphasis on the ideal of poverty is characteristic of the whole of this Gospel.[9] Poverty is again associated with pious devotion in the glorification of the poor in the Sermon on the Mount (Luke 6,20: μακάριοι οἱ πτωχοί). In several speeches and parables (not just in St. Luke) the Lord talks about the life of the poor: the slave, the day-labourer, the sower, the woman without means. In several parables slaves are described as they would have appeared at that time to the Jewish world and to its neighbours, as obsequious and despised men lacking legal rights. Yet precisely because

[8] On the theme of the piety of the poor in the Jewish tradition cf. I. Loeb *La littérature des pauvres dans la bible* (Paris 1892); A. Causse *Les pauvres d'Israel* (*Études d'histoire et de philosophie religieuses* 3: Strasbourg 1922), esp. 81ff.; A. Gelin 'Les pauvres de Yahvé' *Collection Témoins de Dieu* 14 (1953), 98ff. On the history of the concept see Hauck *Theologisches Wörterbuch* VI, 37 (πένης), Bammel *ibid.* 890ff. (πτωχός) and Grundmann *ibid.* VIII, 6ff. (ταπεινός). I have not been convinced by R. A. Gauthier 'Magnanimité. L'idéal de la grandeur dans la philosophie païenne et dans la théologie chrétienne' *Bibliothèque Thomiste* 28 (1951), 376ff., who refers the ideas of poverty and humility in the psalms and in wisdom literature exclusively to an internal condition of the soul unconnected with social realities.

[9] Cf. O. Cullmann in E. Hennecke and W. Schneemelcher *Neutestamentliche Apokryphen* I (Tübingen 1959), 273; Bammel *op. cit.* 904ff.

of this dependence on his master, a slave comes to represent man as such in his dealings with God: through total devotion, through fidelity and love of his neighbour a slave becomes worthy of salvation.[10] In the proclamation of salvation, the concepts of slave and master, poor and rich, are given a religious colouring, but it is impossible to ignore the fact that this message is primarily addressed to the needy and oppressed who have opened their hearts to God, while the rich and powerful find that they are rejected.

The very fact that slaves and the poor occur at all in these comparisons gives them a special status. When the slave has become an image of the man who has devoted himself to God, then this image takes on a life and meaning of its own in the minds of all those who hear it. If a king is described as the shepherd of the people, then some of the royal dignity is reflected onto the concept of the shepherd, on whose care for his flock the comparison is based. If virtue is praised as the armament of God, then arms will be valued more highly than would otherwise be the case. There could hardly be a better example of the independent existence of an image of this kind than the significance given by Paul to the idea of the slave in his doctrine of the incarnation of God and man's destiny of salvation. Since we are here discussing the figure of the *ancilla domini* in early Christian thought, I will only mention accepted theological interpretations. Paul describes Christ 'as he who did not want to manifest his pre-existing "identity with God" in glory during his earthly existence, but took on the humble nature of a slave and accepted an obedience which brought him to death . . . even death on a cross'.[11] By divesting himself of his own nature, the Lord imposes on his disciples an obligation of selflessness, humility and gentleness, of ταπεινοφροσύνη and πραΰτης; these qualities were not recognized as virtues in the ancient world.[12] The service of the Lord is called the service of slaves (δουλεύειν) and Paul refers to himself as the δοῦλος Χριστοῦ and δοῦλος κυρίου (e.g. Romans 1, 1; II Timothy 2,24); δοῦλος comes to be the word which a Christian uses to describe himself—in marked contrast to the usage of the contem-

[10] See p. 143f. above.

[11] K. Rahner *Knechte Christi* (Freiburg, Basel and Vienna 1967), 155 on Philippians 2, 6–8: ὃς ἐν μορφῇ θεοῦ ὑπάρχων οὐχ ἁρπαγμὸν ἡγήσατο τὸ εἶναι ἴσα θεῷ, ἀλλὰ ἑαυτὸν ἐκένωσεν μορφὴν δούλου λαβών, ἐν ὁμοιώματι ἀνθρώπων γενόμενος· καὶ σχήματι εὑρεθεὶς ὡς ἄνθρωπος ἐταπείνωσεν ἑαυτὸν γενόμενος ὑπήκοος μέχρι θανάτου, θανάτου δὲ σταυροῦ.

[12] Grundmann *op. cit.* 17ff.; Bammel *op. cit.* 908ff.; Gauthier *op. cit.* 403ff.

porary Jewish world, whose leaders are no longer found calling themselves the 'slaves of God'. Those who serve God are at the same time those who serve the community, so that their work too is called δουλεύειν or διακονεῖν.[13] Essential to Paul's view is the notion that it is this subjection, this devotion to the Lord, that leads to liberation from the yoke of the old Covenant and allows us to become true children of God (Galatians 4, 21–5, 1 and Romans 8, 15). Thus the group of words based on δοῦλος receives a new meaning in the Christian community without losing its original one. It always describes primarily the status of a slave in civic society, but this slave in the eyes of the world is also called to the service of God and of the community, and as a child of God he stands beside the free man as a brother; like him, he becomes a δοῦλος θεοῦ. These religious experiences and their verbal expression were also transferred to the Latin-speaking world. Pliny's report to Trajan that in the course of his investigations against the Christians he obtained statements by torture *ex duabus ancillis, quae ministrae dicebantur* (*Letters* 10, 96.8) is early evidence for slave-women doing service for the community; within the Christian community, they may well have been called *ancillae Christi*.

Let us take a closer look at what the 'slave of the Lord' and the sacred service and holy poverty associated with this figure meant in the post-apostolic age. From this time on, Christian ideas about Our Lady developed as a reaction against the critical objections of Jews and pagans. The rabbis continued to use the sacred term 'slave of God' for Israel itself and for the heroes of the Jewish past, but Jesus and Mary were excluded from this group. In the Qumran community and in the circles of apocalyptic Judaism, men called themselves 'the humble', and in rabbinical literature too, humility was valued very highly;[14] yet Jesus was not recognized as one of those 'born of the spirit', and there could be no question of comparing Mary with Anna. There are some passages in the Gospels, particularly in that of St. John, that suggest that even in apostolic times the rabbis had found fault with Jesus' low social background and Mary's poverty, or may have made unfavourable comments on these things.[15] It may be that as a result of

[13] W. Brandt *op. cit.* 94ff.; Rengstorf *Theologisches Wörterbuch* II, 276ff. (δοῦλος). This is not the place to consider the general question of the attitude of the early Christians to property and wealth. Among the recent literature on this, see for example P. Christophe *L'usage chrétien du droit de propriété dans l'écriture et la tradition patristique* (Paris 1964), 55ff.

[14] Grundmann *op. cit.* 12ff.

[15] E. Hennecke *Handbuch zu den neutestamentlichen Apokryphen* (Tübingen 1904), 49, 98.

Jewish attacks of this kind, individual Christians, too, were led to ask themselves whether it was worthy of the Son of God that he should take on the form of a slave; this is suggested by the detailed treatment given to this question in the *Shepherd* of Hermas, *Similitude* 5, 5f.[16] Pagan polemics against the Christian doctrine of God's incarnation of the Virgin Mary were of a completely different kind, but just as important. For Greeks and Romans, the terms δούλη κυρίου and *ancilla domini* were at first sight no more than the current ways of referring to the slave-girl of any individual master; in particular, these phrases would be applied to an imperial slave-girl.[17] Was there not a danger that a pagan who in his dealings with Christians heard or read for the first time of the 'slave of the Lord' might be led to think in enitrely profane terms of the slave-girl who was loved by her master and won her freedom through concubinage—an extremely frequent relationship which continued to survive even after society had become Christian.[18] Perhaps he might also be reminded of the ἱεροὶ δοῦλοι, some of them slaves and some free men, who served in certain cults, and could also be found in individual religious communities as holy men ordained by the god.[19] At any rate, he was bound to have heard of examples of amorous associations between individual gods and mortal women from the rich treasury of myths, heroic cycles and historical legends.[20] No doubt he would be surprised at the low status of the bride that God had chosen in the Christian theogony—as low as that of these worshippers of Christ themselves, who go down on their knees in a most undignified fashion, dress in rags and cover themselves with dust (Origen *Contra Celsum* 6, 15).

But there is no need for conjecture about this. We know what the objections of Jews and pagans to the story of the nativity were from

[16] W. Bauer *Das Leben Jesu im Zeitalter der neutestamentlichen Apokryphen* (Tübingen 1909; reprinted Darmstadt 1967), 315f.

[17] Cf. the mass of material assembled in H. Chantraine's *Freigelassene und Sklaven im Dienst der römischen Kaiser* (*Forschungen zur antiken Sklaverei* 1, 1967), 142, 170, 173, 261, 273; and in G. Boulvert's *Les esclaves et les affranchis impériaux sous le haut-empire romain* (dissertation, Aix-en-Provence 1964), 551 n. 555. On the term *ancilla* generally, cf. Klotz *Thesaurus linguae Latinae* II, 27f.

[18] P. Grimal *L'amour à Rome* (Paris 1963), 131, 160f.; F. van der Meer *Augustinus als Seelsorger* (Cologne 1961), 211ff.

[19] Bömer II, 149ff., 179ff.; III, 215ff.

[20] The relevant literature on this much-discussed theme can be found in Schmid's article on 'Brautschaft' *Reallexikon für Antike und Christentum* (Stuttgart 1950–) II, 528ff.

the attempts to refute them made by Christian apologists and scholars of the second and third centuries, and particularly from Justin Martyr's *Dialogue with Tryphon the Jew* and Origen's polemic *Against Celsus.* Justin refers to the hatred Jews felt against Christians, and reproaches the High Priests and teachers of the Jewish people with being responsible for the defamation of the name of Jesus throughout the entire world (*Dialogus cum Tryphone* 134, 6; 117, 3). Tryphon's arguments spring from his consciousness that as a Jew he is superior to the apostate Christians. This so-called Christ, he says, came into the world without honour or glory (ἄτιμος καὶ ἄδοξος γέγονεν). Tryphon compares the Gospel story of Jesus' conception and birth with Greek myths; Zeus fathered Perseus on Danae, Dionysus on Semele and Heracles on Alcmena (67; 69, 1–3; 70, 5). Justin replies with all the conviction of the Christian faith, that he admits to the absence of honour, beauty and fame in the coming of the Lord, indeed, he considers that this abasement was absolutely essential; but he thinks that this is only true of the first coming, which will be followed by a second coming, in glory (121, 3). He describes the Greek myths as caricatures of Christ's incarnation, distortions which the devil has let circulate among the Greeks before the event (69, 1–3; 70, 5). Already in his first Apology, Justin had to some extent recognized that there were certain features common to the origin of the *Logos* Jesus Christ and to Greek mythology, but then went on to stress that it was as a virgin that Mary conceived and bore him, and to repudiate with horror the immoral diversions of the Greek deities (*Apologia* 1, 21; 22; 33).[21] Finally, he states that Christ's Gospel has restored equality between the children of free men and the children of slaves, and that it calls men of every nation, whether slave or free, to be saved (*Dialogus cum Tryphone* 134.4; 139.4f.). This is an essential feature of Justin's explanation of the lowliness of the first coming. This religious proclamation suggests ideas of political equality; indeed the apologist states that all men are brothers by nature (134, 6). He asserts that the Christian community has rejected possessiveness, that it has made the possessions of its members into common property, and that it gives help to those who are in need (*Apologia* 1, 14f.; 67).

[21] Cf. H. von Campenhausen 'Die Jungfrauengeburt in der Theologie der alten Kirche' *Sitzungsberichte der Heidelberger Akademie, Phil.-hist. Klasse* 1962, 3, 24f. Tertullian characterizes love-affairs between gods and mortal women as incest and adultery, and contemptuously says *ista sunt numina vestra* (*Apologia* 1, 21.7–9).

The objections which Justin puts into the mouth of Tryphon must be treated as historical arguments, which were actually used in the course of the controversy between Jews and Christians. The same is true of the Jew's statement of his position in Celsus' work Ἀληθὴς λόγος of which we have some knowledge from Origen's refutation. However much freedom ancient writers may have had when they introduced particular historical individuals into their writings,[22] the content of the words ascribed to them is generally reliable. This is certainly true of the writers we are concerned with here. Thus Origen's polemic gives us a number of new Jewish and pagan criticisms of the low status of Jesus and his mother, while the Christian philosopher's argumentation shows that the virtues of humility and charity were acknowledged stages on the road towards perfection.

Like Tryphon, Celsus' Jew ridicules the virgin birth and brings up the Greek myths of Danae, Melanippe, Auge and Antiope (*Contra Celsum* 1, 37). But he goes much further than this when he contrasts the biblical story of the pretended virgin birth with a story of Jesus' origin and childhood that must have appeared earlier in Jewish circles, and continued to circulate for a long time. According to this version, Jesus was said to have been the son of a poor working-woman from a Jewish village, who had been divorced by her husband for adultery and gave birth secretly to Jesus as she wandered about in dishonour. In his poverty, Jesus went to Egypt as a day-labourer; there he dabbled in Egyptian magic before returning and publicly declaring himself a god with the help of these magic powers (*Contra Celsum* 1, 29). The Jew names a soldier called Panthera as the adulterer (*Contra Celsum* 1, 32f.) and the pagan Celsus accepts this story and concludes that such a situation could certainly not produce a god (*Contra Celsum* 1, 69). Celsus goes further and rejects the belief that this can have been the birth of a god, on the grounds that Jesus' mother was neither propertied nor of noble family; when she was divorced, there was no one to help her, 'for no one knew her, not even a neighbour' (1, 37; 39). Poverty and dishonour again come into play when we hear that as a grown man Jesus went around in misery and need, scraping a wretched living in the company of worthless tax-collectors and boatmen (*Contra Celsum* 1, 61f.). Some essential features of this contemptuous picture of Jesus and his mother found their way into the Talmud. Here Jesus

[22] This is stressed in this particular connection by M. Goldstein *Jesus in the Jewish Tradition* (New York 1950), 33ff., 97.

occurs as the bastard child of a married woman, the son of Panthera and Miriam, who earned her living by making hair-pieces.[23]

Celsus clearly saw the origin of the Christian belief in the virgin birth in the influence of Greek mythology, but then rejected this Christian imitation on the grounds that it was unworthy of the divine spirit to be associated with such a poor and ordinary woman. Origen's arguments characterizing the Christian commitment to poverty are worth looking at in some detail.[24] He accepts that there may be a certain similarity between the aims of these Greek myths and the Christian belief in the virgin birth, in so far as these myths are attempts to explain the divine origin of a particular individual's divine soul, as in the story of Plato's birth from a union between Apollo and Amphictione while she was still a virgin (*Contra Celsum* 1, 37). This idea was later mentioned by St. Jerome with reference to Plato and also to Buddha (*Adv. Jovian.* 1, 42 = *PL* 23, 273). Origen too has no intention of disparaging the value of coming from a noble family or a famous native city. But if it is the case that Jesus, coming from a village, which was not even a Greek village, belonging to a people that was not particularly distinguished and being the son of a working-woman, nevertheless inspired the whole world with his message and was respected because of his wisdom and powers of leadership, it follows that his origin must have been miraculous, since the soul receives a place of habitation commensurate with its worth, as Pythagoras, Plato and Empedocles had also taught. An adulterous liaison should have produced a stupid and harmful human being (*Contra Celsum* 1, 29f., 32f.). Origen defends Jesus' family tree, even if he does not consider that Mary's descent from King David can be clearly proved from the Bible.[25] In contrast to Celsus, he considers it irrelevant whether Jesus' mother was aware of her background or not: 'Or does Celsus think it necessary that the poor should be descended only from poor ancestors, or kings only from kings? . . . Since it is so clear that even in our own

[23] Hennecke *Handbuch* (n. 15 above), 51ff.; H. L. Strack 'Jesus, die Häretiker und die Christen nach den ältesten jüdischen Angaben' *Schriften des Inst. Jud. in Berlin* 37 (1910), 9*ff., 21*ff.; Cecchelli *op. cit.* II, 155ff. The relevant passages from the Talmud can also be found in J. B. Aufhauser *Antike Jesus-Zeugnisse* (*Kleine Texte für Vorlesungen und Übungen* 126, 2nd edition 1925), 44ff. On the name Panthera, which in the first and second centuries occurs especially as a *cognomen* of soldiers, cf. L. Patterson *Journal of Theological Studies* 19 (1918), 79f. and Cecchelli *op. cit.* II, 159 n. 274.

[24] There is a detailed analysis in C. Vagaggini's 'Maria nelle opere di Origene' *Orientalia Christiana Analecta* 131 (1942), esp. 58ff.

[25] Vagaggini *op. cit.* 57.

times some people have been born from rich and respected ancestors who are more poverty-stricken even than Mary, whereas others from the humblest backgrounds have become the leaders of peoples and even kings' (*Contra Celsum* 2, 32).

In his exegetic writings, too, Origen laid great emphasis on Mary's poverty. But here, as a few examples will show, it is quite clear that this Christian Platonist did not associate any ideas of social protest, let alone revolution, with the poverty of the Lord and his mother. What has happened is rather that freely chosen poverty, poverty that has become part of the constitution of the soul, has become an important element in the workings of salvation. Our Lord accepted human poverty as part of the process by which he gave himself up for us: that was why he chose for himself a poor mother, and why he chose to be born in the poor town of Bethlehem.[26] Poverty, if it has been accepted from religious conviction, becomes an important human virtue, pleasing to God. In his commentary on the *Magnificat*, Origen interprets Mary's statement that 'the lowliness of the slave' has been remembered by God as an expression of her humility. He calls to mind Our Lord's words 'Learn from me, my heart is gentle and meek', and he ranks this virtue immediately after the cardinal virtues of Justice, Moderation, Courage and Wisdom. He does not here use the word ταπεινοφροσύνη, which had been current since the time of the Apostolic Fathers to express the idea of humility, but rather defines it in the language of philosophy, as freedom from arrogance (ἀτυφία) and moderation (μετριότης).[27] Considered in these terms, humility is a step on the road to perfection, and precisely for this very reason an opportunity—indeed, the most obvious opportunity—for God to exalt a person: *prima exaltationis occasio apud deum.*[28] This picture of Mary striving towards spiritual perfection is completed by the knowledge of the law and daily meditation on the prophets ascribed to her by Origen; absorption in the sacred writings brings one closer to the Christian *gnosis.*[29]

[26] *In Leviticum homilia* 8, 4 = *GCS* Origen 6, 400.

[27] *In Lucam homilia* 8 = *GCS* Origen 9, 50f.: 'Quod si vis nomen huius audire virtutis, quomodo etiam a philosophis appellatur, ausculta eandem esse humilitatem, quam respiciat Deus, quae ab illis ἀτυφία sive μετριότης dicitur.' Cf. the valuable older work by F. A. von Lehner *Die Marienverehrung in den ersten Jahrhunderten*[2] (Stuttgart 1886), 147f. and Gauthier *op. cit.* 421.

[28] *In Matthaeum Commentarius* 10 = *GCS* Origen 11, 18.

[29] *In Lucam homilia* 6 = *GCS* Origen 9, 37f., also *In Genesim homilia* 10, 2 = *GCS* Origen 6, 95f.; cf. Vagaggini *op. cit.* 59ff.

Mary meditating on the Holy Scriptures: this is a new theme, and it looks forward to the picture of the virgin whom the angel Gabriel visits while she is reading. But before we inquire into the later development of the motifs of service and poverty as associated with Our Lady in the Church Fathers, one more source which enriched the ancient picture of Mary must be pointed out. As well as the speculation of theologians, popular religiosity at a very early date became a creative element in the cult of Our Lady. The general purpose of the apocryphal gospels and lives of apostles was to fill in the gaps in the canonical reports with enjoyable stories. Thus the gospels narrating the childhood of Jesus are more interested in imaginatively embellishing Luke's report than in clarifying questions of theology. Mary and Joseph virtually become the central characters, stories about the sons of pagan gods and about child-prodigies have crept into the developing Christian legend, only to influence in their turn the pictorial representation of Mary and the child Jesus.[30] The impact of the *Protevangelium Jacobi* proved to be particularly widespread in this respect. Its beginnings can be dated to as early as the second century, while its final Greek form probably belongs to the fourth. Apart from individual features which have been borrowed (and occasionally misunderstood) from the Old Testament and the canonical gospels, there are themes from ancient romance and notions originating in the religious syncretism of the period.[31] It is characteristic of the development of the picture of Our Lady which we are trying to trace, that from the first the mother of Our Lord appears exalted in the presence of God and man; the memory of her poverty has undergone a transformation.

The fact that her parents Joaquin and Anna do not belong to the poor is obviously intended to enhance her fame. Joaquin is extremely wealthy, and Anna is served by a slave-girl (1, 1; 2, 1f.). After Anna, who had long remained barren, has heard from an angel that she is going to conceive and bear a child, she at once promises to bring the child to the Lord as an offering (6, 2f.). She fulfils her vow: in the third year, Mary is brought to the Temple, where she grows up (7, 1–3). This dedication of a child in the Temple is reminiscent of the way

[30] W. Bauer *Das Leben Jesu* (see note 16 above), 8ff.; K. L. Schmidt 'Kanonische und apokryphe Evangelien und Apostelgeschichten' *Abhandlungen zur Theologie des Alten und Neuen Testaments* 5 (1955), 78ff.; O. Cullmann in Hennecke-Schneemelcher (see n. 9 above) I, 273ff.

[31] Cecchelli *op. cit.* III, 303ff. The English version is based on the German translation in Hennecke-Schneemelcher I, 280ff.

Samuel was offered as a child to the service of the Lord (1 Samuel 1, 11). But it is surprising that a girl rather than a boy should be serving in the Temple. In ancient Israel, certainly, there was still a preference for women in cult activities, but from the time of the Exile women no longer had any place in cult rituals.[32] This idea of Mary growing up in the Temple and being educated by the priests was clearly felt to be alien by the Church Fathers, too, since they only mention it very rarely. But the child Mary does appear as a Temple-servant in the popular Egyptian *Tale of Joseph the Carpenter*, and there is a strong likelihood that the man who wrote the *Protevangelium Jacobi*, who may have had Alexandrian connections, was influenced by the Egyptian custom of dedicating a girl to Isis until the time of her marriage.[33] We should also take non-biblical prototypes into consideration when the narrator tells us that after being given to the widower Joseph as his wife at the age of eleven, Mary was entrusted by the priests with the task of weaving the purple and scarlet portions of a curtain for the Temple (10–12). The Annunciation takes place while she is thus employed. As she is drawing water from a well, she hears a wonderful voice, and when she returns home, the angel appears to her while she is spinning. She accepts his greeting and his message, and professes herself to be the 'slave of the Lord' (11). Here biblical and foreign elements have been combined: the narrator may vaguely have remembered the story of Rebecca at the well (Genesis 24, 15f.), and perhaps he had heard that the women of Athens wove a new *peplos* for Athena each year.[34] What seems to me quite typical of the tendency towards the exaltation of Mary is that we find her weaving and drawing water, in other words doing tasks which according to the view current in antiquity were those of slaves, and are mentioned along with scouring and grinding grain as laborious chores. Yet because she works for the Temple and because of the miracle that takes place as she works, her activity is regarded as having been divinely consecrated. From the fifth century A.D., this idea that Our Lady has exalted the chores of slaves was illustrated in the visual arts. A mosaic on the triumphal

[32] I. J. Peritz 'Women in the Ancient Hebrew Cult' *Journal of Biblical Literature* 17 (1898), 111ff., esp. 145ff.; M. Löhr *Die Stellung des Weibes zu Jahwe-Religion und -kult* (*Beiträge zur Wissenschaft vom Alten Testament* 4, 1908), 38f., 53; R. de Vaux *Les institutions de l'Ancien Testament* II (Paris 1960), 248f.

[33] S. Morenz *Die Geschichte von Joseph dem Zimmermann* (*Texte und Untersuchungen zur Geschichte der alttestamentlichen Literatur* 56, 1951), 3, 37.

[34] Cecchelli *op. cit.* III, 312.

arch of Santa Maria Maggiore in Rome shows her as a princess at work on the temple curtain; on an ivory relief in the Cathedral Treasury at Milan, the Annunciation is represented as addressed to a girl fetching water.[35] The book of St. James is such a decisive step towards the glorification of the Mother and her Child that we can well understand why it should differ from Luke's account in the information it gives about the site of the Nativity. For the first time a cave is mentioned as the place where the travellers find refuge (17f.), not because of its associations with poverty but in the form of a grotto filled with light, the proper setting for a series of miracles.

Let us now return to the Church Fathers and attempt to survey what they have to say about Mary, keeping in mind the notions of the 'slave of the Lord' and the poor mother, and her consequent appeal to the poor. In the patristic writings, the idea of Christ's self-sacrifice, which had already been formulated theologically in St. Paul, and the association of his self-abasement with the First Coming which we found in Justin and Origen, made it impossible for the historical facts of the real poverty of the Lord and his mother to be lost sight of completely. Tertullian says that he was so poor that at his entry into Jerusalem he did not even possess his own ass (*De Corona* 13 = *CSEL* 70, p. 181). Yet the Christian scholars of the second to the fifth centuries were not concerned with historical reconstructions of Jesus' life, but rather with creating a theology of salvation in their conflict with paganism and Gnosticism and fortifying the Christian communities, which were increasingly coming to accept men from the upper levels of society. Thus it came about that descriptions of Our Lady push the theme of poverty and its associated religious attributes more and more into the background. It continued to be an active force under the surface and became extremely important again later. It is of some historical significance that this should have applied especially to those commentators and preachers who had opted for voluntary poverty or were associated with the ascetic movement.

As works of scholarship on the 'Mariology' of the Church Fathers have recently shown, Mary's vocation within the divine plan for salvation and the exemplary model she became for the realization of

[35] W. Braunfels *Die Verkündigung* (*Lukas-Bücherei zur christlichen Ikonographie* 1, 1949), xif.; M. E. Gössmann *Die Verkündigung an Maria im dogmatischen Verständnis des Mittelalters* (Munich 1957), 35ff.; G. A. Wellen *Theotokos. Eine ikonographische Abhandlung über das Muttergottesbild in der frühchristlichen Kunst* Utrecht and Antwerp 1961), 37ff.

Christian virtue played an important role in theological thinking from Justin to Cyril of Alexandria. Irenaeus points out that because of her obedience, she was able to turn back the vicious circle of evil that began with Eve's disobedience, and thus became the means of salvation for herself and for the whole of the human race (*oboediens et sibi et universo generi humano causa facta est salutis*: *Adversus haereses* 3, 22.4 = *PG* 7, 959 and also 5, 19.1 = *PG* 7, 1175f.). This idea, that the woman's part in the Fall had been counterbalanced by her function in the Redemption, occurs repeatedly in the Fathers and is developed in particular detail by Augustine in his polemic against the Manichees (*per feminam mors, per feminam vita*: *Sermo* 232, 2.2 = *PL* 38, 1108).[36] The connection with Israel's messianic expectations is made through Mary's descent from the House of David, which is repeatedly mentioned; at the end of a lengthy argument Augustine believed that he had been able to show that she was descended both from the royal family and from that of the priests (*De consensu evangelistarum* 2, 2 = *CSEL* 43, p. 84).[37] In particular theologians of the Greek East devoted themselves to the mystery of Mary's virginity and motherhood of God.[38] The last word in this respect may be left to the salutation of Mary by Cyril of Alexandria, in the form in which it was recorded after the Council of Ephesus: 'Hail to you, virgin, mother and slave: virgin because of Him who was born from you, a virgin; mother because of Him who was carried in your arms and nourished by your milk; slave, because of Him who took the form of a slave.'[39] The predicates applied to Our Lady are here derived exclusively from the nature of her son—an exegesis which refines the reality hidden in the metaphor of the 'Slave of the Lord'.

And yet the poor virgin from Nazareth did not disappear from Christian thought and life. She became a model for those select in-

[36] Ph. Friedrich *Die Mariologie des hl. Augustinus* (Cologne 1907), 239ff. On the contrast of Mary with Eve, cf. von Campenhausen *op. cit.* (n. 21 above), 26ff.

[37] Friedrich *op. cit.* 19ff.

[38] I. Ortiz de Urbina 'Lo sviluppo della Mariologia nella Patrologia orientale' *Orientalia Christiana Periodica* 6 (1940), 40ff.; G. Söll 'Die Mariologie der Kappadozier im Licht der Dogmengeschichte' *Theologische Quartalschrift* 131 (1951), 163ff., 288ff., 426ff.; von Campenhausen *op. cit.* 48ff.

[39] Cyril of Alexandria *Homilies* 11 = *PG* 77, 1032: Χαίροις, παρθένε Μαρία, μήτηρ καὶ δούλη. Παρθένε μὲν διὰ τὸν ἐκ σοῦ τῆς παρθένου τεχθέντα· μήτηρ δὲ διὰ τὸν ἐν ἀγκάλαις σαῖς βασταχθέντα καὶ γάλακτι σῷ τραφέντα· δούλη διὰ τὸν μορφὴν δούλου λαβόντα. Cf. A. Eberle 'Die Mariologie des heiligen Cyrillus von Alexandrien' *Freiburger Theologische Studien* 27 (1921), 127ff.

dividuals who chose the perfect discipleship of Christ in poverty, chastity and obedience. From the time of Hippolytus there is evidence for the presence in the Christian community of unmarried women who had taken a vow of chastity. Tertullian calls them *ancillae Christi* (*De virginibus velandis* 3, 3 = *CSEL* 76, p. 82). But in this period pious young girls and virtuous married women were called *ancillae dei* too. It was only in the fourth century that the order of virgins became a regular ecclesiastical institution, the taking of vows was invested with liturgical ceremonies, and the term *ancilla dei* was applied with preference to those who combined their vow of perpetual virginity with entry into a monastic community.[40] In Origen, and later in Methodius and particularly Athanasius, Mary is mentioned as the model of these ascetic women.[41] Then St. Ambrose, in his book *De virginibus* (2, 6–16 = *PL* 16, 208–211) and his other writings, finds in the life of Our Lady a mirror of all the virtues he requires of the virgin who has dedicated herself to God. He also extolls Mary's virtues in his commentary on St. Luke's Gospel. Her words at the Annunciation are praised as evidence for her reverence and prudence, her humility, willingness to serve and complete devotion (*Expositio evangelii Lucae* 2, 7–9, 14, 16–18 = *CSEL* 32, 4, pp. 45–52).[42] It is surprising that there should be no mention in his commentary on the *Magnificat* of the words about the destruction of the mighty and the exaltation of the humble, and it is interesting that on Mary's visit to Elisabeth he should explicitly point out that it was the younger sister who went to the elder one and was the first to greet the other (*op. cit.* pp. 52f.). This sounds like instruction in good manners.[43] The same element is present in the advice he gives to virgins, when he says of Our Lady 'when did she hurt her parents even in the way she looked

[40] Among more recent studies of the *virgines sanctae*, mention must be made of R. Metz 'La consécration des vierges dans l'église romaine' *Bibliothèque de l'institut de droit canonique de l'Université de Strasbourg* 4 (1954), 41ff.; D. S. Bailey *The Man–Woman Relation in Christian Thought* (London 1959). On the subject of nomenclature cf. also H. Leclercq *Dictionnaire d'archéologie chrétienne et de liturgie* (Paris 1903–) I fasc. 7, 1973ff., s.v. 'ancilla Dei'.

[41] Von Campenhausen *op. cit.* (n. 21 above), 48ff.; Ch. W. Neumann 'The Virgin Mary in the Works of Saint Ambrose' *Paradosis* 17 (1962), 8ff.

[42] Cf. von Lehner *op. cit.* (n. 27 above), 156ff.; Neumann *op. cit.* 35ff.

[43] A similar transition from Christian morality to the provision of rules relating to order and decency seems to be implied in Augustine's interpretation of Mary's words to Jesus after he had been found in the temple ('Your father and I have been searching for you . . .') as an example of humility in the context of a universally applicable *disciplina feminarum* (*Sermo* 51, 11, 18 = *PL* 38, 343).

at them? . . . when did she spurn the humble?' (*De virginibus* 2, 7 = *PL* 16, 209). A certain distance between the aristocratic author and the lower classes may be detected in these words. But Ambrose too praises the piety and poverty of the virgin who has absorbed herself in the study of the Scriptures: 'she does not put her hope in the uncertainties of riches but in the prayers of the poor' (*De virginibus* 2, 7 = *PL* 16, 209), and compassion towards the needy and poor, together with affection for one's relatives, is listed among the graces which he begs for those who seek to attain this sanctified status (*circa egenos et pauperes misericordia*: *Exhortatio virginum* 112 = *PL* 16, 332).

The appeal to the poor and humble contained in Luke's account of Christ's childhood was taken up strongly by those of the Fathers who professed the ascetic ideal. The most outspoken voice here is that of Ephraim, the classic poet of the Syrian Church, who remained a Deacon for the whole of his life and was in correspondence with hermits. Leaving aside those of his works which are preserved only in Greek because of doubts about their authenticity, we shall concentrate on his hymns for the Feast of the Nativity and for the Epiphany, which have recently been published in a scholarly edition accompanied by a German translation.[44] Here the notions of wealth and poverty are used unhesitatingly to explain the mystery of the Incarnation. Mary professes poverty in the straightforward sense when she says 'Son of the most rich, who has rejected the womb of rich women, what made you come to the poor? For Joseph is poor and I am poor' (*Hymnus de Nativitate* 15, 3 = p. 73 in Beck's edition). It is the biblical sense of the phrase 'slave of the Lord' that she has in mind when she says that Gabriel's appearance has made her mistress and maid: 'for I am both the handmaid of your divinity and the mother of your humanity, my master and my son' (*Hymnus de Nativitate* 5, 20 = Beck p. 42). The Magi testify in her presence that through her, the mother of the King of Kings, poverty will be glorified.[45] For the poet, poverty understood in a literal sense in this way is 'the soul from which moral beauty

[44] I. Ortiz de Urbina 'La Mariologia nei padri siriaci' *Orientalia Christiana Periodica* 1 (1935), 100ff.; especially E. Beck 'Die Mariologie in den echten Schriften Ephräms' *Oriens Christianus* 40 (1956), 22ff.; and the same scholar's edition and translation of *Des heiligen Ephraem des Syrers Hymnen de Nativitate* (*Epiphania*) (*Corpus Scriptorum Christianorum Orientalium* 186 and 187; 1959). The English version is based on the German translation in volume 187.

[45] Th. J. Lamy *S. Ephraemi Syri Hymni et Sermones* I (Mechlinae 1882), cols. 131–4; H. Barré 'La royauté de Marie pendant les neuf premiers siècles' *Recherches de Science Religieuse* 29(1939), 140.

radiantly blossoms forth'.[46] If he who is rich accepted poverty in the Incarnation, then it is our duty to love the poor and to love poverty (*Hymnus de Nativitate* 1, 84 and 94 = Beck p. 10; 11, 6f. = p. 62; 18, 25 = p. 87).

But Ephraim draws some specific conclusions from his interpretation of the birth of the Lord, which apply to slaves in particular. In one of Mary's hymns, addressed to her son, she says: 'Let the man who owns a slave give him his freedom, that he may come and serve his Lord! The free-born man, my son, who took up your yoke, is given but a simple reward. But the slave, who took up two yokes of two different masters, a heavenly and an earthly one—he receives double compensation and a double reward for his double task. A free-born woman is your handmaid too, if she serves you; and the slave-girl becomes free-born through you. In you she will experience the consolation of manumission. An invisible manumission will lie in her lap, if only she loves you!' (*Hymnus de Nativitate* 17, 8–10 = Beck pp. 80 f.). The slave who serves his heavenly master is here promised a double reward, and an invisible manumission is awarded to the Christian woman in a state of slavery. But Ephraim's first admonition is that a slave should be given his freedom so that he is able to serve the Lord. It is likely that it is formal, legal manumission that is referred to here—at a time when even St. Basil declared (if with some circumspection) that he was prepared to give protection in his monastic community to a slave who had fled as a result of his religious faith.[47] But the statement that he had been raised to freedom and united to the race of the Lord of the Universe also applied to the slave who remained in the state of servitude. Through baptism the slave is set free, the free man made like unto a slave (*Hymnus de Epiphania*, 4, 6–8 = Beck p. 143). This spiritual freedom is particularly true of the virgin who has dedicated herself to God, whom the Lord has taken as his bride: she is entitled to proclaim 'I will be yours, O Lord, and even if my rank is humble, to you I am noble!' (*Hymnus de Nativitate* 8, 21 = Beck p. 54.)

Of the Latin Fathers, it is St. Jerome who comes closest to this

[46] Lamy *op. cit.* II (1896), cols. 1361f.

[47] It is impossible to describe here the practical effects of the Christian attitude to slavery. For a discussion of this question and of Basil's pronouncement I would refer the reader to H. Bellen's recent contribution to the *Forschungen zur antiken Sklaverei* of the Mainz Academy: *Studien zur Sklavenflucht im römischen Kaiserreich* (Wiesbaden 1971). On the way in which the question of private property and wealth was treated by Basil and the fourth- and fifth-century Fathers, see the analysis of P. Christophe (n. 13 above).

Syrian panegyrist of poverty. Here we have a man who was both a scriptural expert who saw clearly the unity of the Old and New Testaments, and also a hermit who withdrew to the solitude of Bethlehem. I shall assemble some of the references that are to be found in his copious writings to the poverty of the Lord and of his mother and to the obligation of service for those who want to emulate Christ. Following Paul, he considers the Incarnation as God's self-sacrifice in taking on the status of a slave. He translates Paul's words (Philippians 2, 7) as *semetipsum exinanivit formam servi accipiens* and several times uses the abbreviated formula *hominem adsumpsit* to express this idea.[48] In this too he follows St. Paul, who ascribes to the service of love the saving act of freeing man from his enslavement to fear (*servitus in timore*). David and Moses, who call themselves the Lord's slaves, are in this state of *nobilis servitus*, and so is Mary when she says *ecce ancilla domini* (*Commentarii in epistolam ad Titum* 1, 1 = *PL* 26, 555ff.). In his Christmas Day sermon, he graphically describes the poverty that attended on the Lord's birth among dust and filth: 'Whoever is poor may find consolation in this. Joseph and Mary, the Lord's mother, owned no slave, no maidservant. They travelled alone from Galilee, from Nazareth, with no packhorse: *ipsi sunt domini et famuli*.' They did not dare to approach the rich, and the best thing that they could find for the birth of the child was a crib. 'The pagan's reward is silver and gold: the reward of Christian faith is that muddy stable' (*Anecdota Maredsolana* Vol. 3, pt. 2 (1897), pp. 393f.). St. Jerome mentions poverty-stricken Bethlehem again and again, with its inn, its cave and its stable. In a letter to Marcella he writes: 'Where are the wide porticoes? Where is the gilded panelling? Where is the palace adorned by the sufferings of the wretched and the forced labour of the condemned?' (*Epistola* 46, 11 = *CSEL* 54, p. 341). The words of the Apostle apply well to this little town: 'God has chosen what is weak in the world in order to confound what is powerful' (*Ep.* 57, 8 = *CSEL* 54, pp. 517f.).[49]

The self-sacrifice of the Son of God, who remained in obscurity until his thirtieth year and acquiesced in the poverty of his parents, calls for self-denial on our part (*Ep.* 22, 39.2f. = *CSEL* 54, p. 206). He himself taught us that 'Whoever has a mind to be the greatest among you must be the slave of all of you.' This is the *nobilis servitus* referred to by the Apostle, the *servitus caritatis*, the service required by love of

[48] Examples can be found in J. Niessen *Die Mariologie des heiligen Hieronymus* (Münster 1913), 105ff.

[49] Further references may be found in Niessen *op. cit.* 134ff.

one's fellow-man, realized by St. Paul, who called himself *servus dei* (as Jerome says at the beginning of his commentary on the Letter to Titus, mentioned above). He writes to Heliodorus the monk that the perfect dedication of the *servus Christi* requires that he should have no other possessions apart from Christ (*Ep.* 14, 6.4 = *CSEL* 54, p. 53), and he promises Heliodorus that at the Last Judgement he will be the blessed slave whom his master finds on the watch—while kings who were once all-powerful tremble and the shortcomings of pagan philosophers are made manifest, you will exult in the vision of your God, who was crucified, laid in a manger wrapped in swaddling-clothes, the son of a labourer and craftsman, who fled to Egypt in his mother's arms, wore a scarlet cloak and was crowned with thorns (*Ep.* 14, 11.1f. = *CSEL* 54, p. 61). Like the monks, female ascetics, too, and particularly the virgins who had dedicated themselves to God, followed the path of total imitation of Christ. For this reason, Jerome calls them *ancillae Christi* (e.g. Eustochium, Fabiola and Laeta's daughter),[50] and it is interesting that the metaphor here develops an existence of its own. In his obituary of Fabiola, he praises her virtues, her fasting and alms-giving, humility and depth of faith, but also her unassuming way of life, plebeian appearance and servile dress; the theme of the *ancilla Christi* formally becomes the leading idea in the *laudatio* of the deceased (*Ep.* 77, 2.1–3f. = *CSEL* 55, pp. 37f.). As the author of the impassioned tract *De perpetua virginitate beatae Mariae adversus Helvidium*, St. Jerome repeatedly brought the example of Our Lady to the attention of these pious slave-women and brides of Christ.[51]

Let us stop at this point in order to review the development we have been considering. The influence which the declaration *ecce ancilla domini* and the hymn to the revolutionary power of God in the *Magnificat* had on the beliefs and practices of the early Christians should be clear. They assimilated the full depth of meaning associated with the notion of the 'slave of God' and with the religious vocation of the poor in Jewish tradition. But because of the Pauline idea that the fulfilment of salvation had turned God's slave into the child of God, and that this applied to free and slave alike, the appeal to exalt the humble lost its literal social meaning, and came to be interpreted in a purely metaphorical sense. Theological speculation devoted itself to the notion

[50] *Ep.* 22, 24.1 = *CSEL* 54, 176; *Ep.* 77, 2.3 = *CSEL* 55, 38; *Ep.* 107, 13.6 = *CSEL* 55, 305.

[51] E.g. *Ep.* 107, 7.2 = *CSEL* 55, 298; *Ep.* 22, 38.3 = *CSEL* 54, 203; cf. *Ep.* 39, 7 = *CSEL* 54, 307.

of the Mother of God, the example of whose humility leads us all to moral perfection, and whose virtues caused her to be chosen as the mediatrix in God's plan for salvation. Popular piety transferred this exaltation of the humble virgin to the realm of historical reality, and made Mary the daughter of rich parents. In the picture of the princess who receives the message of the Annunciation and in the doctrine of the Mother of God (*Theotokos*), these two distinct notions came very close together.

The idea that slavery and poverty should be abolished as conditions of real life in a world that had been saved was expressed only very occasionally. Only the Christian ascetics still responded to this call with total commitment. That the duties laid on Christians by the self-sacrifice of Christ and by the poverty of the *ancilla domini* should have been considered to be fulfilled by the poverty, chastity and obedience of monastic life looks like an extreme solution to this problem.

The teachings of the Fathers continued to be important for many centuries, and indeed they still exercise a powerful influence today. I may end with a reference to the doctrine of Our Lady expressed by the Second Vatican Council in the eighth chapter of the Dogmatic Constitution on the Church (*De Ecclesia*). Article 55 says of Our Lady that she is an outstanding example of the meek and pious who confidently hope for salvation and receive it. In this connection, she is associated with the Holy Ones of Israel, as she had been in the Church Fathers.[52] Article 46 of the same Constitution deals with members of religious orders; on the advice contained in the Gospels it bases a life-style of poverty and chastity which was 'chosen by Christ Our Lord and which His virgin mother made her own'— here, as in the Fathers, Mary is the model for those who choose the ascetic life. On the other hand there is no mention of Mary in a number of contexts where the duty of the Church and of all Christians to come to the help of the poor is given expression, as in article 8 of the same Constitution, or in article 88 of the pastoral Constitution on 'The Church in the world of today' (*De Ecclesia in mundo huius temporis*) and article 12 of the decree on ecumenism (*De Oecumenismo*), which refers to 'the countenance of Christ, servant of God'. As a result of the new movement towards the 'Church of the poor', the social theme of the *ancilla domini* which has sometimes been lost sight of in the past may well come to be emphasized

[52] On this subject see the discussions by R. Laurentin in *Kurzer Traktat der marianischen Theologie* (Regensburg 1959), 129 (before the second Vatican Council) and *Mutter Jesu—Mutter der Menschen* (Limburg 1967), 106f. (after the Council).

more decisively—in the spirit of Charles Péguy,[53] who says of Mary in his poem 'The Gate to the Mystery of the second Virtue':

> Who is Queen for ever.
> For she is the most humble of all creation.
> Just a poor woman, a wretched woman, a poor Jewess from
> Judaea.

[53] Ch. Péguy *Le porche du mystère de la deuxième vertu* (1912). Cf. the quotation on p. 103 of Laurentin's *Mutter Jesu—Mutter der Menschen.*

IX

Research on Ancient Slavery from Humboldt to the Present Day

With the arrival of modern approaches to history and classical scholarship, ancient slavery became a controversial area of research; my survey, therefore, covers a period of a century and a half of scholarship. I wish here to examine only how the problem of slavery has developed in the context of classical scholarship as a whole, how the intellectual trends and social experiences of this stormy period have advanced it, and how it looks now to us as historians and humanists.

In the eighteenth century, scholars of the Enlightenment showed considerable interest in the legal and social structures of ancient peoples and their cultures. Roman law—which in a late form was still in force in some places—held that a slave was a chattel, while at the same time allowing that there were many activities in which he could take part; and it regarded slavery as an institution firmly founded in the *ius gentium*. In 1789, the first year of the French Revolution, Johann Friedrich Reitemeier, a professor of law, published an essay on the subject of slavery in Greece.[1] The author describes the history of servitude among the Greeks, putting it into the context of economic

This chapter is a revision of an address given to the conference of the German Classical Association (*Deutscher Altphilologenverband*) held at Hanover in 1961, published in *Gymnasium* 69 (1962), 264–78. It is dedicated to the memory of acques Moreau.

[1] J. F. Reitemeier *Geschichte und Zustand der Sklaverei und der Leibeigenschaft in Griechenland* (Berlin 1789).

development; he recognizes its advantages and drawbacks and concludes by glorifying freedom and human dignity in general, which he sees realized in more recent states. In Germany, this approach to the subject of slavery lost some of its objectivity when the New Humanism was at its height, because of the widespread belief in the perfection of the Greek ideal. In his essay *On the study of Antiquity and of the Greeks in particular* (1793), Wilhelm von Humboldt describes the aim to 'develop man's potential versatility and the completion of his personality' as the oustanding characteristic of the Greeks, which raises them above other nations and provides a good reason for the study of antiquity. Among the external circumstances which favoured this kind of human development he gives slavery the first place. 'It took from the shoulders of the free man a great part of those labours whose success requires the exclusive application of just one of the corporal and spiritual faculties—mechanical skill.' The free man served by a slave had leisure for athletics, the arts and the sciences; he could take part in politics and defend his state in dangerous and difficult situations 'which the slave did not share with him'.[2] It was this aristocratic prejudice which enabled the humanists of the period to accept the idea that slavery was a circumstance that favoured the development of Greek civilization.

But this kind of study of antiquity also prepared the way for investigations along new lines: it was not long before August Boeckh began to demonstrate 'that the Athenians lived on wheat and barley rather than poetry or philosophy'. Students of ancient history set to work to investigate the idealized picture of the humanists with the aim of critically reconstructing the history and institutions of the Greeks and Romans as they had really existed. We can judge how objective this kind of antiquarian research was from a study of slavery among the Romans by the Scotsman William Blair, which appeared in 1833.[3] His analysis was based on a detailed knowledge of ancient authors, and avoided value-judgements in its reconstruction of ancient institutions. It was not long before these historical investigations were affected by

[2] *Gesammelte Schriften* I, 255ff., particularly 271 (= *Schriften zur Anthropologie und Bildungslehre* ed. A. Flitner (Düsseldorf and Munich 1956), 12ff., esp. 21f.).

[3] W. Blair *An Inquiry into the State of Slavery amongst the Romans from the Earliest Period till the Establishment of the Lombards in Italy* (Edinburgh 1833, 301 pp.). The judgement of Boeckh's work (and in particular of his treatment of the Athenian economy) mentioned above occurs in H. Nissen *Rh. Mus.* 49 (1894), 2. (Cf. K. J. Neumann *Entwicklung und Aufgaben der alten Geschichte* (inaugural lecture as Rector of the University of Strasbourg, 1910), 46.)

the new ideas of the time. In English-speaking countries in particular, the moral and political values of the Enlightenment were winning more and more acceptance; and they had been solemnly proclaimed in the French Revolution. One important result of this struggle for human rights was the battle against modern slavery in colonial territories, particularly in the West Indies. In 1794, the French Convention freed all slaves in territories under French rule. The British Parliament voted to abolish the slave trade in 1807, and in 1833 it put an end to slavery in British colonies. In 1830, Spartacus, whose story had influenced poets from Lessing onwards, was honoured with a statue in the Tuileries in Paris; and in Paris a few years later the Neo-Hegelian democrat Arnold Ruge, inspired by this statue, wrote the text of the opera *Spartacus* for a musician friend of his.[4] This was the intellectual climate at the time when the subject of slavery in antiquity began to arouse widespread interest among historians.

In 1837 the *Académie des Sciences morales et politiques* at Paris offered a prize for an essay on the reasons for the disappearance of ancient slavery and its transformation in Western Europe into feudal servitude. Of the two papers which were awarded prizes, one recorded the evidence for the decline of slavery in the ancient world within the framework of a comprehensive history of this institution from the ancient Orient up to late antiquity. Its author was Henri Wallon, who published his work in three volumes in 1847. During the course of that decade, the final debate about ending slavery in the French colonies was taking place in France. Wallon introduced his book with an analysis of slavery in the colonies; he became a member of the commission which drafted the final Act on the subject, and in the second edition of his work in 1879, he was able to conclude the introductory chapter with the text of the law of 1848 which decreed the abolition of slavery.[5] The immediate relevance of this work on ancient slavery—fundamental even today—to the contemporary political scene influenced the author's methods of scholarship in certain directions. Wallon indulges in polemics against those defenders of the *status quo* who point to the example of ancient society, see the origins of slavery in the family, and would like to justify the institution in general as a form of wardship and an indispensable means of transition from

[4] J. Muszkat-Muszkowski *Spartacus, eine Stoffgeschichte* (dissertation, Leipzig 1909), 95ff.

[5] H. Wallon *Histoire de l'esclavage dans l'antiquité* I–III (Paris 1847; 2nd edn. 1879).

savagery to civilization. Against this defence of slavery on the grounds of natural justice, Wallon objects that slavery originates from evil, from some perverted root of humanity, and that, far from serving to assist progress, it is just as fatal for masters as for slaves; the example of the peoples and states of antiquity should make it obvious that slavery leads to disaster. 'Certainly antiquity has been surpassed by the advances of our own times, but there is still much to be learnt from it on the question of slavery' (I, pp. clxiiif.).

In taking such a resolute stand, Wallon reflects the view that the historian's role is to be judge, not advocate. He brings the institution of slavery in the ancient East, in Greece and in Rome to life again by a detailed and meticulous examination of the sources, in order to prove in his third volume how slavery had to give way to free labour, because of political and economic factors and philosophical and religious trends. It is extremely interesting to follow the author's reasoning. One can feel the self-confidence of a scholar who believes that he is exploring new territory, and is only able to rely occasionally on those who have gone before him. He gives Greece particular attention; for here he senses that the beginnings of political freedom, the fostering of the Arts and intellectual progress, were closely bound up with the existence of slave labour (I, p. 61). He believes that he is able to prove that in the most glorious period of Athenian history, from Solon to Pericles, free labour was respected, and that the use of slaves only became prevalent during the fourth century, when decline had begun to set in. A major part of his argument rests on the size of the Athenian slave population given by Athenaeus, the importance of which had already been recognized a century before by David Hume. Wallon describes the sources from which the Greeks got their slaves, the position of slaves in the family and in the state, manumissions and social theories; and he finally comes to the crucial question of whether slavery, in which his opponents saw an instrument instituted by Providence for the education of the human race, had contributed to the development of Greek culture. His conclusion is that neither directly nor even indirectly did it have any good effects, but rather proved disastrous both for free men and slaves. His portrayal of slavery at Rome is just as detailed; and here too, although compared with Greece there had been far more contacts with peoples at a less advanced stage of civilization, his conclusion is entirely negative. 'Slavery decimated nations rather than saved them, corrupted morals rather than refined them, ruined rather than benefited the family and the state; it did more harm than good for the progress of labour and the development of the intellect. Ancient civilization had its good and its bad points. As we have seen, the bad points were the direct result of slavery, the good ones of freedom' (II, 438). This is followed by an examination of the fundamental transformation of slavery under the Empire. Recognition is awarded to the role of Christianity and Stoicism, with the proviso that the Christian message of equality for all men in the sight of God, first had to change morality before it could reform social realities; while the influence of Stoic thought on Roman law, although it may well have encouraged manumission, did not lead to the abolition of slavery. It was the difficulties which the Empire found itself having to face that led to the approximation of a milder form of slavery to a more restricted form of freedom. But it needed an impetus stronger than the crisis of the Empire, and a power less involved than the Imperial government, to put an end to the slavery of antiquity; it was Christianity that had to complete the task of setting all slaves free. Wallon believes that he is able to prove this on the basis of the teaching of the Church Fathers and Christian influences on Imperial legislation.

I have paid special attention to this outstanding work, not merely because of the important place it holds in the development of historical research, but also because of the comprehensiveness of its documentation and the courage with which it raises new questions. To be sure, some of the opinions it expresses had to be brought up to date in the light of new inscriptions, once the additional evidence of papyri had been taken into account, and once the methods of criticism of ancient texts had become more refined. His value-judgements also needed revision, when people began to realize that it was not just medieval European feudalism and modern colonial slavery which stood in historical succession to ancient slavery, but also the working classes of the industrial era—a point which, incidentally, is occasionally hinted at in Wallon's work.[6] Yet Wallon certainly did give expression to ideas which could never subsequently be ignored.

It was not long before Wallon's views about the influence of Christianity on the transformation of slavery were taken up again and strongly reinforced. In 1876 Paul Allard, later to win fame for his

[6] I, xliv—a reference to the effects of industrialization on European workers; I, 284f.—the deteriorating conditions of contemporary workers, who, however, prefer freedom to a state of subjection; II, 346ff.—a comparison between Roman and English estates with a reference to 'le Dr. Engel'; and particularly III, 440f.—slaves in antiquity and modern industrial workers.

outstanding work on the persecutions of the Christians in the Roman Empire, published a book which received not only the approbation of the Holy See but also an award from the French Academy.[7] After a description of the condition of slavery at the time of the appearance of Christianity which breaks little new ground, the author demonstrates the novelty of the egalitarian ideals contained in the Christian message. From the start, the idea that all men were equal in the sight of God had been realized in community worship; the logical outcome of this idea could only be the abolition of slavery. Yet the religious message did not aim at a social revolution, but rather at a change in moral standards. It was only after society had been Christianized that the Church could start to put the ideal of Christian Freedom into practice and make a major contribution to overcoming slavery. The part Christianity played in this respect is described with the help of a greater wealth of material than had been at Wallon's disposal; but Allard confines himself to religion and morality, and little account is taken of the influence of economic factors on the historical process.

This is surprising when we consider how powerful an impulse Socialism had already given to historical thought and political action by the year in which this book was published. It was as a result of this new movement that ancient slavery came to be examined from a new angle. In sustained analysis of both ancient philosophy and Hegelianism, Karl Marx evolved dialectical materialism and undertook to demonstrate that the means of material production was the condition upon which social, political and intellectual life in general was based. The development of productive forces and the conditions of production corresponding to them were elevated to the status of decisive factors in human history. Ancient society appeared to this single-minded thinker as that stage of historical development in which the last traces of communal property remaining from prehistory disappeared.[8] Now individual owners took possession not merely of the soil but also of the productive human beings who worked it, thereby instituting the system of slavery. But in ancient slave-holding societies the alienation of the subjected slave from his own productive activity and from his

[7] P. Allard *Les esclaves chrétiens* (Paris 1876; 5th edn. 1914).

[8] Among recent studies of the ancient world as seen by Marx and Marxist historians are R. Sannwald *Marx und die Antike* (*Staatswissenschaftliche Studien*, N.F. 27: Zurich 1957); E. Ch. Welskopf *Die Produktionsverhältnisse im Alten Orient und in der griechisch-römischen Antike* (*Deutsche Akademie der Wissenschaften zu Berlin, Schriften der Sektion für Altertumswissenschaft* 5: 1957).

product had not yet been followed through to its logical conclusion; the relationship of dependence was still personal, and the slave-owner did not buy the labour as distinct from the slave, as happened with nineteenth-century capitalism. Marx also held that it was the existence of slaves, those 'machines of the ancient world', that made possible the social structure of the *polis*, with its realization of civic liberties and its fostering among a minority of privileged citizens of that all-round education which the Humanists had celebrated as their ideal. Compared with the social structure of the ancient Near East, classical society, though still based on slavery, could be seen as a decisive step forward. Marx and the Marxists interpreted its later development as the result of the low level of consumption (and therefore of large-scale industrialization) possible in slave-holding societies. The result was economic decline and the impoverishment of the masses, which paved the way for a form of feudalism based on bondage.

At first, this principle which Marx formulated of the economic basis of history had only a limited and gradual influence on historical thought in the Western world. Nevertheless, it provided a great stimulus to economic and social history,[9] as did the explanation of social revolution in terms of the contradictions which had arisen between the means of material production of a society and the conditions of production or property existing in that society, a theory which also attracted the attention of scholars who were not Marxists. It was here that the effect of modern Socialism on the treatment of the problem of slavery in antiquity first made itself felt. The ancient slave revolts, which were for the most part concentrated in the short period from 150 to 70 B.C., were repeatedly explained in terms of the common denominator of some kind of ancient socialism or communism, despite all the apparent differences in the motives and aims of the rebels. The first to make this suggestion was Karl Bücher, who, as an undergraduate at Bonn in the winter of 1869/70, led the discussion of Eunus' Sicilian slave revolt at Arnold Schäfer's history seminars, where the fragments of book 34 of Diodorus were being studied. 'In my investigation of this question', he says in his autobiography, 'I looked at these ancient events in the light of the modern labour movement. My professor, who was not particularly captivated by this approach, let me carry on in the way I saw fit, and I can still remember the astonished faces of my fellow-

[9] Of works written in German, mention must be made of B. Büchsenschütz *Besitz und Erwerb im griechischen Altertume* (Halle 1869), who deals with slavery in Greece on pp. 104–208.

students when my essay came up for consideration by the class. I later revised it when I was in Frankfurt and had it published in the form of a paper. This was the reason why I became interested in economics.'[10] This paper[11] talks of a widespread proletarian movement and of the sudden appearance of socialism, and is the first example of the uncritical modernizing of history that was to lead by way of Robert von Pöhlmann's hypothesis of ancient socialism and communism to Ulrich Kahrstedt's theories about Bolsheviks in Sicily and the existence of a dictatorship of the proletariat in antiquity. The grave misunderstanding that lies at the root of this identification of ancient slavery and the modern proletariat does not have to be refuted here—that has already been done elsewhere.[12]

More important for the advance of scholarship was the fact that not long after, an historian who was a professed Marxist undertook to describe and explain the phenomenon of ancient slavery as a whole in the light of Marxist theories. In 1899, the year after he had been temporarily dismissed from his professorial chair because of his support for Social Democracy, Ettore Ciccotti published a book on the decline of slavery in the ancient world, which was translated into several languages.[13] This book contains a comprehensive history of slavery in Greece and Rome, although, as the title suggests, Ciccotti's main interest is the process by which slavery was superseded. In contrast to the view held by Wallon and Allard, he denies that Christianity or Stoicism played any part in putting an end to the system of slavery; this development can only be explained in terms of changes in economic circumstances. It is on this basis that Ciccotti describes the history of slavery in antiquity. While serfdom was predominant during the archaic period in Greece, the economic revolution brought about by the rise of cities and of industry required a massive increase in the labour force, so that slavery became prevalent. In the heyday of Greek civilization, free labour still seriously competed with slaves, but during the age of capitalism after the Peloponnesian War, the gap between workers and slaves narrowed both in theory and in practice. In the Hellenistic world the contrast was no longer between free man and slave but between capitalist and proletarian, and this prepared the way for the dissolution of the slave

[10] K. Bücher *Lebenserinnerungen* I (Tübingen 1919), 121.

[11] K. Bücher *Der Aufstand der unfreien Arbeiter 143–129 v. Chr.* (Frankfurt a.M. 1874).

[12] Chapter III p. 83ff. above.

[13] E. Ciccotti *Il tramonto della schiavitù nel mondo antico* (Turin 1899).

system. Slavery at Rome developed along parallel lines. Here also in the time of the late Republic—to give only a rough outline—the free workers came to compete with the servile labour force, while slaves were often employed as hired labourers, and were no longer considered as mere chattels in Roman law. The closing of the gap between the free and the servile labour forces was caused less by Christianity than by the decline of the slave trade on the one hand, and the degeneration of free workers to the level of dependants on the other. It was the general economic stagnation of the Empire, which can be seen in agriculture by the rise of the *colonus* system, that caused slavery to give place entirely to serfdom.

It cannot be said that the Marxist Ciccotti satisfactorily solves the problem he has set himself to answer. He is far too ready to force the historical evidence into his preconceived scheme, and his reasoning is inconclusive at exactly those points that are crucial to the development he has traced out. The decline of slave labour, which is assumed to have begun as early as the fourth century B.C. in Greece, and the increase in manumissions and rise of the *colonus* system, require a more detailed analysis based on a greater amount of evidence. But there remains the service which Ciccotti performed of showing that economic phenomena are essential to an understanding of the problem of slavery as a whole.

For specialist historians, however, there was by this time no longer any lack of evidence. Eduard Meyer had pointed the way in two excellent sketches of economic history. These were the lectures he gave during 1895 on the subject of economic development in antiquity and during 1898 on slavery in the ancient world.[14] In the former he emphatically rejects the theory then advocated by Karl Bücher that the economic system of antiquity did not advance beyond the stage of the individual household; in that given three years later Meyer attacks the doctrine that any kind of regular progression can be traced in the way ancient slavery passed via medieval serfdom to the free bargaining of the modern era. He rather sees antiquity as a discrete period which began and ended with serfdom. The rise, predominance and decline of slavery can basically be explained, he argues, with reference to political factors. Among the Greeks it was not the rise of trade and industry but simply the evolution of the constitutional state that paved the way for slavery. That social class which in the Greek world

[14] E. Meyer *Kleine Schriften* I² (Halle 1924), 79ff. and 169ff.

was involved in trade and industry and battled for political power with the landed classes, preferred the cheaper slave workers, thus making them an important source of additional labour, even though competition from free workers always continued to exist. At Rome there was the opposite tendency: the landed classes retained power in their own hands, but they also, after the creation of their world empire, worked their *latifundia* with the masses of slaves who had been obtained in the wars of conquest. The first century B.C. was the heyday of ancient slavery. Two centuries later, the slave system had become insignificant; and because in the following period free workers tended to be bound more and more to the occupation they had inherited, serfdom began to reappear and the whole process started all over again. The salient feature of this argument is that it destroys the notion of the supposedly regular development from primitive communism by way of slavery and serfdom to the proletariat of modern capitalism. Political factors and various other historical forces are placed alongside economic ones, and proper credit is awarded to the unique character of each age and each civilization.

This was the background to the large number of investigations of individual aspects of slavery that were carried out in Europe and America in the course of the following decades, as part of a remarkable upsurge of interest in the social and economic history of antiquity; in this connection one need only mention the names of M. Rostovtzeff, Tenney Frank, A. H. M. Jones, F. Oertel, F. Heichelheim, G. Glotz and E. Cavaignac. These studies could fairly be described as positivist; but there can be no doubt that the far-reaching and fundamental questions which had been asked about the slave system up till then (and in Soviet scholarship at least had often led to over-hasty conclusions) could never have been answered without a methodical clarification of the many controversial points of the institution as a whole. Inscriptions and papyri were now available to supplement the literary evidence which was often so defective or ambiguous. It will be enough to concentrate on a few examples of this type of investigation, which continues in the present day.

The question of manumissions in their various forms and permutations, in Greece from Homeric times up to the Roman Empire, was studied by A. Calderini on the evidence of inscriptions and papyri.[15] From sources which are mainly non-Athenian he is able to explain

[15] A. Calderini *La manomissione e la condizione dei liberti in Grecia* (Milan 1908).

how religious and civil manumission could exist side by side, and from the Athenian evidence he reconstructs the legal and social position of freedmen. While this book occasionally degenerates into a catalogue of references, W. Buckland's great work, which appeared at the same time, does attempt a general reconstruction of the legal system as it applied to slaves in the Roman Empire.[16] He deals with slaves as chattels and as human beings, with all the legal forms of enslavement and manumission and their legal consequences in a methodical way worthy of Mommsen. Other investigators dealt with other historical topics, but without touching on the ultimate question of the importance of the institution for ancient civilization. Historians concerned with the study of population figures looked again at the statistics for Greek slaves, particularly for Athenian slaves of the fifth and fourth centuries.[17] There were detailed analyses of the places of origin of Roman slaves and of the part played by slave populations in the process of blending the various nationalities.[18] R. H. Barrow's monograph, which vividly portrays the life led by slaves, was particularly successful; for it avoids the temptation to make value-judgements and applies the comparison between ancient and modern slavery solely in order to throw light on the question of economic profitability.[19] A. M. Duff's book on freedmen in the Roman Empire, which appeared in the same year, is also a valuable contribution towards an understanding of this social class, and, especially, of the activities of freedmen in the Imperial civil service. In his view the population mixture brought about by the presence of slaves and freedmen was one of the causes of Roman decline.[20] Literary scholars also contributed by examining the important part played by slaves in comedy,[21] and the philosophical

[16] W. W. Buckland *The Roman Law of Slavery* (Cambridge 1908).

[17] R. L. Sargent *The Size of the Slave Population at Athens* (*University of Illinois Studies in the Social Sciences* 12: 1924); A. W. Gomme *The Population of Athens in the Fifth and Fourth Centuries B.C.* (Oxford 1933); W. L. Westermann 'Athenaeus and the Slaves at Athens' *HSCP* Supp. Vol. (1941), 451ff. (= Finley 73ff.).

[18] M. Bang 'Die Herkunft der römischen Sklaven' *Röm. Mitt.* 25 (1910), 223ff.; 27 (1912), 181ff.; M. L. Gordon 'The Nationality of Slaves under the Early Roman Empire' *JRS* 14 (1924), 93ff. (= Finley 171ff.); T. Frank 'Race Mixture in the Roman Empire' *American Historical Review* 21 (1916), 689ff.; his approach is criticized by F. G. Maier 'Bevölkerungsgeschichte und Inschriftenstatistik' *Historia* 2 (1953/4), 318ff.

[19] R. H. Barrow *Slavery in the Roman Empire* (London 1928).

[20] A. M. Duff *Freedmen in the Early Roman Empire* (Oxford 1928: reprint Cambridge 1958).

[21] A few references may suffice: C. O. Zuretti 'Il servo nella comedia greca

theories concerning slavery;[22] they also began the task of examining the plentiful material provided by names of Greek and Roman slaves.[23]

Apart from this activity in specialized fields, there was one scholar who attempted an appraisal of ancient slavery as a whole. This was the American William Lynn Westermann, who came 'ad Germaniam maiorum patriam' in 1899 to study under Diels and Wilamowitz at Berlin, where he graduated in 1902 with a dissertation on the history of medicine in antiquity.[24] In 1923 he was appointed to a professorship at Columbia University. The great acquisitions of Greek papyri made by various American academic institutions encouraged him to study Graeco-Roman Egypt, more particularly slavery in the Ptolemaic period, as well as many individual problems posed by slavery in the Greek and Roman worlds. He also tried to throw light on the various undefined statuses between slavery and freedom. He was commissioned to write the lengthy article on slavery for the *Realencyclopädie der classischen Altertumswissenschaft*, which appeared in 1935 and serves fellow-scholars throughout the world as a mine of information about ancient evidence on slavery (Suppl. VI, 894–1068). This, of course, dealt with slavery in the narrower sense of the word, which meant that the problem of serfdom had to be ignored; but the collection of this huge amount of source-material into chronological order was an achievement of lasting value. Towards the end of his life, Westermann revised the whole of this material, and considered the question of the relation of Hellenistic slavery to the intellectual trends of the period in greater depth; he looked closely at the process by which the differences between free and slave labour disappeared in the Roman Empire, and published this life's work in his book, *The Slave Systems of Greek and Roman Antiquity*, which appeared in 1955, shortly after his

antica' *Riv. Fil.* 31 (1903), 46ff.; P. E. Legrand *Daos. Tableau de la comédie grecque pendant la période dite nouvelle* (Paris and Lyons 1910) [= *The New Greek Comedy* tr. J. Loeb (London 1917)]; C. Langer *De servi persona apud Menandrum* (dissertation, Bonn 1919). Further works are mentioned in P. P. Spranger's study (see above p. 3 n. 4).

[22] R. Schlaifer 'Greek Theories of Slavery from Homer to Aristotle' *HSCP* 47 (1936), 165ff. (= Finley 93ff.); G. Morrow *Plato's Law of Slavery* (*University of Illinois Studies in Language and Literature* 25, 3: 1939).

[23] M. Lambertz *Die griechischen Sklavennamen* (Vienna 1907); J. Baumgart *Die römischen Sklavennamen* (dissertation, Breslau 1936).

[24] Guilelmus Westermann *De Hippocratis in Galeno memoria quaestiones* (dissertation, Berlin 1902).

death.[25] Here, at last, was a book in which all aspects of slavery in antiquity from Homer to Justinian were presented largely from the point of view of economic and social history, and of modern approaches to source-analysis. He covers in chronological sequence the origins of slavery, the many and changing sources for slaves, their numbers and market-price, their legal and social status, their acceptance, normally, of their situation and occasional uprisings, as well as discussing the effects of slavery on morality, philosophical theories, and the equivocal attitude of Christianity in announcing the equality of all men in the sight of God while accepting the existing institution of slavery. When we compare this to Wallon's work of more than a century before, we can see the importance of the additional source-material. But it must be admitted that Westermann not infrequently misinterpreted the evidence, and did not entirely succeed in overcoming the lexicographic character which his work inherited from its original version; he put together a mosaic made up of innumerable tiny pieces, but was unable to achieve the broad vision required on a historical canvas. It is not really surprising that historians and lawyers raised strong objections to some of the points he made. He not only often misunderstood the peculiarities of legal problems, but he also overlooked the connections between the political and social constitutions of individual states and the particular phases of slavery existing in them at the time; the many different grades of bondage and semi-bondage were often simply ignored. The questions that ultimately arise for the historian of slavery in antiquity remained unanswered: the function that the system had fulfilled in fostering and maintaining the position of the ruling classes in ancient societies was not sufficiently investigated; and Westermann clearly tended to underestimate the role of slavery in the conditions of production, and also as a particular type of human existence.

Meanwhile research continued in all fields of classical scholarship. As well as investigations dealing with such important individual problems as the legal position of the unfree rural population in Greece[26] or the importation of slaves from barbarian countries, there was the most important question of all—whether slavery should be considered

[25] *Slave Systems* has a comprehensive bibliography of works dealing with slavery (165ff.); a selective bibliography is also to be found in Finley 229ff.

[26] D. Lotze 'Μεταξὺ ἐλευθέρων καὶ δούλων. Studien zur Rechtsstellung unfreier Landbevölkerungen in Griechenland bis zum 4. Jahrhundert v. Chr.' *Deutsche Akademie der Wissenschaften zu Berlin. Schriften der Sektion für Altertumswissenschaft* 17 (1959); cf. p. 3 n. 5 above.

a fundamental or even the fundamental characteristic of ancient civilization. The work done by English-speaking historians during the last few years is of particular interest in this respect. A. H. M. Jones, in his extremely well-documented analysis,[27] comes to the conclusion that, apart from exceptional circumstances, slaves did not provide effective competition for free labour; and Ch. G. Starr refers to the comparatively small proportion of the total population that slaves constituted in order to correct the nineteenth-century tendency to overemphasize the importance of the slave system.[28] Others uphold the theory that there was a close link between the slave system and the rise of the states of classical antiquity. G. E. M. de Ste. Croix sees slavery as the necessary condition for guaranteeing a surplus of production to a narrow segment of the population, thereby leaving them free to carry on the business of government and gain the opportunities for intellectual speculation.[29] M. I. Finley considers that the slave system, which was universally practised, recognized by philosophers and accepted by slaves, was an integrating factor in society.[30] Similarly, slavery is still seen as a major contributory element in the decline of ancient society, and emphasis is laid on the scant respect awarded to technology, and its decline during the period of the Roman Empire. F. W. Walbank[31] claims that the fact that skilled work was left to slaves prevented advances being made in almost every field of industrial production, and thereby led to the weakening of the upper class itself. In its extreme form this technological emphasis led to the dilettante approach of the French army major Lefebvre des Noëttes.[32] With the help of a wide selection of illustrations, he examined the way in which draught-animals were harnessed in the ancient Orient and in antiquity, and suggested that with such harnesses one animal could not have transported a load of more than 1,000 lb. on a

[27] A. H. M. Jones 'Slavery in the Ancient World' *The Economic History Review* 9 (1956), 185ff. (= Finley 1ff.).

[28] C. G. Starr 'An Overdose of Slavery' *Journal of Economic History* 18 (1958), 17ff.

[29] G. E. M. de Ste. Croix, review of Westermann's book in *Classical Review* NS. 7 (1957), 54ff.

[30] M. I. Finley 'Was Greek Civilization based on Slave Labour?' *Historia* 8 (1959), 145ff. (= Finley 53ff.).

[31] F. W. Walbank *The Decline of the Roman Empire in the West* (London 1946).

[32] R. Lefebvre des Noëttes *La force animale à travers les âges* (Nancy and Paris 1924), republished as *L'attelage. Le cheval de selle à travers les âges. Contribution à l'histoire de l'esclavage* (Paris 1931).

normal road. So there was no alternative solution to the problem of transporting heavy loads, he suggested, but to use human beings as draught-animals. The slave system had to remain until the invention of the collar in the tenth century A.D., which alone enabled the animal's power to be exploited to the full.

No mention has so far been made of the Marxist historians who followed Ciccotti. It ought therefore to be emphasized that since the Russian Revolution, and particularly since the sizeable increase in Communist territory after the Second World War, Eastern European Marxist historians have applied themselves most energetically to the study of slavery in antiquity. F. Vittinghoff has published a critical appreciation of the problems and aims of Soviet scholarship;[33] and slavery has also become a problem of the greatest importance to classical scholars in East Germany, Poland, Czechoslovakia and Hungary.[34] The fact that the purpose and the basic premisses of Marxist historical scholarship in countries under Communist rule have been fixed in advance for all time makes understanding with scholars in the West very difficult. Nevertheless, there are contacts which, it is to be hoped, will continue in the future. At the suggestion of the Association of German Historians, the topic of slavery in antiquity was made the theme of the Eleventh International Historical Congress held at Stockholm in 1960. The talk given there by S. Lauffer, and the contributions of colleagues from Israel, Poland, Yugoslavia, Germany and Britain, impressed on all participants the universal interest and urgency of these problems, even if widely differing interpretations were proposed.[35] New thinking on the subject may be stimulated by one massive task that the Soviet Academy of Sciences is undertaking: the entire history of slavery in antiquity from the Mycenaean age to the fall of the western Roman Empire is to be described in ten volumes

[33] F. Vittinghoff 'Die Theorie des historischen Materialismus über den antiken "Sklavenhalterstaat"' *Saeculum* 11 (1960), 89ff.; id. 'Die Bedeutung der Sklaven für den Übergang von der Antike ins abendländische Mittelalter' *Historische Zeitschrift* 192 (1961), 265ff.

[34] Scholars who have made several individual contributions in this field include R. Günther, G. Schrot, E. Ch. Welskopf; I. Biezunska-Malowist, B. Bilinski, (Bibliography in *Accademia Polacca di Scienze e Lettere: Bibliotheca di Roma, Conferenze* Fasc. 12, 3f.), O. Jurewicz; J. Češka, P. Oliva, V. Vavřínek; G. Alföldy, E. Maróti. Regular reviews of these studies appear in the journal *Bibliotheca Classica Orientalis.*

[35] XIe Congrès International des Sciences Historiques *Rapports* II, 71ff.; *Résumés des Communications* 68ff.; *Actes du Congrès* 87ff.

by experts on the subject. Among the individual volumes that have appeared to date are those of J. A. Lentzman on slavery in Mycenaean and Homeric Greece (1963), L. A. El'nitzkii on the origins and development of slavery in Rome from the eighth to the third centuries B.C. (1964), and E. M. Shtajerman on the developed slave-owning society of the Roman republic (1964). It is to be welcomed that Lentzman introduces his book (and thereby the series as a whole) with a detailed, if often unnecessarily polemical, report on the current state of research on Greek slavery.

As far as I am able to judge the situation in East and West, it would seem that there is still a need for many investigations of individual subjects before a new general survey can be attempted, or before the basic relationship of slavery to ancient civilization can be convincingly demonstrated. There are vast areas yet to be studied. But it is important that each individual monograph should not lose sight of the structure of ancient society as a whole. The functions performed by slavery at every stage of human life will need to be examined in detail before it will be possible to state whether this was a beneficial growth or a malignant cancer on the ancient body-politic. The most diverse branches of classical scholarship in all countries can co-operate in this all-embracing task. I would like to mention here the undertaking begun by myself, and to announce the preliminary results as well as the plans for the future[36] in the hope of arousing not merely interest but also active co-operation among my readers.

Fundamental to all future investigations is the clarification of what the various words used to describe slavery actually mean. The first contribution made by F. Gschnitzer, on linguistic usage in pre-Hellenistic times, has shown us how extensive this problem is, in spite of all that has already been achieved by earlier scholars. The linguistic terminology and legal status of every different kind of slavery and semi-slavery—slave, servant, freedman, hired worker, tied tenant—must be examined within its proper context. The sources from which slaves were acquired, and the different ways slave population numbers were maintained, must be analysed. G. Micknat has made a start by studying war captives in Homer, and H. Volkmann by examining the mass-enslavements of Hellenistic and Roman times. Much interesting information about the slave trade has been produced, but it might perhaps be worth taking a closer look at those countries preferred by

[36] Cf. p. 2 n. 4 above, where those works that have appeared to date are listed. See also the Bibliographical Supplement on p. 211ff. below.]

slave-hunters and slave-traders, and examining the values put on slaves of different nationalities. Above all, however, there is the question of the rearing of slaves at home and in the workshop, which so far has hardly been given any consideration.

F. Bömer has broken new ground with his study of the relationship between Greek and Roman religious cults and slavery, by taking the decisive step of turning the question round, and examining the religious beliefs of Roman and Greek slaves and the many other questions that follow from this. After the early death of Jacques Moreau, H. U. Instinsky and H. Kraft have undertaken to investigate the relationship of primitive Christianity and the early Church to slavery from the same point of view. In the economic field, S. Lauffer, using all the sources now at our disposal, has shown that the slaves in the mines at Laureum were a group of workers essential to the life of the Athenian *polis*. The first of a series of contributions dealing with the activities of slaves of various specialized skills, such as educators, musicians, actors and physicians, have now appeared. They should be followed by studies of architects and sculptors as well as studies of the role of slaves in the world of banking and finance. A paper due to appear in the near future is to consider slaves and freedmen in the service of the Roman emperors. As far as the Roman world is concerned, the sources containing information about slaves in industry have by no means yet been exhausted. A contribution is expected clarifying the crucial issue of whether the stagnation of technological progress in the Empire was general, and whether the slave status of craftsmen was an essential factor in the situation. There will also be a study of runaway slaves in the Roman Empire, which would help to throw some light on the slow transformation which slavery underwent in late antiquity.

As slaves themselves were unable to leave behind any literary documents, we ought at least to listen whenever a poet lets them speak. P. P. Spranger has made a start by considering the slave characters in Plautus and Terence. It might produce some interesting results if classical scholars were to appreciate that the experiences of the ordinary man, both slave and free, as recorded in fables, proverbs and popular farces, represent genuine social comment, and if they were to listen for the voice of the slave world among those literary figures who rose from slave status. Another distinct problem is that of the language used by servants in ancient society.

Archaeologists might examine how slaves are represented in the visual arts, interpreting the characteristic types of so-called barbarians from a historical or ethnographic point of view, and looking for references to unusual individuals from the lower strata of society in the great number of grotesque figures that are found, especially in the minor arts. The theoretical arguments for and against slavery in ancient thought have often been discussed: it is to be hoped that there will soon be a study of the rules of conduct towards slaves contained in the ethical and economic writings of the Greeks, and of the effect that these maxims had on everyday behaviour. And the many ways in which the principle of slavery was overcome, indeed had to be overcome if the system as a whole was to be preserved, will also be given the recognition they deserve. This includes the use of slaves for military service, which occurred so often in times of crisis—slaves fought side by side with free men at Marathon and Cannae, to give only two examples. A prize has been offered for a study of the effects of slavery on relationships between the sexes. This is an area which has not been touched: yet there is no other question which goes deeper into human nature.

Considerations of this kind lead us beyond historical problems to the attitudes we hold towards the ancient world. Any investigation which considers the role played by slavery in the Graeco-Roman world at its height, rather than the way in which slavery disappeared, is sure to come to the conclusion that ancient civilization cannot be imagined without it. The dominance of the ruling classes, their education and wealth required such a system of service. It was a hard solution which can be explained in terms of the vitality and intellectual aggressiveness of the Greeks and Romans, and also by the particular pressures of the place and time in which they lived. The criticisms of philosophers did not stimulate demands for the abolition of slavery; the concepts of *philanthropia* and *humanitas* essentially applied only to the circle of politically enfranchised citizens. We humanists of the twentieth century should not have any reservations in stating this. Today it may be possible, in an age when every man is served by many mechanical slaves, for a far greater proportion of the population to share in the great benefits of a classical education than Wilhelm von Humboldt and his contemporaries thought practicable. Admittedly this goal, if it is ever generally recognized, will encounter its own particular difficulties, but they will be no greater than those of any other intellectual movement in our age. Hippocrates' maxim applies to scholarship as well as to education: 'The lyfe so short, the craft so long to lerne.'

X

Slavery and the Humanists

The term 'Humanist' refers to those European scholars, educators and poets from the fourteenth to the seventeenth centuries who aimed, by studying the ancient Classics, to reach a standard of culture truly worthy of a human being. There are also those philosophers and scholars, artists and writers who followed Winckelmann and Wilhelm von Humboldt in believing that contact with the Greeks would bring about the development of a free individuality, and so the universal aim of mankind. And finally there are the teachers of the last generation, who held that *Paideia*, man's education as a man, was the greatest creation of the Greeks. It would not be improper to consider what position these Humanists (and we ourselves if we wish to be numbered among them) have held on the question of slavery. On the contrary, this is to take them at their word and ask them whether that culture of the individual which, following Cicero's example, they called *humanitas*, can be attained by everyone, whether anyone with the physical characteristics of a human being can reach that goal which in their educational doctrine they honour with the terms *dignitas* and *excellentia hominis*, or whether, like the ancients, their concepts of man and of humanity do not apply to slaves. It might be worth considering that other group of outcasts which in part coincided with them, the barbarians, as another touchstone of Humanism, but this would be too wide a field.

The Humanists of the Renaissance, and in particular the Italians,

This chapter is dedicated to Hermann Dörries.

valued the *studia humanitatis*, the desire to rediscover the Greek and Latin classics, as a sure means to developing one's character as a human being; not merely nobility of speech and good manners were to be learnt from the ancients, but also wisdom, virtue and an unfettered spirit—in a word, the education of the *uomo universale*. This was the common aim they all set themselves, whether they based the *praestantia hominis* on the self-confidence of man in his natural state, or whether their Christian Platonism led them to think that it was founded in the likeness of this last and highest of created beings to God Himself. In practice their doctrine was generally addressed only to the upper levels of society, to princes and their sons and groups of aristocrats, and even when they let young men of other social classes attend their schools and used the vernacular instead of Latin, they still insisted that the *studia humanitatis* were not intended as a means to earning a living but, being *studia liberalia*, served instead to foster virtue and glory.[1]

But it was not only in Italy that Humanist education aimed at the ideal of the true nobleman which was given its canonical form in Baldasarre Castiglione's *Cortegiano* (1528). In every European country influenced by these new ideas, the Humanists turned to kings and magistrates and those who had been selected to serve them. In his letter *De formando studio* (1484), Rudolph Agricola demands that young people should be brought up to behave with modesty, and should be given instruction in the liberal arts.[2] Erasmus, who tried to bring this new intellectual culture into line with the *philosophia Christi*, believed that the only way to attain *humanitas*, to behave in a way worthy of a human being, was that of the *litterae elegantiores*, which were sometimes also called the *litterae humanae* or *studia humaniora*. This literary education was to foster correctness of speech, good manners and a well-balanced character, and, at the same time, serve as an introduction to the study of the sciences .[3] As for the human dignity of the masses

[1] Vergerius can be considered to have represented the views of many when he emphasized the contrast between the liberal and the mechanical arts with great precision in his tract *De ingenuis moribus* (Padua 1402). Cf. G. Toffanin *Geschichte des Humanismus* (Amsterdam 1941), 231ff.

[2] On Agricola, and on Humanist education generally, see H. Woodward *Studies in Education during the Age of the Renaissance 1400–1600* (Cambridge 1906), 79ff.; R. R. Bolgar *The Classical Heritage and its Beneficiaries* (Cambridge 1954).

[3] H. Rüdiger *Wesen und Wandlung des Humanismus* (Hamburg 1937), 103ff.; R. Newald *Erasmus Roterodamus* (Freiburg i. Br. 1947), 137ff., 308ff.; id. *Humanitas, Humanismus, Humanität* (Essen 1947), 23ff.; R. Pfeiffer *Humanitas Erasmiana*

who knew no classical languages and had not studied the liberal arts—the Humanists did not consider this any more of a problem than had the ancients on whom they modelled themselves. The hallmark of the *studia humanitatis* remained aristocratic exclusiveness. Even those manuals dealing with the education of princes themselves basically followed the standards for the ideal statesman that had been laid down in antiquity. Guillaume Budé wrote *L'Institution du Prince* in 1515 (the book did not however appear in print until 1546); Erasmus dedicated his *Institutio Principis Christiani* to Prince Charles—later the Emperor Charles V—in 1516. Budé is rather an isolated figure in his unwillingness to try to show that the teachings of the Gospel are compatible with the natural demands of political wisdom and justice. But both these educators of princes are in agreement when they list the knowledge and virtues expected of a ruler, demanding beneficial legislation and good government and reminding him that he must keep the peace. It is assumed that a prince should be a philosopher. Although Erasmus imposes on him the duty of educating his subjects, this does not alter the fact that the working classes do not share the education or the knowledge contained in the *bonae litterae*.

There was only one man who attempted to draw up a blueprint for a society in which wisdom could be attained by every citizen. In reaching this goal, he was not afraid to follow his arguments through to their most extreme conclusions, and, like an ancient founder of an ideal republic, he introduced communal property on the one hand and slavery on the other. This was Erasmus' friend, Thomas More, whose *Utopia*, an imaginative creation of a rational state, was completed in 1516, the same year in which Erasmus' *Institutio Principis Christiani* and Machiavelli's *Il Principe* appeared. Of course, this book was intended as a *libellus vere aureus nec minus salutaris quam festivus*, as the author implies in the title; any reader versed in ancient literature would have understood this to mean that the book was intended to be read on a holiday such as the Saturnalia, and that it was intended to make him perceive with delight how reason can overreach itself. The author's personal views are to be found in his objections to the narrator, Raphael Hythlodeus, where he expressly states that he is giving us his own opinion.[4]

(*Vorträge der Bibliothek Warburg* 22: 1931), 6ff., also *Ausgewählte Schriften* (Munich 1960), 208ff.; Bolgar *op. cit.* 336ff.

[4] This is quite properly stressed by G. Möbus *Macht und Menschlichkeit in der Utopia des Thomas Morus* (*Schriftenreihe der Deutschen Hochschule für Politik Berlin*

In Utopia, the island of Nowhere, Reason and Justice have created a state in which everything is communally owned and everyone has an obligation to work. But it is sufficient for each citizen to do six hours' work a day; the rest of the day is free for intellectual and cultural pursuits. Leadership of the state is in the hands of the educated (*litterati*) and the magistrates, who are chosen from among their number. This class is exempted from work, but they do not constitute a hereditary aristocracy; rather their numbers are continually supplemented by the inclusion of talented and morally mature citizens. Thus the intelligentsia form the government, but the dignity of manual labour is also respected, as even the rulers and ministers occasionally take part in it in order to set a good example. On the other hand, there are certain low and laborious services that are unworthy of free men; for such tasks forced labour and slaves are employed. Among these are butchery and the menial tasks associated with women's cooking, as well as the driving of ox-carts allocated to those whom the prince has allowed to make a journey; Utopians also include hunting among the butchers' jobs *ut rem liberis indignam.*[5] The inferior status of these slaves is evident to all: they carry chains and fetters made of gold, while Utopian citizens show complete contempt for precious metals.[6] The fact that the *sordida ministeria* are given to slaves reminds us of antiquity; and the ways in which the Utopians maintain the numbers of their slaves correspond to a great extent to ancient methods. They enslave the prisoners they capture in the just wars they wage, and when they conquer a foreign city they execute the leaders and carry off the remaining defenders as slaves.[7] Thus they retain the ancient rights of a belligerent without applying them in their full strictness. The fact that the Utopians reduce to slavery those of their own population who have committed a grave crime is parallel to the Roman practice of sentencing criminals to work in the mines; the Utopians do this on the grounds that it is no less hard on the guilty, and more advantageous to the state, than execution. Further, there is always a chance that, if

10: 1953), who surveys the book's significance in more recent times; cf. the same author's *Europäische Humanität als politische Formkraft* (*Politik der Gegenwart* 8: 1963). The Latin text has recently been published in volume 4 of the Yale edition of Thomas More's *Works*, ed. R. S. Sylvester (New Haven and London 1963), edited with a translation by E. Surtz and J. H. Hexter. An easily accessible English translation is that by Paul Turner in the Penguin Classics series (Harmondsworth 1965).

[5] Surtz-Hexter 138, 140, 146, 170.

[6] More, *Works*, *op. cit.* 150ff., 156.

[7] More, *Works*, *op. cit.* 184ff., 214.

they genuinely repent, they may receive a milder form of enslavement or even a complete reprieve. Then there are criminals who, having deserved the death penalty in a foreign city, can often be bought very cheaply by the Utopians. And when a Utopian has been killed or maimed abroad, the state demands the extradition of the culprits and punishes them with death or slavery. Finally, it can also happen that labourers or poor people in neighbouring countries may prefer to be slaves in Utopia; such people are treated mildly and allowed to leave if they choose.[8]

In Utopia, then, slavery may be either the result of capture in war or a substitute for capital punishment. No one in antiquity would have found fault with such a system. Nor would anyone have disapproved of the law of Utopus that ensured the citizens' freedom of religion by decreeing that those who tried to impose their own religious beliefs on others were to be punished by exile or enslavement.[9] But Thomas More was a Christian Humanist, and so he introduces into his society a group of extraordinary individuals whose voluntary service casts doubt on the whole institution of slavery. These are the members of a religious order who neglect intellectual pursuits and hope to earn eternal bliss solely by serving their fellow-men. They clean out ditches, fell trees and cart timber, they look after the sick and do all kinds of hard work for the community and for individuals. They toil voluntarily and gladly, without grumbling at others or boasting about it. The result is astonishing: 'the more they make slaves of themselves, the more everyone respects them'.[10] We may well ask, if this is the case, what the Utopians really think of hard and unpleasant work. Is it really unworthy of freemen, or is the only thing that matters whether servile work is done willingly or not? And what about slavery as such, in a state ruled by justice and humanity? Ought not the enslaving of prisoners captured in war to be abolished, so that slavery would only occur in the shape of forced labour? These questions remain unanswered; but a reader of *Utopia* must certainly have thought about them.

In order to understand what the early Humanists felt about slavery, we must examine another subject in which they were interested and about which they wrote. For the ancients were not only used as prototypes for oratory and poetry, and to set the standards for education. Together with their public and private institutions, they also

[8] Surtz-Hexter 184, 202. [9] More, *op. cit.* 218ff. [10] More, *op. cit.* 224ff.

became a subject for scholarly study. Interest in antiquity, and primarily Roman antiquity, was aroused as early as the fourteenth century, and was then injected with a new vitality by Erasmus; for some Humanists it soon became an end in itself. Gian-Francesco Poggio Bracciolini (1380–1459), who worked at Rome as a Papal secretary, was filled with sorrow at the sight of the ruins of the city; one of the tracts he wrote was entitled *De humanae condicionis miseria*; it stands out as a strange exception to the general optimism of the age.[11] He laments mankind's misfortunes, which are due to original sin, and composes a kind of chronicle of the calamities of the ancient world from Deucalion's flood down to the last disasters of the Romans. One would have thought that, having observed the misfortunes of each generation and every state, the author might note the distress of those who had been subjugated and enslaved, but his vision does not extend to the lowest levels of society. His contemporary Flavio Biondo (1384–1463) founded the study of antiquities. In his great work *Roma triumphans*, which he dedicated to Pope Pius II in 1459, he describes the beliefs and cults, political and military organization and private lives of the Romans. There is a short excursus on the subject of slaves in the passage about Roman law, but the author does not state his own view on the subject.[12]

The first person openly to give his own opinion was Gioviano Pontano (1426–1503), the head of the Neapolitan Academy. The first of the series of moral tracts in which he dealt with individual virtues was entitled *De oboedientia* (1472), and it contains the earliest Humanist judgement of ancient and contemporary slavery. 'Although slavery contradicts natural freedom, it is certain that it originated in the very earliest times', he says at the beginning of the passage *De servitute*.[13] As evidence for this statement he refers to the wars of the Greeks and the barbarians, and follows classical precedent in explaining the word *servi* as describing those who had been spared in war (*servati*), that is those prisoners who instead of being killed were preserved as part of the property of the victorious side. He contrasts the Roman practice with that of the Assyrians and Persians who procured their slaves *magis e*

[11] Pp. 88ff. in the Basle edition of 1538 of the *Poggii Florentini Opera*.

[12] Pp. 95ff. in the Basle edition of 1559.

[13] *Ioannis Ioviani Pontani opera omnia soluta oratione composita* (Venice 1518), 23: 'Quamquam autem servitus naturali repugnat libertati, initium tamen eius antiquissimum esse constat.' The passage about slavery continues to p. 26, where the author goes on to consider paid labour (*Famuli seu ministri*).

libidine quam ex iusta belli causa, and notes that pirates dealt in slaves. He then passes to the contemporary world and points out that among the Turks and Africans against whom wars were continually being waged, only Christians are to be found as slaves. But, he continues, there are Christian slaves among us, too: these are Thracians and Greeks, Bulgarians and Cercasians who, once owned by Scythians, have been bought by Christian merchants and taken to the West, where they have to work as slaves until they have earned the price of their ransom. This practice is approved in the interests of the name of Christianity. He goes on to say that only the dark-skinned Ethiopians, who live without laws and sell their own children, are to be found as slaves among every nation. So he accepts without comment that it is because of their barbarous nature that Negroes are enslaved. The passage ends with the protestation: 'This grave offence against the human race has been written into the law of nations. Among ourselves it has been restricted to the extent that it is forbidden to castrate boys, as this is an act of extreme brutality.' Although he unequivocally describes the institution of slavery as a *humani generis iniuria,* he is, nevertheless, prepared to acquiesce in it. For in considering antiquity and the present day, Pontano goes on to describe the services done by slaves, and stresses above all that obedience must be enforced by fear. He praises his Roman ancestors for the kind, lenient and just way they treated their slaves, and quotes from the 47th letter of Seneca to prove this. We are told that Roman slaves were even educated in the liberal arts; he mentions Roman poets of slave origin and also the many freedmen in the professions as grammarians, physicians and architects, and finally recalls famous philosophers of the slave class.[14] A brief reference to the powerful positions held by slaves among contemporary Turks and Syrians brings the moralist to some instructions on how slaves and slave-owners ought to behave; the former must show loyalty, honesty and good-will, the latter must let themselves be ruled by considerations of justice. Examples from recent history serve to illustrate these precepts. Here is a Humanist who, although he realizes from his Stoic and Christian viewpoint that slavery is an affront to human nature, nevertheless comes to terms with the practice of the *ius gentium* and follows Seneca in satisfying himself with advising slave-owners to be lenient in the exercise of their rights. The fundamental offence against humanity is to be made tolerable by treating

[14] The theme of *servi philosophi* is reminiscent of Gellius *Noct. Att.* 2, 18 and Macrobius *Saturnalia* 1, 11, to whom Pontano does not, however, refer.

slaves humanely. This is the Humanist position, and it does not advance beyond the doctrines of the ancients.

However, it must be said in exoneration of fifteenth- and sixteenth-century scholars of antiquity that Roman law was then still in force, and had indeed been extended to the countries of Central Europe, and that the institution of slavery was firmly cemented into both the *ius civile* and the *ius gentium*. While those Humanists who entered the legal profession criticized the way jurisprudence had previously been studied in Italy and, in contrast to the glossators of previous ages, went back to the ancient sources of Roman law, they also wanted to prove that these sources were valid and reasonable for all time.[15] This makes it easier to understand why, when they came to comment on the institutions of Roman law, learned antiquaries generally found even fewer matters to question than Pontano had. About a century after Pontano, an important scholar of antiquity by the name of Carlo Sigone (1524–84)—who has been described as the first Humanist to advance from antiquarianism to history[16]—compiled a comprehensive work on Roman legal antiquities. In this, he showed that he knew about the origins and legal position of slaves,[17] but it would seem that he did not consider that the institution of slavery as such posed any fundamental moral problem.

This, however, could not be said of Lorenzo Pignoria (1571–1631), whose literary activity falls within the seventeenth century. After studying law at Padua, he was ordained, and while at Rome became interested in the study of antiquity. He then returned to Padua, where he became a prominent Humanist scholar. His treatise *De servis et eorum apud veteres ministeriis commentarius* (1613) was the first to deal specifically with slavery in antiquity.[18] Already in the introduction, the author expresses his doubts about the morality of the institution. He says that in the good old days there had been few slaves at Rome, and it was only after the destruction of Carthage and Corinth that vice

[15] P. Koschaker *Europa und das römische Recht*[3] (Munich 1958), 110ff.; F. E. Wolf *Grosse Rechtsdenker der deutschen Geistesgeschichte*[4] (Tübingen 1963), 59ff. Cf. also G. Kisch *Erasmus und die Jurisprudenz seiner Zeit* (*Basler Studien zur Rechtswissenschaft* 56: 1960).

[16] U. von Wilamowitz-Moellendorff *Geschichte der Philologie. Einleitung in die Altertumswissenschaft* I, 1 (Leipzig and Berlin 1921), 17.

[17] Carolus Sigonius *Opera*, Milan edition in six folio volumes (1732–7), vol. V, 77, 124, 259, 771 and elsewhere.

[18] My quotations are from the Amsterdam edition of 1674 of Laurentius Pignorius' treatise.

appeared, with an accompanying increase in the number of slaves. He remarks with regret that the contempt of masters for their slaves had not become unfashionable along with the passing of antiquity. As a proper reason why he, as a priest, should concern himself with this subject, he notes that many of the saints had been slaves, and that Christ himself mentions their duties in his parables, to teach us that as Christians, we too must be slaves. We can sense this theological perspective, so obvious in the introduction, again when he comes to explain the name and origin of slavery. Quotations from Genesis and Augustine's *De civitate Dei* date the first occurrence of slavery to the time of Noah and Nimrud, but he also gives an alternative version, which derives slavery from Ninus, who was the first man to wage war against his neighbours. The author then turns to the institution as it existed in antiquity, and notes briefly that a person may become a slave according to the *ius civile* because he has sold himself, or according to the *ius gentium* because he has been captured in war, or because he is descended from a slave-woman. Although this was the accepted Roman doctrine, Pignoria adds: *natura enim servum esse quempiam paucis visum est omnino* (*op. cit.* p. 4), and mentions Aristotle particularly (*Politics* I, 3f.) as one of the authors with whom he disagrees. If nothing more, this at least questions the authority to which those who held that barbarians were slaves by nature had always appealed for support. And, at the beginning of his lengthy discussion of the position and functions of slaves in antiquity, he makes the point that *servitutis autem conditio iniquior fuit, quam ratio humanitatis servo et domino communis exigeret* (p. 6). He thereby admits that even if this institution could be tolerated, it had been applied by the ancients in such a way that it became tantamount to an offence against *humanitas*. For a Humanist to have been so clearly unwilling to offer any extenuation of the ancient practice of slavery is a very positive achievement.

In general, however, Humanist scholars continued to follow the judgements of ancient philosophers about slavery, and only rarely dared to voice mild objections to Aristotle's doctrine of natural slavery. Barbarians and slaves remained excluded from the ideal of man which the *studia humanitatis* propagated. This purely theoretical position led to preconceptions about the problem of the morality of colonialism which arose in the sixteenth century, and even to a failure to try to achieve a complete and universal realization of human dignity under contemporary conditions. In the leading European countries, Humanists were at that time predominant among schoolmasters, preachers and town clerks, some of them becoming the counsellors of kings and educators of princes. They had an obligation to speak and to give their advice on occasions when governments decided not merely to tolerate the continuing existence of traditional forms of slavery in Mediterranean states, but, after the discovery of the New World, even to enslave the defenceless inhabitants of Africa and the West Indies on a massive scale and in the most appalling ways. Yet it was not the Humanists but the last representatives of Scholasticism who tried to check the inhumanity of this new system of slavery and of the wars of colonial conquest.[19]

It is true that the Scholastic view of slavery was also greatly influenced by the ancient philosophers. According to St. Thomas Aquinas, slavery did not originally exist, but the Fall disturbed the natural order with the result that there became human beings of an inferior kind, who had to be guided by force; these are Aristotle's 'born slaves'. But this enforced subjection is only of relevance in so far as the body is concerned; and even in this respect it is restricted by the fact that a slave has to obey God, not man, in anything that pertains to his human nature. This gave Scholastics a more solid basis than Humanists from which to consider the topical question of the enslaving of native populations, even though Scholastic thinkers approved of the statutes of Roman law and recognized that being descended from slaves or selling oneself, as well as capture in war, were valid grounds for being enslaved. In Spain, Scholasticism asserted its intellectual dominance over Humanism in the course of the sixteenth century. It was Scholastic thinkers who discussed the moral problems posed by colonial conquests, when the Portuguese began to import Negroes from the coasts of West Africa, and the Spaniards began to subjugate and enslave the Indians. We will not consider here the various attempts by the Spanish government to give the Indians a certain degree of protection as free subjects of the crown, and the unambiguous if ineffectual condemnation of this new slavery by individual Popes; nor the truly tragic solution proposed by Las Casas—to import Negro slaves in order to save the Indians. A reference to the long-drawn-out controversy about slavery and colonial war among theologians and jurists will be enough to indicate the comparative positions of Scholastics and Humanists.[20] There was no lack of people who wanted to see

[19] On this subject see the informative book by J. Höffner *Christentum und Menschenwürde: das Anliegen der spanischen Kolonialethik im goldenen Zeitalter* (Trier 1947).

[20] Examples are given in Höffner *op. cit.* 175ff.

Aristotle's doctrine of natural slaves applied to the Indians because of their barbarous paganism. Even Juan Gines de Sepulveda, the celebrated Humanist who had studied in Italy and had been appointed the official historian of Charles V after his return to Spain, supported this view. But the Dominican Francisco de Vitoria (1482/6–1546), who at the height of the controversy was teaching at the University of Salamanca, denied the supposed barbarity and insanity of the Indians and undertook to reinterpret Aristotle's theory in accordance with the Church Fathers: the philosopher had not intended to say that one could enslave men of such a low level, but rather that one had a duty to protect them. Arguing from Scholastic principles of Natural Justice, he saw that even heathen states had a right to exist, and made the morality of a colonial war dependent on the condition that the enemy had put himself in the wrong and had shown that his intentions were criminal. A generation later, Francisco Suarez (1548–1617) summarized the political and legal doctrines of the Spanish school of philosophy and laid new foundations for international law. He emphatically dissociated himself from Aristotle and Sepulveda on the question of slavery.[21]

While this controversy was going on in Spain, French and Dutch Humanists had made great progress in classical scholarship. Holland became the centre of humanist studies of antiquity thanks to Joseph Justus Scaliger, who was appointed to the chair at Leiden in 1594, and to his pupils Daniel Heinsius and Hugo Grotius. In addition to his philological and historical writings, Grotius published important legal studies and achieved fame with his treatise *De iure belli ac pacis* (1625), which we may use in order to see what Humanists thought about slavery at the beginning of the seventeenth century, when the slave trade was in its infancy. We should have high expectations of this, since Grotius laid down a new basis for the principles of natural justice and made the social organization of mankind under sub- and supra-national conditions the main subject of his investigations.[22] We may accept the modern view that he based himself essentially on ancient authors, and, in particular, on the Stoic philosophers who appealed so much to Dutch scholars, and also that he consulted the views of Spanish Scholastics.

Grotius sees the creation of human communities as the result of man's urge for togetherness (*appetitus societatis*), with which he had been endowed by God. Society spreads out from marriage and the

[21] Höffner *op. cit.* 228.

[22] P. Koschaker *op. cit.* 249ff.; F. E. Wolf *op. cit.* 253ff.

family to the community and the state, even to all mankind (*societas humana*), which is not organized politically but is founded on natural justice and reason in the same way as the smaller groups are. The rules for intercourse between states are laid down by international law, which has evolved from natural justice and with which Grotius deals in his major work in particular. By looking at things from the viewpoint of natural justice, he was able to apply new standards to Roman law. But the opinions Grotius expresses on the subject of slavery diverge only slightly from the law then in existence. According to Grotius, every man is naturally free; but he also says that every man has the right to renounce his freedom and sell himself into slavery—this recognizes that selling oneself can be a valid cause of slavery. The only restriction to a master's power over his slave is that no one can renounce his right to live, and the life and death of a slave are not therefore at his master's disposal.[23] Capture in war is also accepted as a ground for enslavement; killing or enslaving an enemy are among the acts permitted in conditions of war, and even the killing of innocent people on the enemy's side may be justified.[24] Only among Christian nations has the enslaving of prisoners been replaced by the payment of a ransom. Grotius also considers the question whether kings or nations may declare war on people who have not specifically infringed anyone else's rights but still offend against natural justice, for example by adhering to immoral religious practices. He replies in the affirmative and quotes ancient authors such as Aristotle and Isocrates to describe a war against 'such barbarians as are more like beasts than men' by the term *naturale bellum*; he here explicitly rejects the doctrines of Vitoria and other Spanish moralists and theologians.[25]

Thus, we are forced to concede that in contrast to the late Scholastics, this particular Humanist inherited the extreme view of the ancients on the question of the subjugation and enslavement of primitive races, and that he did this at the very time when the Dutch were already entering into competition against the Spaniards in trade with America, and were beginning to appear in the West Indies with their cargoes of slaves.[26] So it is not surprising that subsequent jurists no longer cared

[23] *De iure belli ac pacis* (*The Classics of International Law* ed. J. B. Scott 3, 1), 2, 5.27f.; 22.11. Cf. P. P. Remec *The Position of the Individual in International Law according to Grotius and Vattel* (The Hague 1960), 70, 106.

[24] *De iure belli ac pacis* 3, 4.3; 20.43.

[25] *Ibid.* 2, 20.40–44–47.

[26] J. H. Parry *The Age of Reconnaissance* (*History of Civilization*, London 1963), pp. 303–319.

to criticize Aristotle's doctrine of natural slavery, and went no further in their comments on the harsh rulings of Roman law than to stress in mitigation that the ancient philosophers described a wise man who had fallen into slavery as free, and that the Romans had not classified slaves with wild beasts.[27]

Perhaps it needs to be stressed here, that our consideration of the Humanists from Poggio Bracciolini to Grotius has been somewhat one-sided. If we wanted to do justice to the historical importance of Humanism, we would also have to bear in mind that it laid the foundations for secular education in modern Europe, and that it not only began the study of antiquity but also provided the first impulses towards modern science.[28] But in spite of this, the fact remains that, fettered by ancient concepts and ideas, the Humanists neglected the reorganization of the political and social life of their own time. If we survey the intellectual and political revolutions of the seventeenth and eighteenth centuries, we cannot but remark the absence of Humanists from the scene of action. We can readily understand why they did not take part in the struggle over class privileges which was fought in England in particular: but it is surprising that they lagged behind in the struggle for the principles of a constitution which guaranteed personal liberty and a new vision of man, an ideal of *humanitas* that was properly understood and followed through to its conclusions, and which was ultimately to lead to the Declaration of the Rights of Man and the abolition of slavery. Certainly individual ideals held by the Greek Sophists and Roman Stoics can still be traced in the philosophy of the Enlightenment, but Plato and Aristotle have faded into the background and the Humanists have had their say. As far as Christian ethics were concerned, it was less the theologians of the great Churches than the champions of small splinter communities and spokesmen of certain sects who carried on the dialogue with the changing world.

The philosophers of the Enlightenment did not claim any metaphysical basis for their ideas of natural justice, but ascribed to Reason alone the power of understanding and forming the world, and of

[27] For example *Georgii d'Arnaud variarum coniecturarum libri duo. In quibus plurima iuris civilis aliorumque auctorum loca emendantur aut explicantur. Accedunt eiusdem duae dissertationes de iure servorum et de his, qui pretii participandi causa sese venumdari patiuntur. Ex auctoris autographo auctae et emendatae. Leovardiae apud G. Coulon 1744*. See particularly 4f., 10ff. of the dissertations.

[28] On the effects of Humanism in this field see the reprint of G. Ritter *Die geschichtliche Bedeutung des deutschen Humanismus* (Darmstadt 1963), and F. Wagner *Die Wissenschaft und die gefährdete Welt* (Munich 1964), 29ff.

achieving human fulfilment. Although it is the theory and practice of slavery with which we are concerned here, it ought to be pointed out that the year after the proclamation of the English Bill of Rights saw the publication of John Locke's *Two Treatises of Government* (1690). The premiss of his argument is that human beings secure their livelihood by working, and he bases the right of property on this as being fundamental to the right of self-preservation.[29] Even the power of the state, which has been established by agreement among men, is limited by the principle that men are free by nature. This freedom is taken to imply that the individual may not put himself in another's power as his slave. The only possible exception is that someone who has forfeited his life through his own fault can be made to serve those into whose power he has fallen instead of being killed.[30] This undermines the legal validity of selling oneself into slavery. There is still, however, the possibility that the victorious party in a just war may subjugate and enslave those who are actively hostile to it, although these victors would do well to let mercy take precedence over justice, and, in any case, they have no authority over merely passive opponents, let alone the wives and children of the conquered.[31] This substantial limitation of slavery had an important effect on libertarian thought in general.

Considering the realities of man's political and social life on earth, however, it was difficult to infer anything from this principle of natural freedom. This can be seen from the 15th book of Montesquieu's *Esprit des Lois* (1748). It contains a detailed discussion of the differences between enslavement according to civil law (*l'esclavage civil*) and the political bondage inflicted by a despotic regime. According to Montesquieu, slavery contradicts civil as well as natural justice; the grounds given for the institution of slavery in Roman law are not reasonable. The doctrine that a religion could justify its adherents in enslaving others who do not profess their faith is rejected with disgust. This leads to the extraordinary fifth chapter in which Montesquieu enumerates a number of reasons for the enslaving of Negroes on the hypothetical supposition that he had to justify this activity. But these arguments are so unreasonable that there can be no mistaking the author's ironical intentions. He says quite clearly that Aristotle's assertion that there are those who are slaves by nature is not based on

[29] *Two Treatises* 2, 5.27; cf. J. Habermas 'Naturrecht und Revolution' in *Die Philosophie und die Frage nach dem Fortschritt* published by H. Kuhn and F. Wiedmann (Munich 1964), 160ff.

[30] *Two Treatises* 2, 4: *of Slavery*.

[31] *Ibid.* 2, 16: *of Conquest.*

sufficient evidence. Coming on to practical considerations, Montesquieu declares that the institution of slavery as a whole is useless, even harmful, as it serves luxury alone—a moral argument adduced a few years later by David Hume in his essay on *The Populousness of Ancient Nations* (1752).[32] But then Montesquieu, who was aware of the colonial policies of his times and of France in particular, goes on half to admit that slavery may be necessary in the tropics. I say only half to admit, because we are immediately told that this consequence of geographical circumstances could be overcome by means of legislation. But it is still surprising that from the eleventh chapter onwards he makes some suggestions on how slavery ought to be regulated in law, and that he here has in mind countries with moderate governments and even republics. So we can understand how it was that at the time of the final struggle to abolish slavery in the nineteenth century, it was mistakenly held that Montesquieu had approved of the institution.

A misunderstanding of this nature was not possible in the case of Rousseau. In his treatise *On the Origins and Causes of Inequality*, he portrays the development of civilization from an original period of bestiality to man's achievement of freedom and equality by means of inventions and social integration. Subsequently the transformation to civic society brought with it private property, and thereby inequality, the rule of the rich, and finally despotism. This suggests that in a state of nature, man is free, but that he is unfree within society. Later, in the *Contrat Social* (1762), Rousseau sketches out a political system in which autonomy and heteronomy are to be brought into harmony in the sovereignty of the General Will, which embodies absolute Reason. In this state, the individual and the community are no longer opposed; freedom and equality are guaranteed as belonging to man by right. In this order of things, political coercion therefore becomes the coercion to be free, which leads man to himself. It has been said with some justice that Rousseau's theory already contains the germ of that concept of man's self-alienation which appears explicitly in Hegel and Marx.[33] As far as our investigation is concerned, we must note that it was Rousseau who pointed this new way towards human self-fulfilment,

[32] *The Philosophical Works of David Hume* III (Boston 1854), 415–29. On p. 416 Hume refers to the customs of antiquity as harsh, even barbarous.

[33] H. Barth 'Über die Idee der Selbstentfremdung des Menschen bei Rousseau' *Zeitschrift für philosophische Forschung* 13 (1959), 16ff.; cf. also M. Rang *Rousseaus Lehre vom Menschen* (Göttingen 1959), 33f.; B. Meissner 'Der Fortschrittsgedanke im Marxismus' in *Die Idee des Fortschritts* ed. by E. Burck (Munich 1963), 108f.

and that his successors did not hesitate to use the term *humanisme* to describe the striving for this highest of aims.[34] This was the origin of the social and political humanism which was to triumph in the following decades. We are more interested here in this new kind of humanism than in the way in which the philosophical theories were put into practice—how the Rights of Man were laid down in the constitutions of the American states, primarily the Bill of Rights of Virginia (1776), and in the Declaration of the French National Assembly of 1789.[35]

The failure of the Humanists to achieve anything in the struggle for human rights must be supplemented by a description of those intellectual forces which after much effort achieved the abolition of the slave trade and ultimately of slavery itself. Considering what has already been said, it was not to be expected that the abolitionists should have enjoyed any special support from Humanists or that they should have based their arguments on ancient writers. Rather, their case was founded on Christian Natural Justice, and later on rationalist views of man's natural rights.[36] The words which John Milton puts into the mouth of the Archangel Michael in *Paradise Lost* are a powerful instance of this Christian viewpoint. When Michael prophesies to Adam that after the Great Flood there will come a person who will subjugate his brother, Adam, appalled at this awful news, exclaims (*Paradise Lost* 12, 64–71):

> O execrable son, so to aspire
> Above his brethren, to himself assuming
> Authority usurpt, from God not giv'n;
> He gave us only over beast, fish, fowl
> Dominion absolute; but man over men
> He made not lord; such title to himself
> Reserving, human left from human free.

[34] On the virtue of *humanité* in Rousseau's educational theory, see Rang *op. cit.* 419ff.; on the history of the rise of the term *humanisme*, C. Dionisotti *Chambers' Encyclopaedia* VII (new ed., 1955), 285.

[35] I would refer the reader to the collection of essays *Zur Geschichte der Erklärung der Menschenrechte* ed. R. Schnur (Darmstadt 1964); G. Ritter's partially revised study of the origins and essence of human rights is on pp. 202ff.

[36] Cf. the description of this development by a contemporary spokesman of the anti-slavery movement, Thomas Clarkson *The History of the Rise, Progress and Accomplishment of the Abolition of the American Slave-Trade by the British Parliament* I (London 1808), also J. H. Franklin *From Slavery to Freedom* (New York 1948), and, more generally, D. Owen *English Philanthropy* (Cambridge, Mass. 1964).

These lines, giving a biblical foundation to the right to freedom, were repeatedly taken up by the opponents of slavery.[37] Sympathy for slaves is found much more widely in eighteenth-century literature, and the rational objections to inequality and lack of freedom begin to have an effect. The privileges of Englishmen were claimed for slaves who had been brought to England and forcibly recaptured after escaping. The Society of Friends achieved the greatest measure of success with its doctrine that all men have an inner light and are therefore equal in the sight of God and man. In America, many Quakers obeyed the precept laid down as early as 1671 by George Fox, and took no part in the slave trade; and where slaves were still being employed they began to treat them as brothers in Christ. After the revolt of the colonies, resistance against British domination proceeded hand-in-hand with opposition to a slave trade which was mainly carried on by England. They did not, however, succeed in incorporating the rejection of slavery in the Declaration of Independence. In England, the Quakers repeatedly made their position clear in resolutions condemning the slave trade, and in 1787, in conjunction with others, they finally caused Parliament to set up a committee charged with preparing the abolition of the trade. This was the turning-point in the long struggle. Perhaps it could be said that Humanist academics joined the movement at the last moment. In 1785, Cambridge University awarded a prize for an essay on the subject *Anne liceat invitos in servitutem dare?* The first prize was won by Thomas Clarkson (1760–1846); and, as he himself recounts, it was as a result of this essay that he came to know William Wilberforce and the other Members of Parliament who were working for the suppression of the slave trade.

It is not our concern to follow in detail the lengthy battles that were fought in the British Parliament before slavery and the slave trade were abolished. But the great speech with which in 1792 the younger Pitt won for the first time a majority for abolition in the Commons is of interest.[38] During a debate on this topic in the previous year, he had branded the awful violation of humanity represented by this 'dealing

[37] These lines are directed against forceful subjugation and tyrannical rule in general, but it is made clear already in line 30 that a despotic government will treat prisoners of war as slaves. It is interesting that in his posthumous work *De doctrina christiana* (2, 15), Milton collects together passages from the Old and New Testaments concerning the position and duties of slaves without himself passing any judgement on the institution of slavery as such.

[38] Hansard's *Parliamentary History of England to the Year 1803* XXIX (London 1817), cols. 1133–58.

in human flesh', and at the same time put forward practical considerations in favour of abolition. Now he demanded that slaves in the colonies should become subjects and citizens 'forming a part of the same community, having a common interest with their superiors in the security and prosperity of the whole' (col. 1138f.). He pointed out with great emphasis that obtaining slaves in Africa necessarily led to internal wars and the criminal treatment of human beings throughout the continent, and publicly stated that 'that nation which calls herself the most free and the most happy of them all' (col. 1149) was sanctioning the most dreadful of all evils. Britain was now called upon to give the African continent the chance to progress by removing the trade. Human sacrifices had been offered up in Britain too, in earlier times, and British slaves had filled the Roman slave-markets: 'There is unquestionably no small resemblance, in this particular point, between the case of our ancestors and that of the present wretched natives of Africa' (col. 1154). But now it was up to them 'by abolishing the slave trade [to] give them the same common chances of civilization with other parts of the world' (col. 1157). At the end of his speech he conjured up a vision of the future, with Africa developing peaceful industry and commerce and accepting Western science and philosophy; and he expressed the hope that these achievements might be connected with the effectiveness of pure religion, and that the continent would graciously render Europe its thanks for all this. Although he concluded the statement of his personal convictions on this fundamental issue with some lines in Latin, these verses had no bearing on the matter under discussion, but were mere oratorical ornamentation. Apart from considerations of political and economic wisdom, the basic intellectual reason for his position was the new idea of what Humanism ought to be; humanity was made to correspond to humaneness, and it was this that led to the 'Ancients' being superseded.

About this time, the intellectual movement that we call the New Humanism had appeared in Germany. Winckelmann had prepared the way for a return to the Greeks; Herder proclaimed a concept of humanity which was to unite the highest ideals of antiquity, Christianity and Idealist philosophy; German classical poetry arose out of a new experience of ancient literature, and Wilhelm von Humboldt laid the foundations for a German system of education which tried to emulate that of the Greeks. We cannot here trace the great influence of the Humanists of this generation on the education and scholarship of the nineteenth century. One of their achievements was the foundation of modern classical scholarship. It has been shown elsewhere to what extent this methodical investigation of the historical realities of antiquity led to the consideration and judgement of slavery during a period when a new kind of humanism, Socialism, was coming into being.[39] We are only concerned here to note such of their evaluations of antiquity as throw light on the problem of slavery. These evaluations can be traced from the beginnings of the New Humanism through the nineteenth century up to the present day, particularly in German literature.

It might have been thought that Herder's conception of humanity would have entailed the utter rejection of slavery both past and present. Although the *Letters for the Promotion of Humanity* (*Briefe zur Beförderung der Humanität*) published during the years 1793 to 1797 do not set up any complete system of philosophy, they do offer a total view of world history, whose meaning is seen as contained in the spread of noble spiritual forces through the whole of the human race. These letters stated that it was the task of every science and art to 'humanize us' and called for tolerance towards every people and language.[40] We must not, he says, be prevented from recognizing what is good in others by our love for our own nation. In his survey of history, Herder expresses the view that every people should be allowed to develop the seeds of its own culture. He considered that migrations, conquests and colonization were generally destructive of civilization. The colonial activity of the Spaniards, English and Dutch had brought them so little honour 'that, if such a thing as a sense of community among Europeans existed elsewhere than in books, we would on the contrary feel shame in the presence of almost every people on earth for these offences against outraged humanity'.[41] It would have been only a short step from such an accusation against colonial policies to criticism of ancient slavery, and it seems quite amazing that Herder did not take this step.

But Wilhelm von Humboldt, who evolved a consistent view of humanity from his idea of the nature of man and his position in the universe,[42] did not become a serious critic of slavery either; and his

[39] See p. 171ff. above.

[40] R. Newald *Humanitas, Humanismus, Humanität* (Essen 1947), 35ff., with references to further reading.

[41] *Briefe zur Beförderung der Humanität* in *Herders Sämtliche Werke* ed. B. Suphan, XVIII (Berlin 1883), 222.

[42] E. Spranger *Wilhelm von Humboldt und die Humanitätsidee* (Berlin 1910); R. Newald *op. cit.* 52ff.

influence on Humanists up to Wilamowitz and Werner Jaeger was far greater than that of Herder. In every period of his life he believed in the ethical ideal of a positively active man who overcomes the barriers between himself and human universality, his individualism purified and sublimated because he has embraced all facets of life. He saw this concept realized among the Greeks; the Greeks had arrived at a set of standards, and 'there is no other way to human fulfilment except by them'.[43] It was this essentially artistic view of man that led him to define humanity in this way and to produce this idealized picture of the Greeks. Man's aesthetic experience could explain why all active and contemplative life had to serve internal enrichment, while only a minor value was put on labour, which served to satisfy merely material needs. Although he could not formally approve of slavery on these grounds, he could accept it. In his essay entitled *Thoughts on the Limitation of State Activity* (1792), Humboldt says: 'The ancients, and the Greeks in particular, considered any activity which was principally concerned with the exercise of physical strength to be harmful and degrading. Even the most philanthropic of their philosophers, therefore, approved of slavery in order, as it were, to ensure the highest power and beauty for one part of mankind, by sacrificing another to an unjust and barbarous system. But reason and experience both expose the error on which this line of reasoning is based. Any activity can ennoble a man and give him an individual role that is worthy of him. . . .'[44] Here he still speaks in terms of 'crimes' and 'error', but in an essay that followed in 1793, *On the Study of Antiquity and that of the Greeks in Particular*, he praises the superiority of the Greeks in having realized man's many-sidedness, and he states without a word of criticism that man's concern for his own development was fostered by external circumstances, and particularly slavery.[45] 'It was from these that there arose that liberal spirit which has not reappeared to a similar extent among any other people, that is to say, the spiritual rule of noble and great attitudes truly worthy of a free man, and the living expression of these in excellence of education and grace of bodily movement.' There is no longer any mention of the lack of humanity and cruelty of the behaviour that David Hume

[43] Spranger *op. cit.* 466.

[44] *Gesammelte Schriften* published by the *Kgl. Preussische Akademie der Wissenschaften*, I (Berlin 1903), 118 [= *The Limits of State Action* ed. J. W. Burrow (*Cambridge Studies in the History and Theory of Politics*: Cambridge 1969), 28].

[45] *Gesammelte Schriften* I, 271; cf. p. 171 above.

associated with slavery; slavery had to be, so that the Greeks could be.

The same tolerance of the inhumanity that enabled the Greeks and Romans to secure their development as human beings occurs repeatedly among Humanist scholars and writers after Humboldt. There is certainly no lack of voices in the nineteenth century criticizing the moral and social conditions of antiquity and condemning slavery together with disdain for the position of women and barbarians;[46] but some who knew and admired the ancient world thought that the negative factor of slavery was more than outweighed by the value of its contribution to constitutional development and culture. Others either did not notice the existence of slavery or kept discreetly silent about it; others again mentioned it in passing and tried to excuse or extenuate it. Even as liberal-minded a person as Acton thought that in the course of history, democracy and slavery had always gone hand in hand; he claimed that Pericles described freedom from manual work as the particular privilege of the Athenians and even said that 'the arguments for and against Abolition have made us all familiar with Burke's words that men only learn how valuable a thing freedom is when they are the masters of slaves'.[47] In his attack on the German 'Socialists of the Chair' (*Kathedersozialisten*), the historian Heinrich von Treitschke goes so far as to describe the introduction of slavery as 'a saving act of civilization' and he accepts the view that 'millions must labour as farmers, smiths and carpenters so that a few thousand may study, paint and govern'; and he celebrates the highly aristocratic society of the Periclean period 'which piled all common concerns of life onto the patient shoulders of their slaves—and surely the price paid by their suffering for the tragedies of Sophocles and Phidias' statue of Zeus was not too high'.[48]

[46] References in G. Billeter *Die Anschauungen vom Wesen des Griechentums* (Leipzig and Berlin 1911), 386f., 392f.

[47] This is the point of view suggested by the essay on Sir Erskine May's book *Democracy in Europe*, which appeared in 1878, reprinted in J. E. Dalberg-Acton *Essays on Freedom and Power* (Boston 1949), 130f.

[48] H. Treitschke *Der Socialismus und seine Gönner* (Berlin 1875), 10, 17, 40. This paper first appeared in *Preussische Jahrbücher* 34 (1874), 67ff. Treitschke's distinction between the millions and the few recalls Dr. Johnson's celebrated *bon-mot*: 'It is better that some should be unhappy than that none should be happy, which would be the case in a general state of equality' (Boswell's *Life of Johnson* ed. G. B. Hill, rev. L. F. Powell, III (Oxford 1934), 26). But it must be borne in mind that Johnson was here thinking of class distinctions within a

Treitschke's ideas were shared by many, even if they were not all able to evaluate debit and credit in such business-like terms. Classical scholars often ignored the institution of slavery altogether. Wilamowitz does indeed reject Aristotle's justification of slavery 'as it introduces the novel supposition, equally inadequate from the logical and from the historical point of view, that apart from the people who constitute the state there exists another, inferior, race of men', but he then contents himself, in his description of Greek society, with a reference to various ways in which the system was alleviated.[49] Again, Max Pohlenz insists in his book on Greek freedom that only the presence of those who were not free, the slaves, aroused an appreciation of freedom in others; he praises the supposedly humane sentiments of owners (there are certainly some good grounds for this) and the frequency of manumissions, but there is no word of criticism when he comes across Plato's remark that slaves are indispensable, or Aristotle's doctrine of natural slavery.[50] And it will have to be admitted that Werner Jaeger did not consider the question of slavery either in his great work on *Paideia* or in his numerous speeches and lectures on Humanist themes. This is puzzling when we bear in mind how much he considered this Humanism of his to be a liberation from rigid conventions and a willingness to accept clear standards, and the decisive emphasis he put on the moral values and educational methods of antiquity as the focal point of his studies.

To try to draw any conclusions for contemporary scholarship and education from these academic approaches to the ideal of Humanism would be an immense task.[51] I will merely say that if the Humanism of classical studies is to survive in our world—a world which has been transformed without the agency of Humanists—it must portray ancient society as it really was without concealing or extenuating its negative aspects, and, in spite of these aspects, it must make the educative values which antiquity possesses accessible to a world in which there ought no longer to be either slaves or barbarians. Perhaps

society of free men, and was in other respects a dedicated opponent of slavery (II, 476f., III, 200ff.), while Boswell defended the institution (particularly III, 204).

[49] U. von Wilamowitz-Moellendorff *Staat und Gesellschaft der Griechen und Römer* (*Die Kultur der Gegenwart* part 2, section 4, 1: Leipzig and Berlin 1923), 33, 37, 195.

[50] M. Pohlenz *Griechische Freiheit* (Heidelberg 1955), 7, 9, 10, 50, 52, 80, 94, 105. [= *Freedom in Greek Life and Thought* (Dordrecht 1966), 3, 5f., 46ff., 74, 88, 98f.]

[51] Cf. H. Rüdiger *Wesen und Wandlung des Humanismus* 296.

it has been left to the Classics to uphold the existence of intellectual standards in all areas of knowledge and skill, under conditions of general equality and universal freedom. That personal merit should take precedence over claims of class, profession or party; that the simple beauty of an artistic form should not be subject to current fashions; that a man's dedication to his life's work should take him so far as to sacrifice himself, and should even lead him beyond himself to the Divine—these are claims that we must be prepared to submit to and act upon. The ideal of classical Humanism will survive in competition with the other great doctrines and principles of mankind if it can give to a new era what Dante, the harbinger of Humanism, summed up as 'the art by which men grow immortal'.[52]

[52] Dante *Inferno* 15, 85: *come l'uom' s'eterna.* It gives me great satisfaction to be able to refer at this point to W. Jaeger *Humanistische Reden und Vorträge*² (Berlin 1960), 264f., 312f.

Bibliographical Supplement

The problem of slavery, which the Mainz Academy of Science and Literature decided to study more than twenty years ago, is being given more and more recognition by classical scholars throughout the world. In socialist countries, where, in accordance with Marxist doctrine, the ancient world is interpreted as a slave-holding society, a great deal of interest is being shown in slavery, the way it arose, the functions it fulfilled and the reasons for its decline. After a number of studies which appeared in the journal *Vestnik Drevnei Istorii*, the section for ancient history of the Historical Institute of the Soviet Academy of Sciences began a series of individual volumes, in which it is intended to describe the entire history of ancient slavery, with the publication in 1963 of J. A. Lentzman's book on slavery in Mycenaean and Homeric Greece. Ancient slavery has become a regular subject for the agendas of national and international conferences held in Eastern Europe—as is shown by the *Neue Beiträge zur Geschichte der Alten Welt* (the publication of the second international conference of the study-group on ancient history of the Association of German Historians held at Stralsund from the 4th to the 8th September 1962), edited by E. Ch. Welskopf (Volume I, Berlin 1964; Volume II, 1965), and *Antiquitas Graeco-Romana ac Tempora Nostra* (report of the international congress held at Brno from the 12th to the 16th April 1966: Prague 1968). Among western historians the general tendency towards the investigation of social structures has led to a particular open-mindedness when dealing with questions of slavery and serfdom. Here too it will suffice to mention a number of representative collections of articles: *Recherches sur les structures sociales dans l'antiquité classique* (Colloques nationaux du Centre national de la Recherche scientifique, Paris 1970), containing papers presented to the conference held at Caen on the 25th and 26th April 1969, including P. Vidal-Naquet, 'Esclavage et gynécocratie' (pp. 63ff.), and *Ricerche storiche ed economiche in memoria di Corrado Barbagallo* I (Naples 1970), with E. Lepore's wide-ranging survey, 'Economia antica e storiografia moderna' (pp. 1ff.); further the informative textbook of M. Austin and P. Vidal-Naquet, *Economies et sociétés en Grèce ancienne* (Paris 1972). J. Gagé *Les classes sociales dans l'empire romain* (Paris 1964) is a useful guide.

Contributions published by the Mainz Academy have been referred to on several occasions; there have been a number of studies in the *Abhandlungen der Geistes- und sozialwissenschaftlichen Klasse* since 1953 and in the series *Forschungen zur antiken Sklaverei* since 1967, as well as several translations into German of Russian works on ancient slavery.

The champion of the social history of antiquity, M. I. Finley, has a bibliographical note on recent publications on ancient slavery in the collection of essays referred to above (p. 4 n. 9). There is also my bibliographical list of the most important works of the nineteenth and twentieth centuries, although it is doubtless neither exhaustive nor free from error: *Bibliographie zur antiken Sklaverei* ed. J. Vogt and N. Brockmeyer; Bochum 1971.

The following pages contain references to the most recent publications and to work relevant to particular themes that I have dealt with which is being undertaken at the moment.

Slavery and the Ideal of Man in Classical Greece (p. 1) and *Slavery in Greek Utopias* (p. 26): on slavery in classical Greece, and especially the question of the origins of slaves, P. Ducrey *Le traitement des prisonniers de guerre dans la Grèce antique* (*École française d'Athènes. Travaux et Mémoires* 17, 1968) is particularly valuable. On the way slaves are portrayed in classical literature see H. Kuch *Kriegsgefangenschaft und Sklaverei bei Euripides* (dissertation, Humboldt University, Berlin 1970); the same author deals with the passage of Euripides' *Cyclops* mentioned above (p. 16f., n. 47) in 'Die Krise der griechischen Polis' *Görlitzer Eirene-Tagung 10.–14.10.1967* I (Berlin 1969), 35ff. Various questions concerning class structure and social movements also occur in *Arbeitsergebnisse der althistorischen Forschung der Deutschen Demokratischen Republik*, submitted to the Twelfth International Congress of Historians in collaboration with the Association of German Historians by J. Irmscher and E. Ch. Welskopf (*Klio. Beiträge zur Alten Geschichte* 43/5, Berlin 1965).

F. Kudlien *Die Sklaven in der griechischen Medizin der klassischen und hellenistischen Zeit* (*Forschungen zur antiken Sklaverei* 2: 1968) is relevant to the use of slaves as physicians mentioned on p. 15. The following two studies dealing with the archaic and classical periods have been completed and will be published in the near future: H. Klees on the theory and practice of Greek slavery in the fifth and fourth centuries, particularly at Athens, and K. W. Welwei on slaves serving in Greek armies.

I have already mentioned the paper by P. Vidal-Nacquet on Greek mythological and utopian thought (p. 32 above). On the importance of technological discoveries for economic and social developments, see M. I. Finley 'Technical Innovation and Economic Progress in the Ancient World' *Economic History Review* 18 (1965), 29ff. Kiechle *Sklavenarbeit und technischer Fortschritt im römischen Reich* (*Forschungen zur antiken Sklaverei* 3: 1969) deals with the question whether slavery contributed to the stagnation of technological progress in the Roman world.

The fact that attention is now being given to slavery by archaeologists too is to be welcomed—cf. N. Himmelmann *Archäologisches zum Problem der griechischen Sklaverei* (*Ak. d. Wiss. u. d. Lit.* 1971, 13).

The Structure of Ancient Slave Wars (p. 39) and *Pergamum and Aristonicus* (p. 93): the slave wars of the second and first centuries B.C. continue to attract detailed examination. M. Capozza's analysis of the unrest among slaves in the period before the great slave wars is extremely useful: *Movimenti servili nel mondo romano in età repubblicana I: dal 501 al 184 a. Cr.* (*Università degli Studi di Padova. Pubblicazioni dell'Istituto di Storia antica* 5: 1966). A. Fuks 'Slave War and Slave Troubles in Chios in the Third Century B.C.' *Athenaeum* 46 (1968), 102ff., suggests that there may be a historical basis to Nymphodorus' story of the rebellion at Chios (Athenaeus 6, 265b–266f.).

P. Oliva 'Die charakteristischen Züge der grossen Sklavenaufstände zur Zeit der römischen Republik' *Neue Beiträge zur Geschichte der Alten Welt* II, 75ff., supplements the interpretation of the great revolts to be found in my essay. M. I. Finley *A History of Sicily* (London 1968), 137ff. and J. Irmscher 'Das antike Sizilien in der Altertumsforschgun der sozialistischen Länder' *Kokalos* 14/15 (1968/9), 272ff., throw light on these revolts in the context of Sicilian history. M. Capozza 'Le rivolte servili di Sicilia nel quadro della politica agraria romana' *Atti del' Istituto Veneto di Scienze, Lettre ed Arti, Classe di Scienze morali e Lettere* 115 (1956/7), 79ff., demonstrates the connections between the revolts in Sicily and Roman agrarian policy. E. Maróti considers the importance of piracy for the slave trade in Sicily and Italy in the second and first centuries B.C. in *Das Altertum* 7 (1961), 32ff. and *Ricerche Storiche ed Economiche in memoria di Corrado Barbagallo* I, 481ff. T. W. Africa 'Aristonicus, Blossius and the City of the Sun' *International Review of Social History* 6 (1961), 116ff. and F. Carrata Thomes *La rivolta di Aristonico e le origini della provincia romana d'Asia* (Turin 1968) express reservations about Aristonicus' 'City of the Sun'. On Heliopolis and other utopias generally, cf. L. Gernet *Anthropologie de la Grèce antique* (Paris 1968), 139ff. G. Manganaro 'Über die zwei Sklavenaufstände in Sizilien' *Helikon* 7 (1967), 205ff., is critical of the suggestion that Syrian nationalism could have been a factor in Eunus' revolt.

Since the publications about Spartacus by A. W. Mischulin and J.-P. Brisson, there has been a new description of the revolt and its historical effects in P. Oliva and V. Olivova's book on Spartacus' rising and the Spartacist tradition (Prague 1960: in Czech). On the rebels' links with Sicily cf. E. Maróti *Acta Antiqua* 9 (1961), 42ff. Z. Rubensohn 'Was the Bellum Spartacium a Slave Insurrection?' *Riv. Fil.* 99 (1971), 290ff., stresses the large proportion of Italians among the rebels.

Human Relationships in Ancient Slavery (p. 103) and *Slaves and the Liberal Arts in Ancient Rome* (p. 122): we are dealing here with professions exercised by slaves which were very important to free society and intellectual life in general. Because of the nature of the work they did, nurses, tutors, secretaries and physicians all had good prospects of gaining their freedom. This situation has aroused the most interest in so far as it relates to the intrusion of Greek ideas of education into the Roman political world. On the slaves and freedmen who represent the sciences and arts in Italy and Rome, see most recently E. M. Staerman *Die Blütezeit der Sklavenwirtschaft in der römischen Republik* (No. 2 in the series of translations of foreign works on ancient slavery undertaken by the Mainz Academy: 1969), esp. 128ff., and S. Treggiari *Roman Freedmen during the Late Republic* (Oxford 1969), esp. 110ff. J. Christes is collating specific references to slaves and freedmen as grammarians, rhetors, philosophers and poets at Rome. On the social status of scholars cf. also R. Müller 'Die Wertung der Bildungsdisziplinen bei Cicero' *Klio* 43/5 (1965), 77ff.

The Faithful Slave (p. 129) *and Ecce Ancilla Domini* (p. 146): the examples of loyal slaves so highly celebrated in the ancient tradition show how personal relationships and bonds of friendship and devotion between slaves and free men often succeeded in overcoming the inhumanity of the slave system. The fact that in oriental religions, including Judaism, man's dependence on God was expressed by the imagery and vocabulary of slavery, could tend towards the same result. Of course the use of the term 'servant of God' by theologians and historians of religion has often had the effect in studies of this subject with regard to the Old or the New Testaments of masking or at least toning down the thought that slavery was a historical reality. Thus A. Weiser's recent book *Die Knechtsgleichnisse der synoptischen Evangelien* (*Studien zum Alten und Neuen Testament* 29: 1971) discusses the master/servant relationship in the Old and New Testaments and the relevant parables of Jesus without making clear the realities of slavery, without, indeed, even making the necessary distinctions between slave, servant and serf.

The attitude of early Christianity to slavery has often been discussed, particularly by theologians, but should be examined afresh by those with some acquaintance with ancient slavery. G. Kehnscherper *Die Stellung der Bibel und der alten Kirche zur Sklaverei* (Halle 1957) gives a somewhat superficial account which is not warranted by the sources or their interpretation. H. Gülzow *Christentum und Sklaverei in den ersten drei Jahrhunderten* (Bonn 1969) is a useful preliminary survey. The much-discussed question of the social orientation of early Christian missionary activity has not been satisfactorily clarified. H. Kreissig 'Die soziale Zusammensetzung der frühchristlichen Gemeinden im ersten Jahrhundert u. Z.' *Eirene* 6 (1967), 91ff., tries to show that the Christian message was addressed not to the proletariat, but to the urban middle classes.

Research on Ancient Slavery from Humboldt to the Present Day (p. 170) and *Slavery and the Humanists* (p. 188). D. B. Davis *The Problem of Slavery in Western Culture* (New York 1966) is a fundamental work about the different judgements passed on slavery particularly in modern America, and about the forces behind the anti-slavery movement, mainly up to about 1770. He also discusses the attitude towards slavery of ancient philosophers (pp. 66ff.) and of early Christianity (pp. 83ff.), as well as the medieval view (pp. 91ff.), Humanism and the Enlightenment (pp. 107ff.). The effect which the historical study of ancient slavery had on the abolition of modern slavery is also shown by I. Biezunska-Malowist 'Les recherches sur l'esclavage ancien et le mouvement abolitioniste européen' in *Antiquitas Graeco-Romana ac Tempora Nostra* 161ff.

Finally, I wish to define some of the questions not already mentioned which, given the state of the evidence, offer the possibility for further investigations.

As far as the origins of slaves are concerned, capture as a result of war has been dealt with in detail. G. Micknat-Wickert is looking at the social conditions of Homeric society. The long-neglected subject of home-bred slaves is being studied by H. Volkmann, who has already produced a description of the mass-enslavement of the inhabitants of cities captured in war. It would be worthwhile examining in greater detail the importation of slaves from the border-areas of the Greek and Roman world, and testing the extent to which slaves from Caria, Phrygia, Thrace and Scythia provided the basis for Greek judgements of these foreign peoples (cf. Καππαδόκες Κᾶρες Κίλικες τρία κάππα κάκιστα). F. M. Snowden's fine book *The Blacks in Antiquity* (Cambridge, Mass. 1970) has little to say about Negroes as slaves.

Given the state of our evidence, the ways in which slaves were used and the professional activities they engaged in can only be pin-pointed with regard to certain specific areas. The functions of state-owned slaves ought to be looked at again; W. Eder has applied himself to this task with regard to the *servi publici* of republican Rome. With respect to the work done by slaves in industry, G. Prachner is producing a detailed evaluation of the craftsmen whose signatures are to be found on terra sigillata. It seems to me that an analysis of the role of slaves in the means of disseminating news would be of some importance. We can also look forward to a portrayal and assessment of slaves and freedmen in the service of the Roman emperors by H. Chantraine.

The Mainz Academy offered a prize some years ago, which has not been awarded, for a study of the effect of slavery on relations between the sexes in the ancient world. H. Cancik has made a beginning with his study of *pueri delicati* in Roman lyric poetry from Catullus to Statius.

Legal historians in particular could undertake further examination of the position of slaves in law, especially to try to define the widely varying statuses that are to be found in the legal codes of different Greek states; and also to clarify imperial legislation on the position of slaves during the Principate and in the centuries from Constantine to Justinian.

Index